Annual Review of Cultural Heritage Informatics

Annual Review of Cultural Heritage Informatics

2014

Edited by
Samantha K. Hastings

ROWMAN & LITTLEFIELD
Lanham • Boulder • New York • London

Published by Rowman & Littlefield
A wholly owned subsidiary of The Rowman & Littlefield Publishing Group, Inc.
4501 Forbes Boulevard, Suite 200, Lanham, Maryland 20706
www.rowman.com

Unit A, Whitacre Mews, 26-34 Stannary Street, London SE11 4AB

British Library Cataloguing in Publication Information Available

Library of Congress Cataloging-in-Publication Data Available

978-1-4422-5011-6 (cloth)
978-1-4422-5012-3 (electronic)

∞™ The paper used in this publication meets the minimum requirements of American National Standard for Information Sciences—Permanence of Paper for Printed Library Materials, ANSI/NISO Z39.48-1992.

Printed in the United States of America

Contents

ARCHI Editorial Board

List of Figures

List of Tables

I

BEST PRACTICES

1

Perspectives on Museum Informatics

Curatorial Voice Reimagined through Gatekeeper Theory; *Museum as Place* Reenvisioned through Nonaka's SECI *ba*

Laura-Edythe S. Coleman

ABSTRACT

The emerging field of museum informatics is more than just an interdisciplinary dialogue with information professionals. The shift of museum missions—from object-oriented to story-oriented approaches, from expert-curated to community-curated exhibits, and from object preservation to promotion of social agendas—demands the skills of information professionals. Recognizing the changing role of museums from information preservation to information provision, information scientists are challenged to study the unique information needs of museum professionals and museum audiences. This chapter attempts to answer that challenge by applying vetted theories from the field of information science to the realm of museums and reimagining two concepts central to museology through the lenses of information science. First, the ubiquitous curatorial voice of a museum exhibit is recast as a gatekeeper, granting the researcher the ability to apply principles of "gatekeeper" theory to this often invisible but always audible voice within an exhibit. Second, the pervasive quandary of museum as place, *or space, is reenvisioned through Nonaka's SECI model as* ba, *the "shared context for knowledge creation" (Nonaka, Toyama, & Konno, 2000, p. 5). Information science research into curatorial voice and museum as place may shed light on these widely accepted and barely understood phenomena, discerning pathways for museums to facilitate their role in society, even as that role shifts.*

INTRODUCTION

At first glance, the emerging field of museum informatics appears to be little more than an effort to bring together information professionals and museum professionals for the purpose of interdisciplinary dialogue. Yet museum informatics is more than an interdisciplinary dialogue. Museum informatics represents the presence of information science in a museum environment. Paul Marty (2009) defines museum informatics as "the study of the sociotechnical interactions that take place at the intersection of people, information, and technology in museums" (p. 3). The importance of museum informatics cannot be underestimated as museum missions shift from object-oriented to story-oriented approaches, from expert-curated to community-curated exhibits, and from object preservation to promotion of social agendas (Chen, 2007). These shifts demand both the skills of information professionals and the recognition of the changing role of museums from information preservation to information provision. Marty speaks to this shift: "Information professionals are not the only ones aware of the growing convergence of cultural heritage organizations in the information age. As users rely increasingly on online information, they will likely expect to find similar types of resources offered by different institutions" (Marty, 2007, p. 104). Pressures from within and without the museum necessitate a "call to arms" for information scientists to study the unique information needs of museum professionals and museum audiences (p. 105). This chapter attempts to answer that call, applying vetted theories from the field of information science to the realm of museums.

In this chapter, two concepts central to museology are reimagined through the lenses of information science. First, the ubiquitous *curatorial voice* of a museum exhibit is recast as a gatekeeper, granting the researcher the ability to apply principles of "gatekeeper" theory to this often invisible but always audible voice within an exhibit. Second, the pervasive quandary of *museum as place*, or space, is reenvisioned through Nonaka's SECI model as *ba*, the "shared context for knowledge creation" (Nonaka, Toyama, & Konno, 2000, p. 5). Information science research into curatorial voice and museum as place may shed light on these widely accepted and barely understood phenomena.

CURATORIAL VOICE

The question arises: What is *curatorial voice*? Peter Walsh (1997) describes curatorial voice as the "Unassailable Voice: an essential part of the museum experience. It is an institutional tone and attitude that pervades museum labels, brochures, exhibitions, catalogues, audio-visual presentations, and now Web sites" (Walsh, 1997). For the museum visitor, curatorial voice is interwoven into the museum experience, providing organization, authority, and authenticity to the "gestalt" (Falk & Dierking, 1992). To the museum visitor, Walsh likened the sound of curatorial voice to the mythical disembodied voice of the Wizard of Oz (Walsh, 1997). How can research investigate curatorial voice? Perhaps the taxonomic model of gatekeeper may reveal a more tangible force or embodiment for curatorial voice.

Why do museums consider the presence of curatorial voice? The museum audience expects to discern a voice of authority, curatorial voice, within an exhibit.

Tony Bennett (1995) postulates that museums can "arrange their displays so as to simulate the organization of the world—human and natural—outside the museum walls" (Bennett, 1995, p. 126). This arrangement of the exhibit is both physical and intellectual, weaving an important tale for the audience. Although Bennett reminds us "the question of how things get displayed in museums cannot be divorced from questions concerning the training of curators or the structures of museum control and management," this is merely a component of the creation of curatorial voice (p. 127).

Multiple aspects of the museum experience, beginning with the original objects and artists, evoke curatorial voice. As an exhibit is developed, the researchers, curators, and designers refine a story line for the public audience. As the audience imbibes the exhibit, it listens to the curatorial voices presented by the docents and museum volunteers. Yet there are more voices involved within the museum context; voices among the family members, friends, and random others who share the museum at that very moment. Ultimately, each individual will gather the swirling voices of those present, both within the exhibit and within themselves, to construct meaning. Curatorial voice is the message received by museumgoers throughout the exhibit, a message that may relay intent or museum authority (Leinhardt, Crowley, & Knutson, 2002). In order to reimagine curatorial voice, to in essence give shape to the formless disembodied voice of curatorial voice, a theory must be introduced: gatekeeper theory.

GATEKEEPER THEORY

Kurt Lewin, researcher and theorist in psychology, coined the term *gatekeeper* in 1947 (Deutsch, 1992). The gatekeeper was an individual considered to have authority or power, and characterized by partiality within a given context (Lewin, 1947, p. 145). Lewin targeted those with "key positions" within a household to examine, dubbing these prominent individuals *gatekeepers* (p. 143). Moreover, he identified these gatekeepers with the intent of developing formats for influencing the entire household through the gatekeepers. His investigation of household food provision led him to identify housewives as the gatekeepers for family nutrition. Lewin articulated his view that, should the government wish to change the nutrition habits of the population, then that change would have to be delivered through household gatekeepers: the housewives (Lewin, 1947). The concept of housewives may seem antiquated in the discussion of national nutrition today, yet the concept of gatekeeper is salient to the continued discussion of the provision of curatorial voice. If museums are to identify the sources of curatorial voice with the intent of influencing and shaping these voices, then a mechanism for identification must be developed. Research into the application of gatekeeper theory for curatorial voice may well lead to practical solutions for museums and society.

In the simplest format, gatekeeper theory describes the processes and players associated with the transfer of information within a given context. In the journey from one individual to another, information must pass through a gate (Barzilai-Nahon, 2008). The presence of a gatekeeper promotes a monitored situation in which the gatekeeper uses gatekeeping mechanisms, such as information selection, deletion, and hoarding, upon the intended recipients. These information recipients are "the gated" ones and may vary in the level of control they have over the information within the context (p. 1496). This information transfer theater, complete with gatekeeping actors and multidimensional relationships, is the basis of gatekeeper theory. Each gatekeeper has a rationale for the approach taken in exercising gatekeeping mechanisms, and much research has been done into these rationales (Barzilai-Nahon, 2009, p. 8). Museums are also theater, complete with actors and multidimensional relationships. It follows logically, then, that there is an application for gatekeeper theory within a museum context.

Gatekeeper theory may serve as a framework for evaluation of curatorial voice within a museum context. In using gatekeeper theory, caution should be applied to the interpretation of its usage. All too often, gatekeeper theory is associated with theories of social domination. However, the true power of gatekeeper theory is to reveal the influence of individuals within a context. A museum context will benefit from the application of gatekeeper theory for the evaluation of curatorial voice only if the theory is used for the revelation of relationships, not the exploitation of individuals. This usage draws upon the theoretical refinements made by Cheryl Metoyer-Duran. She traced gatekeeper theory (Lewin, 1947) through its use by Kurtz (1968) and by Monroe throughout the 1970s (Metoyer-Duran, 1991). Metoyer-Duran explored gatekeepers in ethnolinguistic communities, exploring their role as "persons who help individuals gain access to resources needed to solve problems" (Metoyer-Duran, 1991). Metoyer-Duran's ethnolinguistic gatekeepers acted as a bridge between distinctly different communities. The actions and motivations of these gatekeepers became the starting point for the development of a taxonomic model of gatekeepers. Metoyer-Duran's gatekeeper taxonomy, when charted, reveals the spectrum of possible gatekeeper roles: positive, negative, and neutral. Beyond the theoretical revelations, this taxonomy has applications for social inclusion/exclusion, information poverty, digital divide, information policy, and museum informatics.

As a continuation of this line of research, the development of a taxonomic model of curatorial voice is underway, applying gatekeeper theory as appropriate. An analysis of curatorial voice benefits from gatekeeper attributes such as the "facilitator," as described by Metoyer-Duran. She portrays the "facilitator" as having "internalized a set of experiences, attitudes, and values that are more positive than negative. The individual believes that information and information providers can make a positive contribution to his or her ability to affect change" (Metoyer-Duran, 1991, p. 333). Museum professionals are the guardians and presenters of information; it naturally follows that the ultimate goal of museum professionals is to facilitate the transfer of information from object to museum visitor. As the role of museums transforms from object oriented to story oriented, understanding the gatekeeping nature of curatorial voice, especially in a facilitating role, becomes essential. Gatekeeper theory regarding the facilitator may be applied to the practical application of evaluating curatorial voice. Insight into the intention and rationale of gatekeepers may be gained by the usage of qualitative techniques such as interviews, focus groups, and self-reflection journals. The more clearly museum gatekeepers can articulate their rationale and mechanisms, the more accurate the evaluation of curatorial voice will be.

The *facilitator* functions in a positive manner within the gatekeeper theory. Yet development of a taxonomic model of curatorial voice will also benefit from Metoyer-Duran's *the impeder* gatekeeper profile. As the name implies, the impeder uses gatekeeper functions to control, or block, the flow of information from the gated. The impeder views his or her "primary role as that of guarding cultural values and ensuring the maintenance of traditional social institutions and forms of interaction" (p. 334). Gatekeeper theory reveals a spectrum of individuals functioning as gatekeepers: the facilitator functions in a positive manner; the impeder functions in a negative manner; and *the unaffiliated* uses gatekeeping mechanisms in a neutral way. Metoyer-Duran's profile of the unaffiliated, gatekeepers who "lack formal affiliations to either local institutions or agencies," could further museum research into participatory museum visitors, as well as curatorial voice (p. 336; Simon, 2010). Gatekeeper profiles such as *the broker*, "facilitators who concurrently function in two cultures," linking two groups without adding value, are extremely valuable in a museum context (Metoyer-Duran, 1991, p. 337). Understanding roles and relationships among the sources of curatorial voice will assist in the promotion of practical solutions for museum community relationships. For example, another role is that of *the affiliated*, a gatekeeper that is "formally linked to other institutions, agencies, organizations," and could be identified as associated with local community groups (p. 338).

Of particular interest to the field of Library and Information Science, and in particular Museum Informatics, is Metoyer-Duran's gatekeeper profile of *the information professional*. The traditional role of many museum professionals is that of preservationist: collecting, curating, and displaying the objects of significance. The curatorial voice of archivists, librarians, and docents may be associated with the information professional, who is a trained individual, or representative of "professional knowledge workers and institutionally based information providers" (p. 338). However, the mission of museums is changing, and as museums move from object preservation to promotion of social agendas, an examination of curatorial voice should include the gatekeeper profile *leader/executive* (Chen, 2007). Metoyer-Duran also describes leaders who "facilitate change, and develop and implement strategy" (1991, p. 340). As museums hope to construct a socially relevant curatorial voice, practical evaluation strategies should include an examination of the leader profile, granting powerful insights for museums.

As museums struggle to understand their communities and their shifting role within society, the application of gatekeeper theory to museum community evaluation is salient. Museum researchers can apply gatekeeper profiles to the sources of curatorial voice that have been identified and give practical community insights to museums. A possible application could include qualitative studies of museum professionals, based on a taxonomic model of curatorial voice. In the milieu of the museum, multiple agents can perform gatekeeping: curators, exhibit designers, docents, volunteers, and the museum visitors. It is important to note that curatorial voice may also exist in the community gatekeepers who use their joint roles of museum volunteer and community leader, exercising mechanisms of connection. In this capacity, community gatekeepers act "as information intermediaries who move between cultures, linking their community members with alternatives or solutions" (Agada, 1999, p. 75).

Museums are as unique as the communities in which they exist. Their gatekeeping mechanisms most likely vary considerably from one museum to the next, reflecting this uniqueness. However, generalizable characteristics of these gatekeeping mechanisms exist; for example, curatorial voice is altered by the mechanism of object selection on the part of curators, curatorial voice is altered by the mechanism of text choice on the part of exhibit label designers, and curatorial voice is altered by the docent's attempt to explain an academic subject in layman's terms. Whether the curatorial voice resides in the museum professional or the community, certain general characteristics apply: curatorial voice can be directly expressed to the gated, reinterpreted for the gated, or blocked completely from the gated. For the purposes of reimagining curatorial voice in gatekeeper theory, and ultimately a new taxonomy, the gated should refer to the intended audience of the museum, the museum visitor(s). It is assumed that museum agents, such as docents, and curators do not function as gated in this scenario.

A major factor in understanding curatorial voice, gatekeeping, and museums is the changing nature of technology. The advances in technology impact studies in gatekeeping, and the pervasiveness of these technologies has created an unusual conundrum. Essentially, technology has changed the balance of power for curating. Previously explored concepts in museology, such as indigenous curation, have been reborn under the banners of "collaborative annotation," "crowd cataloguing," "crowd sourcing," and tagging (Bearman & Trant, 2005). As people and technology meet to curate, does curatorial voice become a shared role? And as curatorial voice metamorphoses, how does it act as a gatekeeper for the exhibit? Walsh foresaw a problem with the continuous existence of curatorial voice in a networked world, and described a world in which the gatekeeper role of the institution and curator is diminished by the democratic nature of the Internet (Walsh, 1997). The expansion of technology has created a linkage between curation, communication, and democracy. Examples of these connections are evidenced in the use of Twitter in the Arab Spring in 2011, and the creation of the "Activist New York" exhibit at the Museum of the City of New York (Herther, 2012, pp. 36–37). As technology empowers the masses to curate, how do we identify the curatorial voice? In an odd twist of fate, identification of curatorial voice is exceptionally more difficult to obtain today than it was a generation ago, as the disembodied voice is spread among a greater number of individuals.

Prior gatekeeper models have extracted the core attributes of gatekeepers for a given situation; Barzilai-Nahon (2008) has proposed a Network Gatekeeper Theory (NGT), in which traditional models of gatekeeping are recast for the modern networked world. In this model, the process of gatekeeping involves not only the selection of information, but an entire spectrum of information control processes (Barzilai-Nahon, 2008). These gatekeeping processes that are applicable to the role of curatorial voice include "selection, addition, withholding, display, channeling, shaping, manipulation, repetition, timing, localization, integration, disregard, and deletion" (Barzilai-Nahon, 2005, p. 249). Practical application of NGT is found at multiple points in the curation process; for example, an exhibit curator selects the objects for display only after an original selection process was made by the museum to collect certain items for preservation. The rationale for gatekeeping may be practical; for example, because museums have the ability to display physically only a small portion of their collection, it is inevitable that certain objects must be withheld from exhibit display. The act of choosing objects to be withheld is a gatekeeping process. Channeling of the intended message through the shaping of the exhibit story is an essential gatekeeping process performed by curators and docents. Repetition of important themes and the timing of the presentation of objects is an inherent part of the storytelling role of curators and a gatekeeping process. Interestingly enough, these gatekeeping processes may be visible not only in the physical museum but in the digital museum as well. As museums struggle to recreate themselves in the digital realm, an understanding of network gatekeeping processes of curatorial voice will be necessary.

Traditional gatekeeping models focus on the individual gatekeeper, yet NGT realizes that the mere possession of necessary attributes does not make an individual a gatekeeper. The role of gatekeeper is divided by Barzilai-Nahon into two dimensions, "authority and functional" (Barzilai-Nahon, 2005, p. 249). In disbursing the role of gatekeeper along the dimensional lines of authority and function, research may then examine the gatekeeping role of curatorial voice as it moves among people and institutions. In Network Gatekeeping Theory (NGT), the role of gatekeeper is not permanently established and may in fact move throughout the context. Nahon (2011) states, "even if one has the discretion to control information, the context determines the role" (p. 758), suggesting that at times the gated choose to be gated and designating an individual to be their gatekeeper. In stark contrast to traditional gatekeeper models, Nahon ventures to suggest "the emergence and maturity of the life cycle of gatekeepers in networks depend on a recursive relationship with the gated" (p. 761). Implications for research are drawn from examples of social media movements in which the gated have crowned their gatekeeper, essentially substituting one gatekeeper for another. Examples of gatekeeper exchanges are the Arab Spring use of Twitter in 2011 and the alignment of the gate by the gated through the use of Facebook's liking function (Nahon, 2011).

Nahon proposes that the widespread use of technology has granted researchers the opportunity to see the transformation of the transient elites, the dynamics of power, and the "duality of dependency and control" (p. 765). If Nahon is correct, the technology that distributes curatorial voice among the masses also grants researchers a new vantage point in the discovery of networks and power, and that the unit of analysis in gatekeeping is at the community level. The usage of NGT allows for the justification of analysis at the community level rather than the individual level.

MERGING OF CURATORIAL VOICE AND GATEKEEPER THEORY INTO A TAXONOMIC MODEL OF CURATORIAL VOICE

In the traditional gatekeeper theory, examination of communication channels was of prime importance, and the gatekeeper functioned as a producer and sender of information. An emphasis was placed upon the individual gatekeeper, their power, and the mechanisms they employed. This traditional view of gatekeeping may have proven useful in the analysis of individual museum settings, ones in which the only identified curatorial voice belonged to the original exhibit designer. However, the traditional view of gatekeeping no longer permits sufficient understanding of our intricately networked world. If Barzilai-Nahon is correct, and "information science's contribution to gatekeeping research is the conceptualization of gatekeepers as being immersed in communities whose voice they represent," then the application of gatekeeping theory to curatorial voice is valid (Barzilai-Nahon, 2009, p. 8). As the development of a taxonomic model of curatorial voice proceeds, research will draw upon the power of NGT.

MUSEUM AS PLACE

As institutions, museums have functioned as places of safety and voices of authority within society. Museums provide a public sphere for society both to observe and participate in a spectacle. In Bennett's genesis of the modern museum, panopticism is the primary goal: museum exhibits exist to instill desired behaviors in the lower, "less civilized" classes (Bennett, 1995). A museum visitor is observed by society and is observing society as he interacts with the exhibit. In a small way, Bennett alluded to the importance of the space between the exhibit and the visitor, and that in reality the museum visitor is part of the exhibit. John Falk divides the museum context into three different planes: the personal context, the sociocultural context, and the physical context (Falk & Dierking, 2000). For Falk, museums are spaces of situated learning in which individuals are impacted upon multiple levels. Falk declares "that the museum visitor experience is neither about visitors nor about museums and exhibitions, but rather is situated within that unique and ephemeral moment when both of these realities become one and the same—visitors are the museum and the museum is the visitor" (Falk, 2009, p. 35). In order to reenvision museum as place, in essence to capture a snapshot of that "unique and ephemeral moment," a theory must be introduced: SECI *ba* theory (p. 35).

KNOWLEDGE MANAGEMENT: SECI *BA*

Library and Information Science has made contributions to the field of knowledge management, especially in the arena of organizational and community knowledge. Knowledge management focuses on the creation and effective usage of organizational knowledge and attempts to regulate the knowledge of an organization, both explicit and tacit (Davenport & Prusak, 2000; Davenport as cited in Rowley, 1999). Tacit knowledge is generally considered to be internal to the individual, located within one's mind, and not easily articulated or externalized (Dalkir, 2005, p. 8). Explicit knowledge is typically regarded as knowledge that has been externalized from the individual and documented, often in a tangible format such as written or audio language (p. 8). According to Dalkir, knowledge exists in a powerful paradox; "the same content may be explicit for one person and tacit for another" (p. 8). This paradox is amplified by the fact that tacit knowledge is often perceived to be more valuable than explicit (p. 8). Explicit knowledge may be formatted for organization, transmission, and replication. Yet tacit knowledge has the unique "ability to collaborate, to share a vision, [and] transmit a culture" (p. 8). As museums seek to go beyond the basics of preservation and exhibition, research turns to knowledge management to focus on the ability to transmit culture.

Knowledge management enjoys the limelight, in part, due to the writings of Ikujiro Nonaka, famous for his development of the Socialization-Externalization-Combination-Internalization (SECI) model. In SECI, knowledge moves from tacit to explicit to tacit in a continuous knowledge-creation spiral (Nonaka, Toyama, & Konno, 2000). Starting with *socialization*, Nonaka proposes that tacit knowledge is shared between individuals through socialization, a process in which individuals "share personal knowledge and create a common place—or *ba*" (Nonaka & Konno, 1998, p. 43). As individuals create a shared space, tacit knowledge becomes articulated, and the process enters the *externalization* mode. During externalization, raw tacit knowledge becomes accessible, often documented, and translated into terms another individual can understand (Nonaka & Konno, 1998). The externalized knowledge of different individuals, now articulated, can be combined. *Combination*, as described by Nonaka and Konno, "involves the conversion of explicit knowledge into more complex sets of explicit knowledge" (Nonaka & Konno, 1998, p. 44). The final conversion process of SECI is *internalization*, a point in which explicit knowledge is now internalized. Individuals capture this new, often combined, explicit knowledge and place it into the category of tacit knowledge (Nonaka & Konno, 1998). Nonaka and Konno proposed that this SECI process occurs not only on the individual level but also on the corporate level. Communities, organizations, businesses, and societies all experience the SECI process as they create shared histories.

Nonaka and Konno explored the management and creation of knowledge as it is applied to business and industry settings, centering on an examination of the concept of *ba*. *Ba* is an ancient Japanese philosophical construct, an idea of "place," upon which Nonaka and Konno discern *ba* as "thought of as a shared space for emerging relationships" (Nonaka & Konno, 1998, p. 40). This existential concept, *ba*, can be physical, virtual, or a combination, leading the authors to stress that *ba* is not limited to traditional Western notions of place. More importantly than the boundless nature of *ba* is the sense that *ba* is steeped in meaning: *ba* is more than a neutral place, it is a "shared space that serves as a foundation for knowledge creation" (Nonaka & Konno, 1998, p. 40).

For Nonaka and Konno, knowledge is inseparable from *ba*, and should knowledge be removed from *ba*, "it turns into information, which can then be communicated interdependently from *ba*" (Nonaka & Konno, 1998, p. 41). How might museum as place be reenvisioned as *ba*? And what are the implications for such a reimagination of museum as place? Suspending the tangible portion of museum as place, *ba* signifies the horizon upon which knowledge may rise as the sun. What could be more significant to the understanding of museum context than to see it as the horizon upon which knowledge may rise?

Additionally, Nonaka and Konno believe that *ba* is a place of self-reflection: "*ba* is the world where the individual realizes himself a part of the environment on which his life depends" (p. 41). When visitors recognize themselves individually and collectively, have they not found the very essence of identity? Understanding the museum as place to be, *ba*, may lend insights into museum visitors' identity discovery process. In the research of museums and identity creation, Falk has generated a preliminary "identity-related visit motivation" model for predicting the museum visitor experience (Falk, 2009). Among his reasons for creating the new model, Falk felt the need to mitigate the traditional limitations concerning "temporal and spatial perspectives of the museum visitor experience" (Falk, 2009, p. 34). SECI *ba* may grant new understandings of these temporal and spatial perspectives within the museum experience. As identity is interconnected with both tacit and explicit knowledge, as well as individual and collective knowledge, it is important to recognize the all-too-silent partner in knowledge: place.

The historical and philosophical hallmarks of Nonaka's SECI *ba*, such as his views on explicit/tacit knowledge relationships, reveal the theory's ties to Japan. It is understood that the concept of *ba* distinctly reflects Nonaka's Japanese background, and this has brought criticism of Nonaka's work. This inherent cultural bias has also brought research into "the underlying sources of cultural embeddedness and the implications for their global diffusion" within the SECI *ba* model itself (Glisby & Holden, 2003; Hong, 2011, p. 199). In an ironic twist, these same cultural areas that constitute weakness for SECI *ba* lead directly to generating the strengths of the theory: in order for SECI *ba* to be transplanted across cultures, local personnel must play a prominent role in the maintaining of *ba*. An area of overlap between *ba* and gatekeeper theory is evident in Hong's description of the strength/weakness duality of the SECI model:

> The spread of knowledge needs to pass through successive stages of dis-embedding translation and local institutionalization, but it is the local actors who would undertake a more salient and performative role by acting as knowledge agents and re-embedding

> the ideas and materializing them into specific actions, which involves creativity, improvisation, enactment, blending and transformation of the taken-for-granted cultural rules since "to set something in a new place is to construct it anew." (Hong, 2011, p. 101)

In describing a weakness of the SECI model, local participation, Hong reveals the presence of information gatekeepers in the place *ba*. Despite criticisms, SECI *ba* has emerged in the business world as a key model for knowledge management. Understanding the context, or *ba*, of knowledge is a key element in the development of a model for the museum experience. The question arises: How will that model change as the museum becomes digital, and museum experience is no longer within the physical museum walls?

Knowledge management, as gatekeeper theory, has been impacted by rapidly changing technology (Blair, 2002). This influence comes at a cost, as the increased use of technology separates knowledge from the social context of its creation (Blair, 2002, p. 1024). This objectification of knowledge into information is a mirror image of the "museum effect," by which an object is created anew by its placement within the museum walls (Casey, 2003). Nonaka and Konno see technology in a more positive light, suggesting that technology has actually accelerated the knowledge process. According to Nonaka and Konno there is a digital form of *ba*, *cyber ba*, which occurs during the combination phase (Nonaka & Konno, 1998, p. 47). In the domain of *cyber ba*, a "combination of explicit knowledge is most efficiently supported in collaborative environments utilizing information technology" (p. 47). If knowledge management incorporates museum as place, *ba*, in both the physical and the cyber realms, and has gatekeepers of knowledge, there are significant implications for the view of curatorial voice within an exhibit.

CONCLUSION AND IMPLICATIONS FOR FURTHER RESEARCH

A museum exhibit is an engaging collection of social actors: it is an illusion of the cessation of time. The spaces created to tell the stories of the world appear static, consisting of glass-encased objects and formalized explanatory texts. Yet despite the attempt to yield authority to the voice of the museum through architectural design, museum docents, and security guards, museums are in fact a place of constant, irrepressible change. How better to capture this dynamic environment than to understand the museum as place in terms of *ba*, the shared space for knowledge creation and transfer, and the invisible omnipresent curatorial voice in a gatekeeper taxonomic model?

Further research in museum informatics will go beyond understanding the exchange of information in museums and seek to examine the co-construction of knowledge within the museum context, *ba*. Generation of a more holistic model of the museum experience will require the examination of the co-construction of identity within the museum context. This chapter is specifically related to the ongoing investigation into the role of information in the creation of individual and collective identities as a product of the museum experience. The ultimate goal of this research is to discern pathways for museums to facilitate their role in society, even as that role shifts.

REFERENCES

Agada, J. (1999). Inner-city gatekeepers: An exploratory survey of their information use environment. *Journal of the American Society for Information Science, 50*(1), 74–85.

Barzilai-Nahon, K. (2005). Network gatekeeping. In K. E. Fisher, S. Erdelez, & L. McKechnie (Eds.), *Theories of information behavior* (pp. 247–53). Medford, NJ: American Society for Information Science and Technology.

Barzilai-Nahon, K. (2008). Toward a theory of network gatekeeping: A framework for exploring information control. *Journal of the American Society for Information Science and Technology, 59*(9), 1493–1512. doi:10.1002/asi.20857

Barzilai-Nahon, K. (2009). Gatekeeping: A critical review. *Annual Review of Information Science and Technology, 43*, 433–78. doi:10.1002/aris.2009.1440430117

Bearman, D., & Trant, J. (2005). Social terminology enhancement through vernacular engagement: Exploring collaborative annotation to encourage interaction with museum collections. *D-Lib Magazine, 11*(9). doi:10.1045/september2005-bearman

Bennett, T. (1995). *The birth of the museum: History, theory, politics*. London; New York: Routledge.

Blair, D. C. (2002). Knowledge management: Hype, hope, or help? *Journal of the American Society for Information Science and Technology, 53*(12), 1019–28. doi:10.1002/asi.10113

Casey, V. (2003). *The museum effect: Gazing from object to performance in the contemporary cultural-history museum*. Paris, France: Archives & Museum Informatics Europe. Retrieved from http://www.archimuse.com/publishing/ichim03/095C.pdf.

Chen, H.-L. (2007). A socio-technical perspective of museum practitioners' image-using behaviors. *The Electronic Library, 25*(1), 18–35. doi:10.1108/02640470710729092

Dalkir, K. (2005). *Knowledge management in theory and practice*. Amsterdam; Boston, MA: Elsevier/Butterworth Heinemann.

Davenport, T. H., & Prusak, L. (2000, August). Working knowledge: How organizations manage what they know. *Ubiquity, 2000*, 2–es. doi:10.1145/347634.348775

Deutsch, M. (1992). Kurt Lewin: The tough-minded and tender-hearted scientist. *Journal of Social Issues, 48*(2), 31–43. doi:10.1111/j.1540-4560.1992.tb00881.x

Falk, J. H. (2009). *Identity and the museum visitor experience*. Walnut Creek, CA: Left Coast Press.

Falk, J. H., & Dierking, L. D. (1992). *The museum experience*. Washington, DC: Whalesback Books.

Falk, J. H. & Dierking, L. D. (2000). *Learning from museums: Visitor experiences and the making of meaning*. Walnut Creek, CA: AltaMira Press.

Glisby, M., & Holden, N. (2003). Contextual constraints in knowledge management theory: The cultural embeddedness of Nonaka's knowledge-creating company. *Knowledge and Process Management, 10*(1), 29–36. doi:10.1177/1350507611428853

Herther, N. K. (2012). Content curation: Quality judgment and the future of media and web search. *Searcher, 20*(7), 36–37.

Hong, J. F. L. (2011). Glocalizing Nonaka's knowledge creation model: Issues and challenges. *Management Learning, 43*(2), 199–215. doi:10.1177/1350507611428853

Kurtz, N. (1968). Gatekeepers: Agents of acculturation. *Rural Sociology, 33,* 64–70.

Leinhardt, G., Crowley, K., & Knutson, K. (Eds.). (2002). *Learning conversations in museums.* Mahwah, NJ: Lawrence Erlbaum.

Lewin, K. (1947). Frontiers in group dynamics: II. Channels of group life; social planning and action research. *Human Relations, 1*(2), 143–53. doi:10.1177/001872674700100201

Marty, P. (2007). The changing nature of information work in museums. *Journal of the American Society for Information Science and Technology, 58,* 97–107. doi:10.1002/asi.20443

Marty, P. (2009). An introduction to museum informatics. In P. Marty & K. B. Jones (Eds.), *Museum informatics: People, information, and technology in museums* (pp. 3–8). New York: Routledge.

Metoyer-Duran, C. (1991). Information-seeking behavior of gatekeepers in ethnolinguistic communities: Overview of a taxonomy. *Library and Information Science Research, 13,* 319–46.

Nahon, K. (2011). Fuzziness of inclusion/exclusion in networks. *International Journal of Communication, 5,* 756–72. Retrieved from http://ijoc.org/index.php/ijoc/article/view/1119/552.

Nonaka, I., & Konno, N. (1998). The concept of "ba": Building a foundation for knowledge creation. *California Management Review, 40*(3), 40–54.

Nonaka, I., Toyama, R., & Konno, N. (2000). SECI, ba and leadership: A unified model of dynamic knowledge creation. *Long Range Planning, 33*(1), 5–34. doi:10.1016/S0024-6301(99)00115-6

Rowley, J. (1999). What is knowledge management? *Library Management, 20*(8), 416–20. doi:10.1108/01435129910291175

Simon, N. (2010). *The participatory museum.* Santa Cruz, CA: Museum 2.0.

Walsh, P. (1997). The web and unassailable voice. Paper presented at Museums and the Web: An International Conference, Los Angeles, California, March 16–19, 1997. Retrieved from http://www.archimuse.com/mw97/speak/walsh.htm.

2

Restaging the Record

Opportunities for Collaboration in Event-Based Archivy

Tonia Sutherland

ABSTRACT

Bounded by and framed within the question of the role of contemporary archives in preserving performed expressions of cultural heritage, this chapter investigates the ways performance and intangible cultural heritage are fixed and represented in archives; offers new ways of thinking about the points in which archives and intangible cultural heritage intersect; and analyzes three distinct efforts to safeguard performative practices. Using case studies representative of digital humanities, local praxis, and international policy, the chapter identifies and explores existing approaches to documenting and safeguarding human performances as expressions of cultural heritage and offers three distinct solutions to the problem of archives and performance: a reframing of archival custody, creating tangible infrastructures for intangible cultural heritage, and supporting cultures of collaboration. This chapter argues that inherent tensions between the archives and the repertoire, while complex, are mitigable. Although archives and performance operate at opposite ends of temporal spectrums, the spaces between them are full of potential. These liminal spaces offer information professionals and performers compelling opportunities for creative engagement and collaboration, and this study sets the proverbial stage for these future undertakings.

INTRODUCTION

Bounded by and framed within the question of the role of contemporary archives in preserving performed expressions of cultural heritage, this chapter investigates the ways performance and intangible cultural heritage are fixed and represented in archives; offers new ways of thinking about the points in which archives and intangible cultural heritage intersect; analyzes three distinct efforts to safeguard performative practices; and offers three unique solutions to the problem of archives and intangible cultural heritage. Using case studies representative of digital humanities, local praxis, and international policy, the chapter identifies and explores existing approaches to documenting and safeguarding human performances as expressions of cultural heritage.

With an eye toward archival theory and practice, as well as an understanding of "the archive" grounded in performance studies, the cases discussed in this paper are: the Live Performance Simulation System's Virtual Vaudeville prototype; the Katherine Dunham Archives and the Dunham Technique; and the implementation of the United Nations Scientific, Educational and Cultural Organization's (UNESCO) 2003 Convention for the Safeguarding of the Intangible Cultural Heritage. These three cases, considered collectively, shed light on the perceived boundaries between archive and repertoire, allowing for a robust discussion of how contemporary archives can best support the documentation and preservation of performance as intangible cultural heritage. At the same time, each individual case provides a unique opportunity to interrogate event-based archivy and speak to a need for shifts or adaptations in archival theory and practice that better support documenting and safeguarding performance as a means of cultural expression.

The chapter therefore discusses issues of ownership; makes claims about the evidentiary properties of records; recommends implementing holistic, decentralized records policies and revisiting rigid custodial archival mandates; examines the cultures of collaboration that emerge around event-based archivy; and, finally, suggests tangible infrastructures for intangible cultural heritage. The chapter draws on data from interviews, archival records, historical newspapers, internal project documents, national and international grant proposals, international policy documents, and an array of secondary sources.

ARCHIVES AND PERFORMANCE

Existing research suggests that although archives provide societies with an opportunity to preserve cultural evidence, the preservation of temporal, event-based, and intangible cultural heritage such as performances, oral traditions, social practices, and festive events poses an ongoing challenge. While archives and other memory institutions tend to navigate the needs of those who work with intangible culture in traditional ways, such as the preservation of documentary evidence (photographs, audio and visual recordings, scripts, and other mediating artifacts), literature in the disciplines of anthropology, cultural studies, and performance studies suggests that these methods are both inadequate and exclusionary. For example, because Western archivists and archives tend to privilege tangible—and often text-based—records, cultures that rely on oral or other intangible modes of communication are often underrepresented in the archival corpus.

To work toward an understanding of how archivists and archival scholars approach matters of performance, it is necessary to define the scope of performance as it relates to modern archivy. The performing arts have traditionally been defined in academic circles as theater, dance, and music. Most fine arts schools and departments in higher education offer these three options as majors in their performing arts programs, which is to say that one can be a theater major, a dance major, or a music major. As a result, many university archives are familiar with the detritus of these kinds of performances and have developed systems with which to appraise, preserve, represent, and arrange provisions of access to those materials. The realm of performance studies, however, encompasses much more than the "traditional" modes of performance inherent in theater, dance, and music.

Emerging as academic departments in the mid-twentieth century, performance studies as a discipline challenges the boundaries of traditional performance and expands the definition of performance to include such things as oral traditions, rituals, commemorative rites, festivals, carnivals, and parades; the performance studies view of performance explodes the limits of performance to embody all of humanity's performative qualities and occasions. Performance studies, then, is based on the premise that anything can be studied as performance. As performance studies scholar Richard Schechner (2002) suggests, the methods and tools used in performance studies are derived from the social sciences, history, gender studies, psychoanalysis, semiotics, game theory, popular culture studies, and media studies.[1] Moreover, Victor Turner, whose work in the anthropology of ritual, symbols, and performance has inspired myriad scholarly interventions on the intersecting performative modes of play, drama, and community, posits that performance is critical to the reproduction of culture (Turner, 1990). Turner's cultural processualism recognizes that societal reproduction is dependent upon "organized moments" during which culture emerges or is produced. These generative moments speak to the temporality of cultural production; performance, as a mode of cultural production, is also defined by its temporal traits.

The temporal nature of performance naturally raises questions about the ability of archivists to capture and preserve performed works. Even though challenges arise when attempting to document performance in archives, many performing arts archives have been established through direct working experience with artists and live arts collections. As such, the materials that generally comprise their collections are related to the performance professions and do not have their counterparts in standard print collections. If, however, the archivally captured performance simply reflects tangible artifacts (e.g., costumes, scripts, light plots, and choreographic notation), to what extent can these records be considered an accurate record of the performance?

Simultaneously, because the archives only reflect tangible artifacts, there is a gap in the body of research that addresses archival theory outside the realm of cultural heritage that can be deemed tangible. Ephemeral art and cultural events have enormous social and cultural value, yet archives and other memory institutions do not have robust theoretical frameworks that support the preservation of event-based cultural heritage. Discussions about archives in the performance studies literature focus primarily on an "embodied archive," suggesting that modes of reception and transmission are best used to ensure the permanence of event-based cultural heritage. For example, performance studies scholar and New York University professor Diana Taylor, in her seminal book *The Archive and the Repertoire: Performing Cultural Memory in the Americas*, draws attention to what she deems a radical difference between archival traditions and what she calls "the repertoire," an aggregate of embodied gestures and practices. This chapter hypothesizes that while such a disconnect might currently exist, contemporary archivists might reconceptualize archival traditions such as custodial relationships with records creators, as well as embrace emerging fields such as the digital humanities, creating new possibilities for archives and archivists to embrace the work of preserving or safeguarding event-based and other intangible cultural heritage. Performance, as a temporal mode of cultural production, is particularly at risk for loss over time. Reframing performative acts as archival evidence mitigates concerns about the completeness of the record. Working with performers as communities of practice to better understand the evidentiary properties of performed records also addresses concerns about loss. Taylor's work lays a foundation for understanding the gaps between the archive and the repertoire. Furthering Taylor's analysis, this study maps the gaps between archive and repertoire, finding points of connection and opportunities for intervention.

THE EVIDENTIARY PROPERTY OF RECORDS

Traditionally, *evidence* in the archival sense has been defined as "the passive ability of documents and objects and their associated contexts to provide insight into the processes, activities, and events that led to their creation for legal, historical, archaeological, and other purposes" (Gilliland-Swetland, 2000, p. 10). The concept of *evidence* in archival discourse appears as early as Hilary Jenkinson's description of the archivist as one committed to the "sanctity of evidence." Archival pioneer Theodore Schellenberg's articulation of evidence recognizes a distinction between the evidential and the informational value of a record, suggesting that the evidential value of a record lies in the documentary significance of the circumstances of its creation while its informational value is more closely tied to its content.[2] Throughout the 1990s and during the early part of the twenty-first century, confronted with the advent of electronic records, many archival scholars argued that preserving a record's evidential value was the primary role of the archivist as recordkeeper.[3] Contemporary archival scholars have problematized the discourse on records and evidence, suggesting that a preoccupation with evidence and reliability in archival records has inappropriately narrowed the lens through which archival work is viewed.[4]

Jeannette Bastian (1999) proffers a theoretical framework that creates a space wherein performed cultural events (such as pre-Lenten Carnival celebrations in Central America and the West Indies) are signifying objects and, by extension, documents. Simultaneously, archival scholar and educator Richard J. Cox (2000) suggests in his book, *Managing Records as Evidence and Information*, that "the physical entity of the document, which in the past dictated aspects of access, security, and maintenance, has so changed as to call all such functions into serious re-evaluation as to their applicability" (p. 6). Although Cox is referring to electronic records, the assertion holds true for event-based records: the physicality of the record is secondary to its function as evidence of a transaction or activity. Extending the scholarship of Bastian and Cox, this chapter argues, in part, that that the evidentiary qualities of a record supersede its need to be text based. The Virtual Vaudeville prototype is one example.

CASE ONE: VIRTUAL VAUDEVILLE

This case study investigates one early digital humanities project that sought to revolutionize present-day representations of past performances by moving a historical performance into a digital environment. The objective of the Virtual Vaudeville project was to use digital technology to address a problem fundamental to performance scholarship and pedagogy: how to represent and communicate the phenomenon of live performance using media. For the project team, led by University of Georgia professor David Saltz, this problem was especially pressing because the objective was to represent a performance tradition from the past (Saltz, 2001).

The Virtual Vaudeville project, then, was conceived as a response to the problem of performing arts archivy. A prototype of the Live Performance Simulation System, it is the product of collaboration among a diverse group of U.S. scholars, including computer scientists, 3D modelers and animators, and theater practitioners and historians of both theater and music. The prototype is, in essence, a single-user 3D computer game that allows users to enter a virtual theater to watch a simulated performance. Funded by a sizeable three-year grant from the National Science Foundation in 2001, the project sought to use digital technologies to answer the question: "Is it possible to archive a live performance?" Using motion capture technology—among others—the project aimed to represent a historical performance tradition using a virtual reality environment to simulate the experience of attending a live performance. These scholars, without the benefit of an archivist among them, wanted to proffer an archive of experience, one that would incorporate not only elements of sight and sound but also the interactive nature of a live audience. Scholars immersed in the Virtual Vaudeville project were, in part, testing hypotheses about historical performance practices and engaging with historical performance traditions as performance rather than through the mediation of scripted theater or film.

The Virtual Vaudeville project aimed to test the potential of virtual environments to provide truly high-quality theater experiences to remote audiences. The central objective of Virtual Vaudeville was to simulate a feeling of "liveness" in a virtual theater environment: the "sensation of being surrounded by human activity onstage, in the audience and backstage, and the ability to choose where to look at any given time (onstage or off) and to move within the environment" (Saltz, 2001). In what was a radical departure from existing methods, the Virtual Vaudeville team proposed using motion capture technology to capture real-world performances by professional, highly skilled actors, singers, dancers, acrobats, and musicians, thus re-creating a historical performance for a digital environment. In so doing, they hoped to make important advances in the design and implementation of virtual environments, advances that would build on prior successes in creating photo-realistic simulations of real 3D environments by introducing a large quantity of complex human performance data. Virtual Vaudeville was intended to constitute an invaluable work of applied scholarship, and provide an "unprecedented resource for visualizing past performances and testing hypotheses about historical performance practices" (Saltz, 2001).[5]

The prototype successfully demonstrates, in a historical snapshot, the potential of motion capture technology and digitizing historical performances. It has proven its educational value as it has been used in introductory theater courses at the University of Pittsburgh and the University of Georgia. At the same time, Virtual Vaudeville can, itself, be read as an archive of a point of view locked in time of historical work done in the 1990s. Virtual Vaudeville is also an archive of the questions people were asking at the time—questions about acting, historical spaces, and richer learning experiences. The website is the only place where all of this information is collocated, making it at the very least a digital repository of vaudeville materials. Virtual Vaudeville is an artifact of what was technologically available at the time.[6] Historically, particularly with the theater architecture, the prototype arguably takes on additional archival qualities. The model itself is evidence, as the blueprints that were created and the photographs that Saltz took were then mapped into the virtual reality of the prototype.

The archives that supported the creation of the Virtual Vaudeville prototype were the Library of Congress, the Harvard theater collection, the performing arts library at New York Public Library/Lincoln Center, and finally, the archives of the University of Illinois at Urbana-Champaign Library. These collections, all print and digitized artifacts, do not capture or represent vaudeville in the same visual, experiential way that the Virtual Vaudeville prototype does. Although Virtual Vaudeville is mediated through the lens of theater and music historians, 3D animators, game designers, and the content police at the National Science Foundation, it nonetheless provides an aggregated view, based on historical, archival evidence, of the cultural artifact that is American vaudeville.

Although performing arts archives supported the creation of the Virtual Vaudeville prototype, its creators were, from the outset, dissatisfied with the existing archival artifacts available to them. That a group of performance studies scholars sought to create their own archive, without the benefit of an archivist, speaks perhaps to the inadequacy of the archival endeavor where event-based cultural heritage is concerned.

Virtual Vaudeville is an example of a nontextual record that has clear and specific evidentiary properties and exists outside a custodial archival paradigm. How, then, can contemporary archives, archives that are perhaps less constrained by an insistence on the custody of records, reposition themselves to support the preservation of performed culture? Some compelling examples already exist.

CASE TWO: THE KATHERINE DUNHAM ARCHIVES AND "THE DUNHAM TECHNIQUE"

Known through journalistic common coinage as "Katherine the Great" or "Anthropological Katie," Katherine Dunham was born in Chicago in June 1909. She completed her PhD at the University of Chicago in anthropology—focusing on the dances of the African diaspora—in 1936. Her first dance company, Ballet Nègre, was established in 1930 as the first Negro ballet company in the United States.

Dunham was trained in classical ballet, with her formative training influenced most by artists such as Ludmilla Speranzeva and Vera Mirova. Speranzeva, who had come to America with the Chauve-Souris, a Franco-Russian vaudeville troupe, was one of the first ballet teachers to accept black dancers as students. Dunham was particularly interested in dances and rhythms as they applied to her own ethnic and cultural background, and upon entering the University of Chicago she began teaching her own style of dance, in part to explore her theoretical beliefs about the rhythms of the Negro people and in part to meet the financial demands of private university education.

By 1932, Dunham had consulted with her former ballet teacher, Ludmilla Speranzeva, about her desire to open a school for young, black dancers where she would teach them about their African heritage. Speranzeva advised her to forgo ballet, to focus instead on modern dance, and, most importantly, to develop her own style (Library of Congress, *Special Presentation: Katherine Dunham Timeline: 1932*). In 1935 Dunham was awarded a Julius Rosenwald Fellowship to conduct fieldwork in the Caribbean, where she studied the survival of traditional African dance in the face of European colonization and acculturation. Nervous about the disappearance of dances from many "tribal" and "folk" communities, Dunham constructed new kinetic models that tested traditional paradigms of "high" cultural expression (Johnson, 2005). The Dunham Technique, Dunham's unique dance pedagogy, emphasizes cultural contextualization in movement. Sharing the principles of this technique was among the primary objectives of the Dunham School in New York City—established at the end of World War II, the Dunham School offered an extensive curriculum in the humanities that combined dance, drama, languages, philosophy, and anthropology.[7] This pedagogical attention to culturally informed movement, also evident in later Dunham institutions, forms the basis of the Dunham Technique.

Katherine Dunham died in 2006 at the age of ninety-six after a long and celebrated career. One of the primary ways in which Dunham-trained dancers seek to continue her legacy and preserve the Dunham Technique is through codification. In 1986, Albirda Rose, cofounder of the Institute for Dunham Certification, spent six months with Katherine Dunham poring over her materials in preparation for writing *Dunham Technique: A Way of Life*, a book that codifies the Dunham Technique through choreological notation. As part of this process, Rose endeavored to work with master instructors of the Dunham Technique to attain a level of fixity for both the terminology and movements associated with the Dunham Technique (A. Rose, personal communication, November 19, 2013). For example, Joyce Aschenbrenner's book *Katherine Dunham: Reflections on the Social and Political Contexts of Afro-American Dance*, a critical study of Dunham's work, was published through the Congress on Research in Dance in 1981; Rose used Aschenbrenner's choreographic critiques of Dunham's work from the 1940s through the 1960s, along with drawings and descriptions of the Dunham Technique done by Dunham dancer Lavinia Williams, as a foundation on which to build her attempts at codification. Rose also looked to Dunham's lesson plans and the curriculum from Dunham's Performing Arts Training Center in East St. Louis, Missouri. Finally, she incorporated data from moving images of instruction in the Dunham Technique and of Dunham Company rehearsals.

Ensuring that the Dunham Technique endures is now handled by committee; Theo Jamison, Keith Williams, and Rachel Tavernier, all trained by Dunham at the Performing Arts Training Center, currently head the Institute for Dunham Certification. There is also a DVD of the Dunham Technique housed at the Library of Congress. Together with Rose's book, the DVD and the embodied knowledge of Dunham's dancers create additional layers of codification. Codification is an attempt to bring all of Dunham's work under the same umbrella: it is a way to make it last and to perpetuate the work. As Dunham-trained Point Park University dance professor Ron Hutson suggests, to properly safeguard the Dunham Technique, a marriage of archive and repertoire are essential:

> I think that the written word has value, I am a scholar, but I think some people who are in the field of dance are totally body-oriented and I think some of us, and I think that we are fortunate, are physically as well as verbally oriented and expressive. The scholarly aspects, the written aspects, are important. It helps people who haven't danced—and even people who have danced—understand dance. That's one of the things that gives ballet and modern dance such dignity, is that there is this whole body of recorded information on them. They are all codified. And people don't look at Afrocentric dance forms, art forms, as having this kind of codification. There's a place for that. But there's a transference of information from body to body that's very much like oral traditions. Oral tradition has been important since the dawn of time, and even though we write things down now, we codify, the oral tradition still works. From body to body as a learning tool, that still works too. (R. Hutson, personal communication, October 2, 2013)

Around the globe one can find examples of codified gestures that, with the proper visual literacy, can be read, understood, and used to transmit knowledge. Sign language is one such example, and, as Hutson suggests, ballet is another. Like sign language, ballet is comprised of a set vocabulary of movements that can be combined in varying ways to convey meaning and transmit knowledge. When archives take custody, however, performed art is flattened and becomes two-dimensional, often being relegated to folders, boxes, and shelves. To have performance endure, information professionals need to allow artists to maintain their own work in the most appropriate ways. In the case of the Dunham archives, archival repositories maintain these two-dimensional traces of Dunham's work, while the broader cultural dimensions of Dunham's work survive in the minds and bodies of her dancers. The apparent duality between archive and repertoire meet here: Dunham's work endures because of *both* archive and repertoire, each informing the other and tempering any gaps between them. Taking an advisory rather than a custodial role and providing the necessary infrastructures—such as standards and built systems—is one way that archives can help to safeguard performed acts and other articulations of intangible cultural heritage. The United Nations Educational, Scientific and Cultural Organization has modeled this noncustodial relationship in the policy document that is the 2003 Convention to Safeguard the Intangible Cultural Heritage. One can see evidence of this relationship at work in the countries that have ratified and deployed the convention.

CASE THREE: THE UNITED NATIONS EDUCATIONAL, SCIENTIFIC AND CULTURAL ORGANIZATION'S (UNESCO) 2003 CONVENTION TO SAFEGUARD THE INTANGIBLE CULTURAL HERITAGE

Using three global examples—Belgium, Newfoundland and Labrador (Canada), and Trinidad and Tobago, this case study investigates the role archives play in safeguarding performance as intangible cultural heritage. Intangible cultural heritage is a term that has emerged out of the varying proclamations, recommendations, conventions, charters, and codes addressing cultural heritage issues over the past century. As the significance of human interaction with cultural heritage "objects" became more apparent, the language of cultural heritage documents shifted to include considerations of more ephemeral notions of heritage, such as performance. UNESCO defines intangible cultural heritage (ICH) as "a living form of heritage which is continuously recreated and which evolves as we adapt our practices and traditions in response to our environment. It provides a sense of identity and belonging in relation to our own cultures" (UNESCO, 2003). UNESCO's concept of intangible cultural heritage encompasses oral traditions and expressions, performing arts, social practices, rituals, festive events, knowledge and practices concerning universe and nature, and traditional craftsmanship.

In 2003, UNESCO adopted the Convention for the Safeguarding of Intangible Cultural Heritage. The convention is an interventive tool; it is a normative model that at the same time raises issues of value, threat, and moral obligation and informs people's relationships to their own cultural practices. As such, the ICH convention was conceived as a "permissive document." Much of the language in the text of the convention is nonprescriptive; this was designed to allow national governments flexibility in their approaches to implementation. However, the convention does require ratifying states parties to adopt "appropriate measures" at the national and international level to "encourage and foster all forms of international cooperation aimed at safeguarding intangible cultural heritage" (UNESCO, 2003). The convention, in part, mandates that state parties pursue policies that value intangible cultural heritage because, per UNESCO, intangible cultural heritage is a *mainspring* of cultural diversity and a guarantee of sustainable development. Each country has chosen to deploy the convention differently. A key component of the convention was the mandate that requests for inclusion and consideration for safeguarding an intangible cultural heritage element originate from the group or community in whose hands care of the cultural "object" currently fell. In this way, UNESCO hoped to remove the possibility of cultural appropriation and the intentional misuse of cultural heritage.

Belgium

In Belgium, heritage is considered collective property. Heritage communities must come to a consensus on the meaning and function of their cultural expressions. The designation of a cultural expression as "heritage," then, is temporally fixed and defined by both geography and community. This conceptual fluidity allows for subsequent generations to reconsider the value of a given cultural expression, thereby meeting another requirement of UNESCO's ICH convention: that communities be responsible for designating their own heritage and determining its cultural value.

In deploying the 2003 ICH convention, the government of Flanders, Belgium, began with a national inventory. Flanders responded to the UNESCO ICH convention by introducing regulations, such as the Flemish Parliament Act, on the basis of which the *Inventaris Vlaanderen voor Immaterieel Cultureel Erfgoed* (Inventory of the Intangible Cultural Heritage in Flanders) could be created. The *Inventaris Vlaanderen* (Flanders Inventory) served as an awareness-raising mechanism in regard to the communities, groups, and individuals concerned.

The Flemish Parliament Act introduced a practical and theoretical model whereby one designated organization is subsidized and serves to anchor a heritage community; that is, to guide the heritage community and to maintain and disseminate knowledge and expertise. Archives, libraries, and museums, as cultural heritage institutions, are expected to fulfill this function, and they are mandated to make available the disciplinary knowledge they have at their disposal. In Flanders, the government aims to create a network of cultural heritage organizations that addresses all aspects of preservation and access, and that negotiates the relationship between heritage communities and the general public (Government of Flanders, 2010). The organizations within this network prepare and draft application files for inclusion in the Flemish ICH inventory and on UNESCO ICH lists and registers. As such, Flemish cultural heritage centers, organizations for popular culture, and nationally recognized museums and archives are required to share their knowledge and expertise with heritage communities, fulfill the aforementioned anchor function, and develop activities that are culturally relevant for all of Flanders. There is an additional *international* education and outreach mandate as well; these institutions are expected to elaborate ICH activities in an international context, provide heritage communities with access to international expertise, and encourage the heritage community to develop best practices (Government of Flanders, 2010).

To achieve these goals, the Government of Flanders (2010) has proposed creating an ICH database. This relational database would house inventories, place a central focus on interaction, allow for the exchange of knowledge and expertise, and emphasize individual elements as well as relationships between and among ICH elements. As it is currently conceived, data entry would fall to the heritage communities, assisted by cultural heritage organizations. Archives, libraries, and museums are expected to support heritage communities' safeguarding decisions, establish links with experts, identify other elements with similar characteristics, and work with heritage communities to "transmit processes that belong to the same heritage group." At the same time, these institutions will be expected to define projects based on data in the database and ensure an appropriate clustering of elements and best practices. The database is expected to be managed by a consortium ("whether or not with its own legal personality"), and the Flemish community has been designated as the owner of the database. This proposal is based on an existing, successful model; *Archiefbank Vlaanderen* (Archives Database Flanders) is organized in this same way, and experience with this database offers sufficient evidence for the government of Flanders that such a system of decentralized entry and joint management is effective.

Newfoundland and Labrador, Canada

In 2006, The Heritage Foundation of the Canadian province of Newfoundland and Labrador held an intangible cultural heritage conference that was followed in 2008 by the establishment of an intangible cultural heritage office and codified strategies for the preservation of living heritage. At the time, however, the initiative lacked the personnel to oversee and enact the new strategies. When Dale Jarvis, a folklorist in the province who is now the Intangible Cultural Heritage Development officer, was installed in the ICH office of the Heritage Foundation, programming workshops and community events such as festivals were established to promote ICH in the province (D. Jarvis, personal communication, January 30, 2014).

Newfoundland and Labrador considers the work of safeguarding intangible cultural heritage "public sector folklore." As such, the province has adopted a strategy for safeguarding that is aligned with the UNESCO ICH convention, but remains unique to Newfoundland and Labrador. The strategy has four components: *inventorying*, as is mandated by the convention and is effectively an act of records creation; *celebration*, such as festivals and other programs that draw attention to traditions and/or tradition bearers; *transmission*, or projects that encourage the transmission of skills and knowledge between generations and within communities; and *cultural industry*, or building a sustainable environment for intangible cultural heritage. Each program that originates in the ICH office is designed to incorporate as many of these four elements as possible. A celebration, therefore, might also include an opportunity for skill building and will be recorded as part of the province's ethnographic record (D. Jarvis, personal communication, January 30, 2014).

Among the successes of the Newfoundland and Labrador ICH program is an annual folklife festival, modeled after the Smithsonian Folklife Festival that takes place annually on the National Mall in Washington, D.C. (D. Jarvis, personal communication, January 30, 2014). Similarly, the Heritage Foundation has established a festival centered on the Christmas tradition of Mummering. Mummering is a disguise tradition wherein celebrants travel door to door during the twelve days of Christmas in disguise, in the hope of fooling their neighbors. Mummering was a popular tradition in rural Newfoundland and Labrador, the decline of which was spurred by population decline, an aging population, and the effects of urbanization. The Heritage Foundation chose to reinvigorate this dying tradition through creating a festival. In the 1800s, Newfoundland and Labrador province was known for their Mummer's parades; however, prior to this intervention, a parade had not been held in over a century. The decision was therefore made to run a month-long festival celebrating the Mummer tradition, including lectures, workshops, costume parties, and, of course, a parade.

Despite successes, however, scope remains an issue; without national government buy-in, the ICH office in Newfoundland and Labrador remains small, as does their budget. They are, therefore, heavily reliant on community organizations and other heritage organizations. They maintain strong partnerships with umbrella groups such as the museums organization and the archives organization. Depending on the project, the nature of the collaboration might be with an individual archive, museum, historical society, town council, food security network, or community center. If a community organization is interested in a living heritage project, the Heritage Foundation is willing to work in partnership with them, offering interventions and support as they are able.

In Newfoundland and Labrador, the ICH office works collaboratively with the archives association (The Association of Newfoundland and Labrador Archives—ANLA). Recently, ANLA conducted a collections survey that uncovered unexpected ethnographic material, including oral history and video collections. The ICH office worked with ANLA to develop a workshop that they titled "Boxes Under the Bed." The central idea behind the workshop was that archives "had these boxes of stuff that they had collected over time that had been just gathering dust, no one was actually seeing it." For Dale Jarvis, whose mantra was that in order for stories to live they "can't just be in archives, they need to be back out in the community," this level of access was insufficient (D. Jarvis, personal communication, January 30, 2014).

Digitization is the primary means of preservation and access that countries appear to be undertaking to safeguard the archival detritus of ICH expressions. For example, the Heritage Foundation reports working with a local historical society archive that had received a donation of a large audio collection. The donor had been a former broadcaster from the 1950s to the 1980s and had done hundreds of hours of interviews with people in small communities. The Heritage Foundation worked to secure funding for a co-op student to digitize and make available this large oral history collection. This kind of collaboration between local archival institutions and the ICH office extends to ICH projects as well.

Trinidad and Tobago

Trinidad and Tobago has interpreted the convention to mean that they must create an enabling environment in which intangible cultural heritage can flourish. For them, ratifying the convention, agreeing to the provisions of the convention, and creating this enabling environment are all synonymous: by signing the convention they have agreed to create an enabling environment for individuals, communities, and groups for the continuity of their intangible cultural heritage (A. Blake, personal communication, October 31, 2013).

Faced with the knowledge that existing records such as documents and recordings are underpublicized and the public is unaware of their existence, Trinidad and Tobago's Cultural Research Unit, housed within the Ministry of Arts and Multiculturalism, has proposed an institute—the Remember When institute—to make provisions for public access to the country's intangible cultural heritage. Although the physical entity has not yet been established, the proposed institute will work in partnership with the country's other cultural establishments: the National Library, the National Museum, the National Art Gallery, the National Carnival Commission, the Carnival Institute of Trinidad and Tobago, and the National Archives. The Remember When Institute is intended to function as a "repository for the memories of Trinidad and Tobago"; in its current incarnation (a website), it holds information about the Cultural Research Unit's extensive audio-visual library that contains audio recordings, video recordings, and oral histories (A. Blake, personal communication, October 31, 2013). The National Culture Council was responsible for creating the recordings, of which there are thousands, now housed in the offices of the Ministry of Arts and Multiculturalism, rounding out what the Cultural Research Unit calls their "cultural archive." These recordings are slowly being digitized, but the process is a minute-by-minute transfer, and one man does all of this digitization work.

The Remember When Institute is intended to be an instrument that will reflect Trinidad and Tobago's intangible cultural heritage; as such, its creators sought to model it after an existing international policy, consulting with cultural resource managers at the Smithsonian Institute and the Jamaican Memory Bank. The goal for the institute is to be semiautonomous, although it will remain under the purview of the Ministry of Arts and Multiculturalism (A. Blake, personal communication, October 31, 2013).

ANALYSIS

The following section considers the cases above and discusses three distinct themes that have emerged as solutions to the problem of archives and intangible cultural heritage. The first is a renegotiation of the custodial relationship between archives and heritage communities. Next is the recognition of a need to create tangible infrastructures for intangible cultural heritage. Finally, there is a discussion of the cultures of collaboration that have developed in each of the case studies above.

Heritage Communities and Archival Custody

In each of the cases selected for this study, archival institutions maintain a portion of the record while the community or community of practice retains another: the repertoire of embodied practices that form the remainder of the complete record. This study has evidenced that the traces of performance that remain in archival repositories are those that can be read as fixed text or fixed images; the repertoire, by contrast, is a living and mutable archive of the identifying characteristics and, often, the cultural inheritances of a given community. For some communities these inheritances may come in the form of narrative or music traditions. For others, it may be a traditional dance. For others still, the inheritance may be a "low art" form of variety theater that allows for an escape on a Friday afternoon. Regardless of the form of the cultural inheritance, these communities, who perform, operate without traditional archival intervention. Nonetheless, they have found solutions to problems that archivists consider uniquely archival. Issues such as preservation and provisions for access are at the center of discussions about the "repertoire" in each of the three case studies. These issues are, indeed, archival. They require a renegotiation of a traditional archival paradigm: archival custody.

Fifteen years ago, in 1999, Jeannette Bastian, then a doctoral candidate in Library and Information Science at the University of Pittsburgh, wrote a dissertation that interrogated issues of archival custody and access in the Danish West Indies. Bastian noted then, at the turn of the twentieth century, that for colonized people, ownership of their records assists in negotiating identities and forming collective memories. Extending this argument to address concerns generated by what was already an escalation in the production of electronic records, Bastian (1999) concluded, in part, that "solutions to [dilemmas of archival custody] depend on redefining the principle of custody itself in broader more inclusive terms that will accommodate societal needs for access to collective memory."[8] This study, building on Bastian's work, further suggests that not only are provisions of access to the records of one's past critical to developing stable social and cultural societal structures, the act of ownership itself is closely linked to some communities' experiences of agency and justice.

In the United States, for example, slavery remains an issue fraught with complex feelings and deeply held beliefs. It is an undisputed fact, nonetheless, that slaves were property, and as such, they could not themselves own property. When freed, African Americans were legally enabled to exist politically and economically; one of the ways this new freedom was expressed was through the simple act of ownership. Owning things was a means by which to prove one's existence, to work against the notion that a person could have so little economic control as to effectively disappear.

Discussions about ownership, custody, and access converge in archival thinking where definitions of "archival" mandate the physical custody of records in an archival repository. Custody, in U.S. archivy, means the assumption by archival repositories of both physical possession (physical custody) and legal responsibility (legal custody) of records from the records-creators. Despite debates over the appropriateness of custodial archival relationships in the face of mounting pressures to manage an ever-increasing influx of electronic records, this custodial standard persists in North American archivy.

Electronic, digital, and digitized records are not the only record type, however, that resist traditional custodial solutions. Performed acts—whether they be traditional performing arts, expressions of intangible cultural heritage, or other modes of performance—also resist the custodial paradigm. In part as a result of the temporal nature of performance, determining which part(s) of the record should cross the archival threshold becomes a complex negotiation between record-creator and archivist. How, for example, does one decide which is the true representation of any given performance?

Each of the cases in this study details a relationship between the archive and the repertoire and suggests a scholarly need to critically disrupt issues of archival custody. In the case of Virtual Vaudeville, the project team found it difficult to locate archival materials because capturing popular entertainment was not an archival priority in the United States during the vaudeville era. Project team members differentiate vaudeville as "popular" theater rather than "legitimate" theater, further suggesting that at the turn of the century vaudeville would not have been considered important enough to cross an archival threshold (S. Kattwinkel, personal communication, August 7, 2013). That the Virtual Vaudeville team, with the benefit of hindsight, would recognize the breadth and depth of cultural expression inherent in vaudeville performances as an educative tool in a culturally charged moment (the U.S. "culture wars" of the 1990s) could never have been predicted by turn-of-the-century American archivists—of whom there were few and whose mandate was largely the care of historical manuscripts and government records. Vaudeville performers, likewise, were too busy traveling and performing—*creating art*—to be concerned with preserving their work for future generations. Vaudeville, then, is effectively a lost cultural moment, the value of which took a million dollars in federal and state funding to reclaim and reinvigorate.

Similarly, Katherine Dunham's anthropological recordings and the origination of the Dunham Technique are one woman's efforts to avoid the same cultural obsolescence for an underserved community. Dunham's attempts to educate African Americans in the United States about their own cultural inheritances through performative practices were, in effect, her efforts at creating an archive. Although Diana Taylor's framework relegates the Dunham Technique to the realm of repertoire, in the absence of archival intervention the Dunham Technique functions effectively as a repository of cultural knowledge: each codified, culturally informed movement contributes to a gestural language that, with the proper visual literacy, can be read, understood, and transmitted. The more recent addition of the Dunham archives adds an additional layer of documentation and codification; the Dunham Technique, however, is the primary repository. This repository exists outside the framework of traditional archivy. There is no custodial relationship between dancers' bodies and archives, nor is a relationship such as this necessary for the continuation of the Dunham Technique. Rather, Dunham Masters (those certified to train others in Dunham Technique) work collaboratively with archivists to maintain the Dunham archives that *support the continuity* of the Dunham Technique.

This noncustodial, advisory arrangement is echoed in the countries that have deployed the Convention to Safeguard the Intangible Cultural Heritage. In each of the sites in this study (Belgium, Newfoundland and Labrador, and Trinidad and Tobago), national and private archives work to provide advisory support to heritage communities in safeguarding their own traditions. The detritus of these traditions already appear infrequently in archival repositories; working collaboratively with heritage communities increases the scope of traditional archival documentation and, at the same time, provides crucial professional expertise in information management and stewardship to communities who lack this knowledge. For example, the Heritage Foundation of Newfoundland and Labrador works closely with communities to teach basic technical skills such as digitization, while in Trinidad and Tobago, the Ministry of Arts and Multiculturalism offers training in conducting oral histories and video documentation. This new documentation contributes substantially to the archival record and helps to address existing gaps and vagaries.

Noncustodial agreements do not necessarily require archives and archivists to abandon notions of public access. In each of these three cases, provisions of access were paramount to the communities working with performed acts. For Virtual Vaudeville, improving education about the sociocultural aspects of vaudeville and providing for broader access to more performance-based archival materials were among the most important project goals. For Katherine Dunham, creating the Dunham Technique was, in large part, about providing future generations of African Americans with access to their own cultural inheritance. Finally, for UNESCO, ensuring access to intangible cultural heritage is embedded in the language of the convention itself.[9] How, then, do archivists, cultural resource managers, and other information scientists provide this support and ensure access without maintaining physical custody? This study suggests that one solution is for information scientists to provide tangible infrastructures for performed acts and other intangible cultural heritage.

Tangible Infrastructures for Intangible Cultural Heritage

Understanding how cultural knowledge is produced, transferred, and maintained is not only the purview of archival studies but is also closely tied to the broader information profession. One way that cultural knowledge is transferred and maintained is through human interaction. Seminal historian and philosopher Walter Ong suggests that valuable cultural information is available in sound, bodies, and performances through fixed, formulaic phrasings that aid memory. Ong (1982) asserts that the knowledge stored in bodies passes from generation to generation through performance; he further maintains that the way a culture stores and retrieves its valuable information is specifically tied to how individuals in that culture think.

In the case of Virtual Vaudeville, the sensors used to create a visual representation of a past art form were placed on a human actor, who was then responsible for breathing life into vaudeville as a performed art. Without the benefit of a human actor's corporeal knowledge of the large, broad movements associated with vaudeville acts, the archival data that the team collected could not have been translated to a format that effectively reanimates a rich and diverse cultural tradition.

Ong's assertions become particularly apparent when considering the ways that the Dunham Technique—as it continues to be codified both in bodies and in more fixed formats such as DVDs—creates an infrastructure of both cultural knowledge acquired by Katherine Dunham and of her distinctive dance work. Dunham's dance work requires the same visual literacy to be read as cultural information as does a similar dance form—ballet. Each dance form consists of a series of specific, codified gestures that can be combined and recombined to tell a history. For Dunham, these movements combine to create physical narratives of stored cultural information important to restoring cultural identity for African Americans and Caribbean Americans.

Similarly, heritage communities partnering with states parties who have ratified the 2003 Convention to Safeguard the Intangible Cultural Heritage are charged with finding best practices for safeguarding their performed acts. For many of these performed traditions, the primary safeguarding tool is human transmission with institutional support providing a necessary, but secondary, tangible infrastructure. Ensuring that a tradition is passed from one generation to the next and understanding how this transmission occurs is one way information professionals help sustain and protect human-rooted cultural knowledge or intangible cultural heritage.

Cultural knowledge is transferred and maintained through systems and structures that capture that knowledge and through the information stewards who maintain those systems and structures. Importantly, archivists and other information professionals are qualified to define, build, and develop policies for tangible infrastructures to support the preservation and safeguarding of intangible cultural heritage. Information professionals and information scholars tend to work specifically within contexts that are substrate bound, tied to underlying systems and structures. Providing this structure for performers and heritage communities allows for performed acts and other intangible cultural heritages to shift and change as necessary while still offering frameworks within which they can function and be preserved.

In the case of Virtual Vaudeville, sensors were used to capture human movement that was then stored as data points for future manipulation and animation. This motion capture data, the archival data, and the Gamebryo game engine were used in combination to create the Virtual Vaudeville prototype. These stores of data and the mediated, visualized data that comprise the prototype's website are not currently being managed by an information steward and are considered at risk for loss by project team members. Information stewards and data curators have already created systems that would help the project team manage and preserve this data. Here, there is an opportunity for intervention: information professionals can and should be called upon to create a tangible infrastructure for the preservation of this data artifact.

The Library of Congress provides this necessary infrastructure for the Dunham Technique. Codification of the Dunham Technique takes two concurrent and corresponding forms: the archive and the repertoire. The institutional structures of the archive offer a stable environment for the tangible detritus of Dunham's work. Dunham's dancers, however, work closely with the Library of Congress to provide crucial supporting cultural information in the form of metadata, personal narratives, choreology, photographs, and moving images.

Similarly, national databases of intangible cultural heritage elements around the world offer a stable system in which an accounting of the ICH can take place. That countries have identified digitization as a primary means of preservation is a problematic notion in archival studies and the broader information fields. Here, too, is an opportunity for intervention. Information stewards are equipped to assist states parties in finding more suitable methods for preserving and safeguarding intangible cultural heritage. Heritage communities around the globe have begun conducting oral histories and recording instances of performed cultural heritage as another safeguarding tool. With the benefit of institutional support and advice, these communities are successfully navigating the spaces between the tangible and the intangible.

As such, cultural knowledge is also transferred and maintained through the institutions that support culture bearers—information systems and the information professionals who manage those systems. From the Library of Congress to UNESCO and the cultural heritage institutions that partner with states parties, institutions play a significant role in safeguarding performed acts and intangible cultural heritage. It was, for example, an initiative by the National Science Foundation that created the opportunity for Virtual Vaudeville to exist. Without physical archival spaces, such as those at the Library of Congress and Southern Illinois University, aspects of the Dunham Technique might not be legible to future generations. Finally, national archives, libraries, and museums create a vital and tangible infrastructure for the world's intangible cultural heritage.

This study, in part, elucidates the ways that people, systems, and institutions form tangible infrastructures that support the longevity of performed acts and other forms of intangible cultural heritage. Similarly, the networks created by these infrastructures among heritage communities and heritage institutions such as archives, museums, and libraries illuminate existing cultures of collaboration.

Cultures of Collaboration

Information professionals increasingly work with communities to manage large and disparate data sets. Policy as well as best practices impact how those data sets are managed. Nonetheless, at the center of each of these interactions is a culture of collaboration. Each of the cases in this study exemplifies a distributed model where nodes of knowledge come together under a single policy umbrella. Sometimes the policy itself is responsible for creating these nodes. Such is the 2003 UNESCO convention, which is effectively a policy instrument. Sometimes the nodes create policy, as with Virtual Vaudeville. The Virtual Vaudeville case study is an example of different centers of knowledge—both across the country and across disciplines—working collaboratively to create a single, unified vision of a vaudeville act. Similarly, Katherine Dunham's dancers collaborated with her and now work with archivists to codify the Dunham Technique and to make arrangements for its continuation. It is the UNESCO case study, however, that is the best example of how cooperative work requires and leads to cultures of collaboration.

As with Virtual Vaudeville, the UNESCO case study is an example of how performed culture, no matter how distributed, comes together in a unified narrative through collaborative means. Two clear illustrations of this convergence can be found in Trinidad and Tobago's Remember When Institute kickoff and Newfoundland and Labrador's folk dance safeguarding initiatives. In both cases, teams collaborated across disciplines and geographical distance to create and implement a safeguarding plan that included tradition and/or culture bearers, archival repositories, museums, government organizations, and nongovernmental organizations. Through events designed to be both collaborative and celebratory, the knowledge and expertise of each group was collocated, allowing a robust presentation of the ICH element and an opportunity to transmit collective cultural knowledge to younger Trinbagonians and Canadians.

CONCLUSION

The cases in this study bring to light cultures of collaboration that are worthy of deeper investigation and interrogation than is possible here. Examining and analyzing these collaborative networks for safeguarding performed and event-based art and intangible cultural heritage is one possible area of future study. A deeper analysis of collaborative cultures may address itself to systemic inequities, to the genesis of more tangible infrastructures, or to conditions of collaborative possibility.

This chapter challenges inherent tensions between the archives and the repertoire and argues that these tensions, while complex, are mitigable. Although archives and performance operate at opposite ends of temporal spectrums, the spaces between them are full of potential. These liminal spaces offer information professionals and performers compelling opportunities for creative engagement and collaboration. This study sets the proverbial stage for these future undertakings.

NOTES

1. Archival scholar Francesca Marini echoes this sentiment in her 2007 article, "Archivists, librarians and theatre research," in *Archivaria, 63*, 7–33.

2. For more on this distinction, see J. Furner, "Conceptual analysis: A method for understanding information as evidence, and evidence as information," *Archival Science, 4* (2004): 233–65.

3. See for example: S. McKemmish, & F. Upward, *Archival documents: Providing accountability through recordkeeping* (Melbourne, National Library of Australia, 1993); T. Eastwood, "Educating archivists about information technology," in *American Archivist, 56* (1993): 458–66; W. Duff, "Ensuring the preservation of reliable evidence: A research project funded by the NHPRC," in *Archivaria, 42* (1996): 28–45; and S. Mason, "Authentic digital records: Laying the foundation for evidence," in *Information Management Quarterly, 41* (2007): 32–40.

4. Terry Cook offers a discussion of the history of diplomatics and the authenticity of the record in T. Cook, "Evidence, memory, identity, and community: Four shifting archival paradigms," in *Archival Science, 13* (2012): 95–120.

5. The Virtual Vaudeville Project Summary submitted to the National Science Foundation goes on to elaborate that the technologies and strategies developed through Virtual Vaudeville have applications that extend well beyond the simulation of theatrical performances; the same requirements and obstacles arise in the attempt to simulate any kind of performative event, including political congresses, coronations, parades, festivals, battles, rituals, riots, and so on.

6. The Virtual Vaudeville team used Maya for the animation and Filmbox for the motion capture.

7. The Dunham School of Dance and Theater was established in 1945 in New York City and operated there until 1957. Sara E. Johnson argues that the Dunham School anticipated (by decades) the interdisciplinary, historically grounded discipline of cultural studies that emerged in institutions such as the Birmingham School in the 1970s.

8. See also J. Bastian, *Owning memory: How a Caribbean community lost its archives and found its history* (Westport, CT: Libraries Unlimited, 2003); J. Bastian, "A question of custody: The colonial archives of the United States Virgin Islands," in *American Archivist, 64* (2001): 96–114; and J. Bastian, "Taking custody, giving access: A postcustodial role for a new century," in *Archivaria, 53* (2002): 76–93.

9. Article 13 of the 2003 Convention to Safeguard the Intangible Cultural Heritage mandates: "(ii) ensuring access to the intangible cultural heritage while respecting customary practices governing access to specific aspects of such heritage; [and] (iii) establishing docu-

mentation institutions for the intangible cultural heritage and facilitating access to them." Retrieved from http://www.unesco.org/culture/ich/index.php?pg=00006.

REFERENCES

Bastian, J. (1999). *Defining custody: Archival custody and its impact on the relationship between communities and historical records in the information age: A case study of the United States Virgin Islands*. Unpublished doctoral dissertation. University of Pittsburgh, Pittsburgh, PA.

Cox, R. J. (2000). *Managing records as evidence and information*. Westport, CT: Greenwood Press.

Gilliland-Swetland, A. J. (2000). *Enduring paradigm, new opportunities: The value of the archival perspective in the digital environment*. Washington, DC: Council on Library and Information Resources.

Government of Flanders. (2010). *The Government of Flanders' policy on safeguarding intangible cultural heritage: A current state of affairs with regard to the policy for the intangible cultural heritage in Flanders*. Flanders: The Government of Flanders, Belgium.

Johnson, S. E. (2005). Introduction: Diamonds on the toes of her feet. In K. Dunham, V. Clark, and S. E. Johnson (Eds.), *Kaiso! Writings by and about Katherine Dunham* (pp. 3–18). Madison, WI: University of Wisconsin Press.

Library of Congress Performing Arts Encyclopedia. (2013). *Special presentation: Katherine Dunham timeline: 1932*. Retrieved from http://lcweb2.loc.gov/diglib/ihas/html/dunham/dunham-timeline.html.

Ong, W. (1982). *Orality and literacy: The technologizing of the word*. London, UK; New York: Methuen Press.

Saltz, D. (2001). Project summary. *A Live Performance Simulation System: Virtual Vaudeville*. National Science Foundation Grant Proposal.

Schechner, R. (2002). Performance studies in/for the 21st century. *Anthropology and Humanism, 26*, 158–66.

Turner, F. (1990). Hyperion to a satyr: Criticism and anti-structure in the work of Victor Turner. In K. Ashley (Ed.), *Victor Turner and the construction of cultural criticism: Between literature and anthropology* (pp. 147–62). Bloomington, IN: Indiana University Press.

UNESCO. (2003). *Intangible heritage: What is intangible cultural heritage?* Retrieved from http://www.unesco.org/culture/ich/index.php?pg=00021.

3

Technicolor Shades

Considering Privilege in Modeling of Information Behavior

Simon Tarr

ABSTRACT

Existing models of information behaviors have served well to describe and predict practice, but they do not adequately account for the effects of culture or privilege in these behaviors. By interviewing a group of undergraduate students before and after they engage in a new self-directed learning process (in this case, how to use professional video editing software), this study attempts to establish preliminary findings about how existing models of information-seeking behavior may be affected by aspects of participants' backgrounds.

INTRODUCTION

Modeling is an important process in the development and articulation of theory as it relates to information behavior. Bates aptly identifies modeling as "proto-theory," an intermediary prototype that can withstand testing and evolve on the way to becoming settled theory (2005). But models are not just a critical way station on the road to developed theory. Once a model has been tested and retested, and has ripened into a widely accepted theory, the model upon which the theory was based is not discarded. It remains as a road map or a central metaphor, serving as an emblem of the theory itself.

MODELING AS NARRATIVE

There is certainly no shortage of theories of information behavior available to guide researchers in description and prediction. Fisher, Erdelez, and McKechnie's simply and aptly named *Theories of Information Behavior* describes no fewer than seventy-two—perhaps every field-tested theory in information behavior at the time of its publishing (2005). Some of the accompanying models have such striking profiles that their mere shape can evoke the entire theory. Krikelas's model of information seeking (figure 3.1) evokes the image of a watershed, beginning at the top with a churning pool of exigencies, funneling through a channel of source preference before expanding into a wide array of pathways to knowledge (1983).

Wilson's revised general model (figure 3.2) has a more computational feel, resembling a standard loop of a piece of software during its execution (1997). Perhaps the most instantly recognizable metaphor is the "information gap" (figure 3.3) in Dervin's sense-making (Dervin & Frenette, 2001), which succinctly depicts an information seeker attempting to traverse a chasm of nonknowledge to get to the eventual information goal.

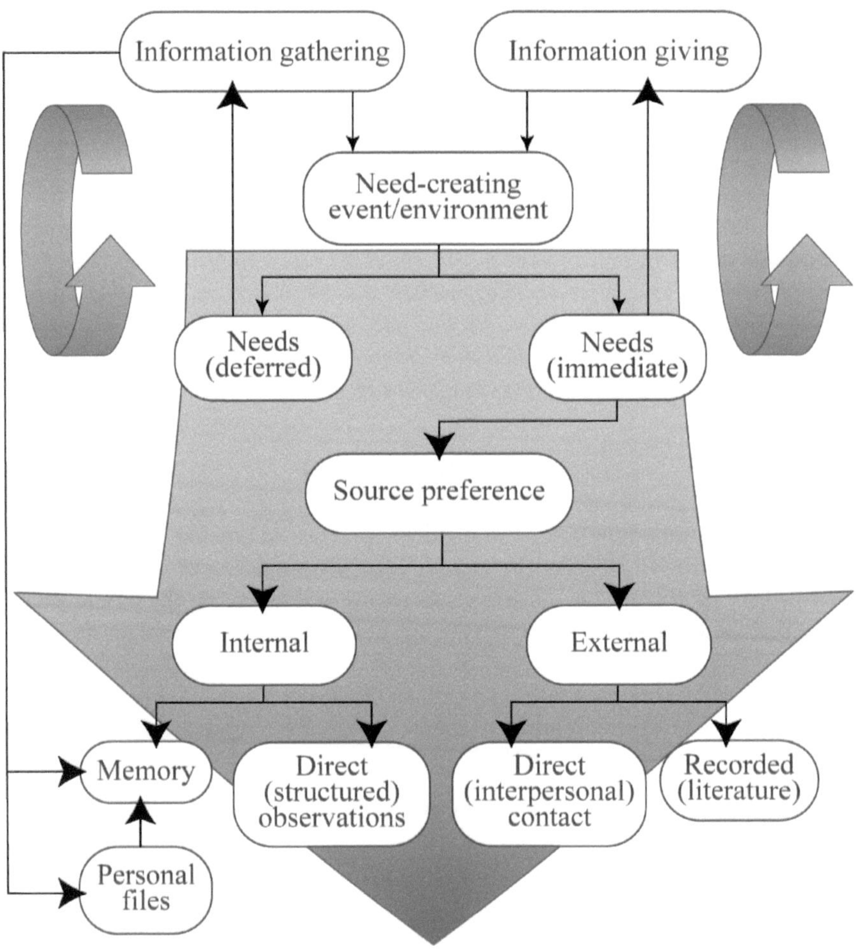

Figure 3.1. Illustration of narrative flow in Krikelas's 1983 model of information seeking. Adapted with permission.

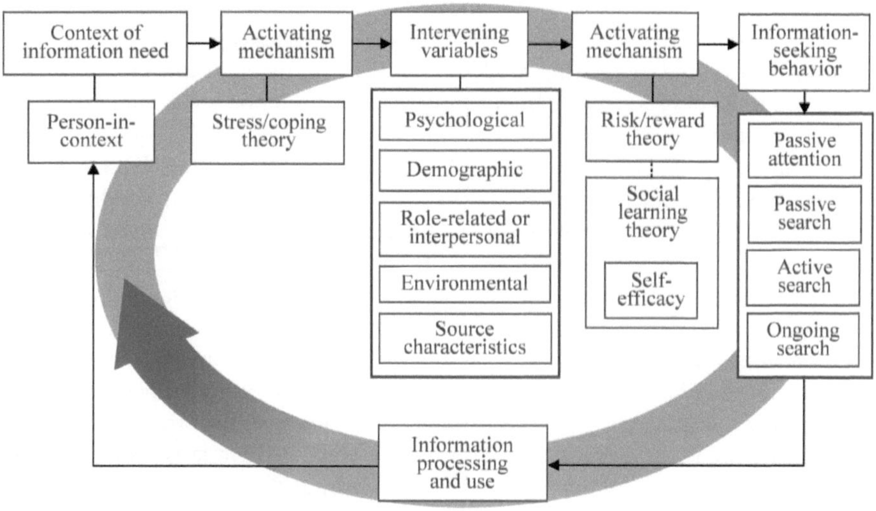

Figure 3.2. Illustration of narrative flow in Wilson's 1997 revised model of information-seeking behavior. Adapted with permission.

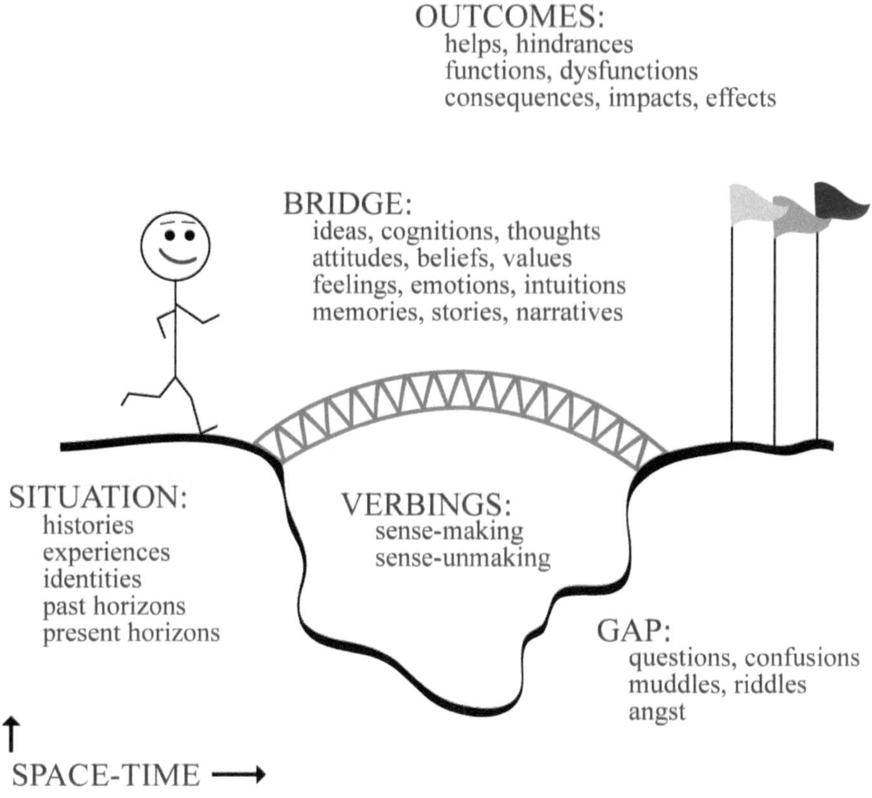

Figure 3.3. Illustration of Dervin's 2001 sense-making metaphor. Adapted with permission.

In the stories told by existing models, aspects of culture are depicted as discrete, contained units of experience. "Intervening variables" is a node with subnodes such as "demographic" and "environmental" in Wilson's model (1997). Nodes such as "needs (immediate)" or "needs (deferred)" play that role in Krikelas's (1983). While Dervin does take specific care to explain that moment-to-moment conditions are fluid and changing, aspects of culture in the sense-making model consist of headings such as "context" and "situation," with bullet points such as "power structures and dynamics" and "identities," words that are floating outside or layered upon the clear metaphor underneath (2001). These are not unique examples; Belkin's model of anomalous states of knowledge has a node called "user's image of the world, problematic situation" (1980), Chang's refined framework of browsing has "context (environment, display, etc.)" as a large node resting above all the others (2001), and Savolainen's model of everyday life information seeking has a large node running parallel to the main model that contains "values, attitudes," "material capital," "social capital," "cultural and cognitive capital," and "current situation of life" (1995).

Models craft a narrative of the information seeker, and we who read about these models are placed in a spectating position, observing the seekers' stories from a perspective orthogonal to the experience of the narrative itself. But in fact, culture is not perpendicular to experience, nor does it exist outside of experience. How might future versions of models reflect this?

CULTURAL FILTERS AND METAPHORS OF VISION

As disciplines have borrowed concepts from contemporary literary theory and criticism in the last thirty-five years, the metaphor of a "lens" has become popular in many fields to describe critical and theoretical approaches to literature, media, and data. Variations on this theme have emerged, with "critical lens" spiking in the 1980s, to "cultural lens" in the 1990s, to "theoretical lens" in the 2000s (figure 3.4).

The photographic concept is helpful, especially for those who may be new to using theory as a tool, since it is simple to imagine using different tools for different applications (a feminist lens, a postcolonial lens, or a Marxist lens) to achieve nuanced results. One photographer might prefer a particular lens to bring a shallower depth of field and separate a subject from a background, while another might choose a different lens to gain a wider view of the very same scene but at the expense of detail on an individual element in that scene. It is an elegant metaphor that requires the individual choosing the theoretical lens to consider their perspective and position as a fundamental aspect of their thought process. The lens metaphor's limitations extend gracefully to explain limitations of critical perspectives; lenses necessarily refract light and distort how subjects are seen to observers, and everything that is framed in a scene through a lens is at the expense of what is left outside of the lenses' view.

If it is common practice to consider theory by declaring our lenses up front, then perhaps by considering culture as a function of vision and perspective, not merely

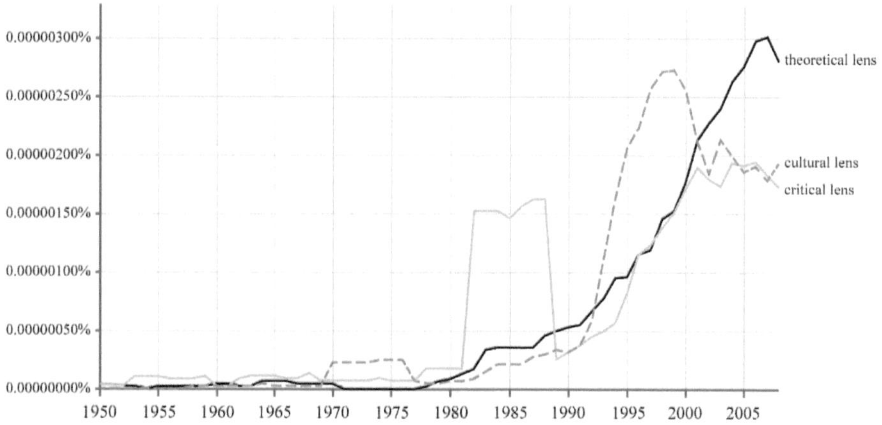

Figure 3.4. Frequency of phrase occurrence in published English language books, 1950–2008. Corpus: English One Million. Generated with Google Books Ngram Viewer (books.google.com/ngrams).

situationality, we might better understand how deeply aspects of culture can alter behavior. There is precedent for this from anthropology: Hall likened culture to a screen through which an individual sees the world (1976). I propose to extend the photographic metaphor a bit further by building onto the concept of a theoretical lens, quite literally, with the addition of a "cultural filter." When using a normal camera, a photographer might place a filter in front of the lens to alter aspects of light, perhaps to reduce ultraviolet light that might cast a haze on the image in the camera or augment how certain colors are seen. Indeed, its effects would take place before any information reaches a lens (optical or theoretical). A popular common use of the term *filter* in smartphone applications (such as Instagram or VSCO Cam) refers to effects that are digitally added after the camera sensor receives an image, but this is a misuse of the term.

To envision the metaphor of a cultural filter, consider the following thought experiment based on Dervin's model. Imagine two information seekers, call them Paul and Ringo, facing a typical information gap. In this experiment, each was born with a pair of sunglasses permanently over their eyes. Paul's are colored magenta, and Ringo's are green (figure 3.5).

Both Paul and Ringo live their lives completely accustomed to their sunglasses. Imagine further that in addition to the visible goal on the far side of the gap, a thick, lush, green vine has grown down from above, hanging over the gap. Paul, with his congenital magenta glasses, approaches first. When Paul sees the green vine through his magenta glasses, it appears to him to be a deep black (figure 3.6), obviously darker than anything else around. Naturally, he grabs the opportune vine and swings over to the other side of the gap, and being a good citizen, Paul throws the vine back over to the other side for future seekers. Ringo, sporting his

Figure 3.5. Our information seekers, with colored glasses, in view of the vine over the gap.

Figure 3.6. Paul's perspective of the green vine through magenta filters.

green glasses, approaches the gap next. The green vine matches the color of his glasses, therefore it is invisible to him. All he sees is a gap and Paul, already on the other side. Paul calls to him, telling him to use the vine. Ringo looks around, sees no vine, and becomes frustrated at Paul for giving him useless advice (figure 3.7). Paul becomes frustrated at Ringo for not taking the vine that he made the effort to throw back for him, and he eventually leaves Ringo behind, while Ringo begins to look for the materials that are visible to him so that he can build a bridge to cross the gap.

We leave the thought experiment with not just two different results, but two dramatically different experiences of the exact same model. If we were to interview the participants, they would recount the same information geography in space and time, but the two descriptions would bear little resemblance to each other based solely on the cultural filters that were each seeker's birthright. The phenomenon of the technicolor shades in this thought experiment could be called by its more common name: *privilege*.

Figure 3.7. Ringo's perspective of the green vine through green lenses.

RESEARCH QUESTIONS, METHODOLOGY, AND *GUNSMOKE*

In order to move beyond speculation, it is necessary to design a study to begin to identify and perhaps operationalize how privilege or at least culture might reveal itself in information behavior in order to address two main questions emerging from a reconsidered perspective of culture's impact:

1. In what ways do culture and privilege affect information behavior?
2. How might conditions of privilege be taken into account using existing models of information behavior?

Site Selection

I am the professor of a one-hundred-student undergraduate course called Digital Media Art Fundamentals, where novice students learn how to become proficient users of highly complex professional software applications to solve specific problems. A subset of this class serves as the site of this pilot study, using an action research approach that intends to improve understanding of the conditions surrounding practice (Kemmis & McTaggart, 2009), in this case the information-seeking behaviors of novice users who are seeking to learn a new piece of software.

During one segment of this course, students must learn how to use professional digital nonlinear editing (DNLE) software, which is used to edit motion picture footage into completed films. The specific professional DNLE software chosen for this study is Adobe Premiere Pro.

The act of editing a motion picture is conceptually very difficult, and the software used to perform that conceptual task is similarly complex. Facing both of these tasks for the first time presents a formidable information gap for a new user.

Action research notwithstanding, there are several criteria a site would need to have to be ideal for this study, which were prioritized using Patton's criterion sampling selection criteria (2007). An ideal site would have a large number of people of relatively heterogeneous racial and class demographics, actively attempting to learn a similar professional skill that could be perceived as critical to future success, with access to the technological material to do so. A large course at a public postsecondary institution fits that bill and provides a large potential pool of participants to apply further criterion sampling.

Participant Selection

In order to focus the pool of candidates, participants were invited to be a part of this study based on two intersecting gauges using criterion sampling (Patton, 2007). The first is that a participant must have had little to no prior experience with the software, and the second is a previously articulated desire to specifically learn motion picture editing. Some students might have had opportunities to become familiar with professional media software through school or workshops, and some students may only be taking the course to fulfill a general education requirement in arts and humanities. Either a standing level of expertise or a disinclination or ambivalence toward the specific skill would make for less ideal participants. Written introductions of the students posted to the class Facebook group served to identify potential participants, and their experience and goals were confirmed in preliminary informal conversations. There were ten people fitting both criteria; to increase confidence in the data, reasonably describe the phenomenon (Patton, 2007), and to include potential subgroups that may introduce variations for future research, all were invited and went through the informed consent process of IRB. Nine participants ultimately decided to join the study. These participants chose their own pseudonyms, which were used throughout the study to maintain confidentiality.

Of the nine participants, there were six women and three men. Five participants were white, one was Indian, one was Japanese, and two were African American. Two participants were exchange students, one from Japan and one from Scotland. Five participants were born and raised in the southern United States.

Methods

With the intent to investigate and interpret a complex set of phenomena, this study used multiple qualitative methods so that the data might complement each other (Greene, 2007). This study combined interviews and document analysis, with memos collected immediately after interviews based on observations therein.

Each participant was interviewed before they were given a motion picture editing task (the task is a normal part of the class, the participants would have done it anyway, and it was no different from the work anyone else in the class did). Initial interviews were loosely structured, focusing on collecting participants' stories about their backgrounds, both in general and as they related to computers and technology. Participants then had two weeks to learn to use the software, and then to complete the assigned task. Afterward, during closing interviews I collected their expressed thoughts, experiences, and emotions that resulted from the process of undertaking the editing task and learning the new skill, including questions about their process in deciding to make their specific video. To increase validity, participants received transcripts of their own interviews with an opportunity to give feedback as a member check early in the process.

The Exercise

Every participant was given the same footage to work with: fourteen minutes of black-and-white film from a 1958 episode of the television show *Gunsmoke*, titled "Buffalo Man" (figure 3.8). The American Cinema Editors, a professional society for motion picture editors since 1951, has sold the footage of this scene as a package called *Basic Principles of Film Editing* since the early 1960s (1961).

Figure 3.8. Adobe Premiere Pro motion picture editing software, with artist's rendition of a Western-style scene like those used in this study. Adobe® product screenshot reprinted with permission from Adobe Systems Incorporated. Illustrations by Simon Tarr.

Editing this particular scene from the iconic Western has been a rite of passage for thousands of film students for decades, sparking discussions among students and aficionados seeking input about their interpretation on Internet forums (Ashreipinkus, 2013), as well as between teachers comparing notes on its use as a tool (Dwiggins, 1994). Though there have been complaints in higher education in film concerning the continuing effectiveness of using a fifty-year-old scene instead of "exciting, high-end footage" to teach new practitioners (Hollyn, 2014), there is clearly a long-standing affection toward the exercise, with one Academy Award–winning editor even likening the experience to removing scales from one's eyes (Cunningham, 2005).

The *Gunsmoke* scene was originally intended to be edited as a prototypical Western, where U.S. Marshall Matt Dillon (played by James Arness) confronts the feared buffalo hunter Ben Siple (John Anderson) to stop him from absconding to the frontier with his former ward/girlfriend Abby (Patricia Smith). Siple strikes Abby in the middle of the main street in Dodge, and Dillon intervenes before the situation escalates. After an extended standoff where the men posture with dialogue, Dillon and Siple fight. The ensuing brawl extends through the street, with props (a knife, barrel, and wagon), and townsfolk both watching in amazement and shoving the fighters back into engagement with each other, with the upper hand shifting back and forth several times. Dillon eventually beats Siple into submission, leaving the bad guy to be carted out of town never to return. The scene ends with Dillon engaging in silent, bashful flirtation with Abby, who had been watching the entire time. Of course, the footage provided contains all the material to complete the scene, but the footage also contains everything not normally seen in a final edited film: lines spoken off camera, pauses while actors wait for instruction, flubbed lines, and slate clappers that labeled each new shot at the beginning.

Though it is a straightforward four- or five-minute scene, it is very complex and time-consuming for the first-time editor. Moreover, building the scene as it was intended to be edited is an exercise for a specific film production class later in the curriculum; that task is out of scope for first-year students in this particular class. Instead, this class and the participants in this study are presented with a simpler task using the footage, designed to test the most basic proficiency in DNLE workflows. Using only the provided footage (no additional music, effects, or visuals), participants were instructed to create a sequence no longer than thirty seconds, export the sequence as a new video with proper settings and specifications, and upload it to an online video streaming service such as YouTube.com or Vimeo.com.

Content-wise, participants could do anything they want with the *Gunsmoke* footage: create a section of the original scene, ignore the scene's intent altogether and create something different, even exhibit total disregard for spatial, temporal, or dramatic logic. The grading rubrics for this particular exercise included only elements specific to proficiency with the tool; mastery of the more advanced topics such as nuanced visual storytelling or sophisticated dramatic pacing happen later in the curriculum once basic proficiency is assured.

This task takes place in the context of a course that meets in a large auditorium, not in a computer lab; in-class time is used for critique and for background and contextual instruction while students do the work of the course outside of the classroom. It is clear from existing literature that learning a technology-based skill is an evolutionary process of accustomization (Peterson et al., 2002), that this process works better when active rather than abstract (Bonwell & Eison, 1991), and when the process is outside a traditional classroom setting (Reber, 2004). Wiedenbeck and Zila further demonstrated that combining a directed exercise with users' exploration of a new software application increased the users' success in learning (1997). Therefore, the specific implementation of this editing exercise is on firm ground as a learning tool, even beyond its storied lineage in the film industry.

DATA ANALYSIS

Interviews were transcribed and coded along with observations using a thematic analysis process to identify patterns and prevalent themes inductively (Braun & Clarke, 2006). The approach seems like a grounded theory approach on the surface in that it seeks to derive patterns from the data by induction, but because this is a pilot study designed to investigate existing models but not yet fully generate theory from that data (Holloway & Todres, 2003), grounded theory does not fit this analysis.

In the document analysis, participants' exercises were coded according to a rubric to analyze both the dramatic/thematic content and the sophistication of craft of the scenes. Since participants were only being evaluated as students for proficiency, not for content or sophistication, participants were free to experiment with the content or craft any way they wished without risk of a grade penalty if their experiments did not go well.

There were four codes for dramatic/thematic content. The highest-level code was "transformed," for scenes where participants took the footage and created something completely new—a scene whose meaning went beyond the original intent. Next highest was "mimetic with transformative elements," for scenes that mostly tried to imitate the story as written but contained parts with new interpretations that altered the scene in those places. The code below that was "mimetic," for scenes where participants just tried to replicate the story precisely and follow visual storytelling conventions that they knew. The lowest level was "basic," for scenes that were neither replicating the intended structure of the scene nor transforming the content.

There were also four codes for the sophistication of craft in the scenes. The lowest level was "metric," which refers to what Eisenstein identified as the most simplistic form of montage, where the editing decisions are based merely on physical length of each shot (1949). The second level was "sutured," a film theory concept that refers to techniques used to "stitch" the audience into the story of the film; in other words, to forget that the real looking is being done by a camera intervening between the action on the screen and the spectator (Silverman, 1983). This is the prevalent mode in American narrative media. Above that was "sutured with transformative elements" for scenes where the participant mainly tried to edit seamlessly and hide any artifice, and it took the form beyond that in parts. Again, the highest level was "transformed," for scenes that had been edited in a way that transcended the way the shots were intended to be cut together.

RESULTS

All nine participants completed the editing exercise in the two weeks allotted, and all nine successfully fulfilled all of the measures of basic proficiency in professional DNLE software. All but one of the participants reported that they found the exercise to be enjoyable, even easy. The one participant who expressed difficulty with the exercise was the Japanese exchange student who was facing steep language barriers all semester; the language of the software interfaces were typically in English, but even when they were not (she used a Japanese localization of Adobe Premiere Pro for this exercise), most of the learning materials, books, videos, and websites that she used were all in English. The main frustration shared by the other participants related to the mechanics of exporting their final video (an annoyance shared by professionals as well). Since the experience was consistently positive across participants, any patterns and variations would need to be found in the edited scenes, examined as a function of data from the interviews.

Table 3.1 shows how the videos submitted by participants measure. In both content and craft, participants tended to rank at the lower two levels, regardless of variations in the backgrounds.

Participants gave extensive descriptions of their pasts in the loosely structured interviews. Six participants indicated that they had access to computers in school, while only three had no access or poor access in school. Only two participants had their own personal computer at home during childhood, but that number increased to six as they became teenagers. Six had access to a shared family computer; one did not have computer access at home until late childhood. Five participants have had a specific college and career path planned since high school and have not deviated from this plan; the rest have switched majors, and may have no idea or only a vague idea about what they want to do after college. Three participants regularly attended large churches that had media production as part of their services and sometimes interned with their places of faith, three attended churches that had no media component to their services, and three did not attend services regularly. All of the participants reported playing video games as their earliest memory of being exposed to computer technology. Four participants described situations in which they became local experts in computer and technology matters at home. Four participants grew up in households with one stay-at-home parent; two had parents who are educators. Three participants moved frequently due to one or more parent serving in the military. Two participants grew up in households with three generations living together under one roof. None of this data correlates with participants' abilities to successfully complete the exercise, or the complexity of sophistication of their approach to how they created their videos. However, there are two outlying events that deserve a closer look.

Table 3.1. Participants' Scenes Coded for Craft and Content

Participant	*Content Level*	*Craft Level*
Abigail	Basic (level 1)	Metric (level 1)
Alestar	Mimetic (level 2)	Sutured (level 2)
Darnell	Mimetic (level 2)	Sutured (level 2)
Elizabeth	Basic (level 1)	Metric (level 1)
Etsuko	Mimetic (level 2)	Metric (level 1)
Michelle	Mimetic (level 2)	Sutured (level 2)
Mop	Basic (level 1)	Sutured with transformative elements (level 3)
Paige	Transformed (level 4)	Sutured (level 2)
Tachabel	Mimetic (level 2)	Sutured with transformative elements (level 3)

Outlier 1: Intensive Hobbyists

When examining sophistication of craft, only two participants ventured into experiments with form. Mop created a video that, while extremely simplistic in its approach to content, was very complex in its craft. Throughout Mop's video, the cowboys engaged in a sort of temporal fugue where the marshal and outlaw would punch each other, but at every moment where a fist would land on an opponent, the video would shift into reverse at that instant and bring both fighters back to their starting point. This would repeat and become more and more frantic before eventually stopping at the end of the thirty-second time limit. While the content of this interpretation of the scene does not make much narrative sense, manipulating the footage in this way is much more difficult and requires more precision than editing the scene normally might. Looking at a graphical overview of how the film is laid out (figure 3.9) to see what Mop would have seen while he cut the footage, the timeline has a visual cadence and patterned aesthetic that other participants' scenes do not (figure 3.10).

The scene cut by Tachabel takes a different approach. In her scene, the marshal, the outlaw, and Abby are locked in a sort of staring contest, gazing back and forth at each other. As Abby shifts her attention from one man to the other, the entire scene takes on an apocalyptic orange cast, and the color contrast increases to give the scene a supernatural, horrifying look. The scene flashes to pure white several times, giving an impression that Abby might be unleashing her wrath on the town. Then, the color goes away, Abby walks off with a smile, and the marshal proceeds to punch out the bad guy. Though shifting for a moment from Western to science fiction tropes, Tachabel's new story still has the feel of a scene that could pass for something one might typically see on screen. But her choice to craft the story almost entirely with color effects is a significant conceptual advancement for a novice, even if inconsistently applied and only partially successful.

During their respective interviews, both Mop and Tachabel described the all-consuming pursuit of hobbies in their childhoods. Mop is an engineering major

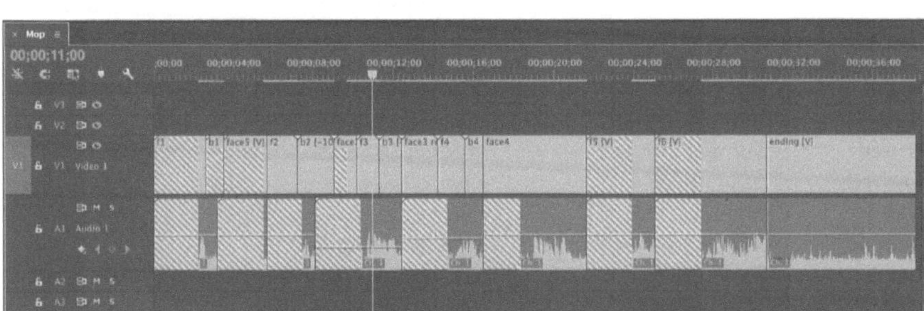

Figure 3.9. Mop's complex editing timeline window from Adobe Premiere Pro. Adobe product screenshot reprinted with permission from Adobe Systems Incorporated.

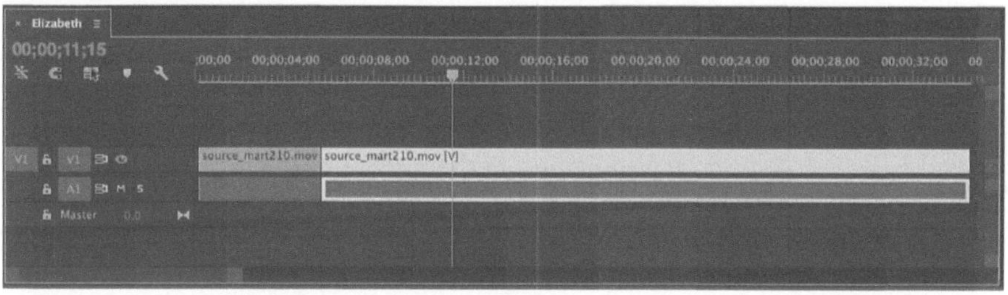

Figure 3.10. A simple metric editing timeline example from Adobe Premiere Pro. Adobe product screenshot reprinted with permission from Adobe Systems Incorporated.

whose family immigrated to the United States from India when he was in elementary school. As a child he watched his grandmother solve Rubik's cubes. After watching and learning from her he began solving them himself, eventually deducing the solution algorithms and applying those to different puzzles. Mop became so accomplished at solving puzzles of all kinds that he challenged speed records, solved puzzles blindfolded, and started a YouTube channel where he would share his solutions online with thousands of subscribers.

During her childhood, Tachabel wrote fan fiction that imagined scenarios of her favorite boy band in the 2000s. She spent so many hours crafting stories that her mother ended up buying her a computer of her own so other family members could use the shared computer. She later expanded the stories, outsourcing different character's arcs from the boy band to her friends so she could weave together a larger and more complex fan fiction. She describes the corner of her bedroom as being buried in dirty dishes, since she'd take all her meals at the computer as she wrote.

It would be a stretch to try to assign relevance to particular hobbies. However, while all of the participants described their childhood pastimes, Mop's and Tachabel's stories stood out as particularly intense, even all-consuming.

Outlier 2: Secret Stories

Looking at the content of the scenes, only one participant's endeavor could be considered "transformative"; that is, fundamentally changing the meaning of the scene even while using the same footage. Paige's edited scene begins over a black screen, and we hear the actress's voice say "I never want to see him again as long as I live," followed by white text that appears, reading "brought to you by women against violence." The action of the scene proceeds quickly. We see Siple strike Abby in the very first visual, then the shots that follow are a flurry of men's characters rushing through the town toward the event. There is no standoff, no macho posturing. The marshal swiftly knocks out the outlaw and instructs Siple's henchman to "get him out of town and don't ever come back." In the final shots of the scene, the wagon departs, revealing Abby watching it go. Text appears again, reading "domestic violence, it CAN be stopped," then the video ends on a black screen again. When it was screened before the entire class, there was a long silence before applause. Not only was Paige the only participant in the study who brought this interpretation to the scene, she was the only one in the class of one hundred to do so.

At the end of our follow-up interview, Paige explained that she had originally wanted to have a comedic interpretation of the scene, but she kept coming back to the scene where the outlaw hits Abby and it "just clicked," but she did not know why it read as domestic violence to her. "I'm not one for feminist rights and all that stuff," she continued. "I've never been one to like dedicate my time to a certain group, I've never found a group that I was really passionate about." Then after a pause she added, "I know my sister used to be in a domestic violence relationship, that was a long time ago." She recounted the story of how her adult sister moved back home, with a child of her own, when Paige was eight. She did not learn that her sister had been in an abusive relationship until only a few years ago, and when further considering her interpretation of the scene, Paige mused "that could have, you know, psychologically had an effect on it too."

IMPLICATIONS AND FURTHER STUDY

This study suggests that culture may play a deeper role in information behavior than considered in current models. I attempt to account for this role by adding the concept of "cultural filters" to these models—conditions that fundamentally alter how the models behave when activated by the culture and/or privilege of information seekers.

Several participants in this study grew up in households that allowed for or actively supported certain highly focused hobbies, regardless of how directly applicable those may be to academic success or career paths. Even though all participants had a similar lack of experience with the new tool and process to be learned in the study, were given the same amount of time to complete the exercise, and reported spending generally the same number of hours working directly on editing the scene, the two participants with histories of an intensive pursuit of hobbies showed significantly more experimentation and complexity in the craft of their work. Did they learn more quickly and then spend more time trying new things, or was their process basically the same as all the others but with a higher quality of work? Had they acquired filters that circumvented hindrances that plagued the other participants, or did the other participants have filters through their own cultures that created hindrances?

Another participant had a very specific cultural filter: her familial experience with domestic violence triggered a leap in sophistication as she interpreted a scene that was, to all other eyes, a run-of-the-mill television Western. Or put more aptly, the rest of the participants had filters of a particular privilege that allowed them luxury to see film footage of a man hitting a woman as a simple plot device to advance the hero's story in a television show. In this particular information-seeking event, Paige was able to wield a new tool at a far more advanced, nuanced level than her peers with the same background experience, precisely because she was able to see a story that no one else did, converse to the hypothetical Paul in the earlier thought experiment, who was able to see the vine to his advantage that was invisible to those with filters that rendered the vine invisible. This is not to say, of course, that any experience with domestic (or any) violence could be read as an advantage under any circumstance. My argument is that when considering models of information behavior there are different conditions, attributable to culture, that lead to fundamentally different ways of perceiving, approaching, and therefore navigating the same information event.

Indeed, privilege and culture are complex and unpredictable, and in this study there were no cut-and-dry instances where one might point to one person who had every advantage and therefore did well while another lacked in many ways and fell behind. This research suggests that privilege exists and may have an effect on information behaviors, but it raises much messier questions. On what does privilege take root, what are its antecedents, what does it distort, and what does it render visible or invisible?

REFERENCES

American Cinema Editors, Inc. (1961). *Basic principles of film editing.* American Cinema Editors.

Ashreipinkus. (2013, February 9). Have you ever edited "Gunsmoke"? *Reddit.* Retrieved from http://www.reddit.com/r/Filmmakers/comments/1884ba/have_you_ever_edited_gun smoke/.

Bates, M. J. (2005). An introduction to metatheories, theories, and models. In K. E. Fisher, S. Erdelez, & L. McKechnie (Eds.), *Theories of information behavior* (pp. 1–24). Medford, NJ: Information Today.

Belkin, N. J. (1980). Anomalous states of knowledge as a basis for information retrieval. *Canadian Journal of Information and Library Science, 5,* 133–43.

Bonwell, C., & Eison, J. (1991). *Active learning: Creating excitement in the classroom.* Washington, DC: George Washington University.

Braun, V., & Clarke, V. (2006). Using thematic analysis in psychology. *Qualitative Research in Psychology, 3*(2), 77–101. doi:10.1191/1478088706qp063oa

Chang, S.-J. L. (2001). Browsing and communication. In R. E. Rice, M. McCreadie, & S.-J. L. Chang (Eds.), *Accessing and browsing information and communication* (p. 255). Boston, MA: MIT Press.

Crutchfield, L. (Writer), & Post, T. (Director). 1958. "Buffalo Man" [Television series episode]. N. MacDonnell (Producer), *Gunsmoke.* Los Angeles, CA: CBS.

Cunningham, M. (2005). Editing for entertainment value. *Editors Guild Magazine.* Retrieved from http://www.editorsguild.com/v2/magazine/archives/1105/features_insidehbo.htm.

Dervin, B., & Frenette, M. (2001). Sense-making methodology: Communicating communicatively with campaign audiences. In R. E. Rice & C. K. Atkin (Eds.), *Public communication campaigns* (3rd ed., pp. 69–87). Thousand Oaks, CA: Sage.

Dwiggins, S. (1994, January 3). Re: ACE "Gunsmoke" sequence. *SCREEN-L Listserv.* Retrieved from https://listserv.ua.edu/cgi-bin/wa?A2=SCREEN-L;906724ee.9401.

Eisenstein, S. (1949). *Film form.* Orlando, FL: Harcourt.

Fisher, K. E., Erdelez, S., & McKechnie, L. (Eds.). (2005). *Theories of information behavior.* Medford, NJ: Information Today.

Greene, J. C. (2007). *Mixed methods in social inquiry.* San Francisco, CA: Jossey-Bass.

Hall, E. T. (1976). *Beyond culture.* Garden City, NY: Doubleday.

Holloway, I., & Todres, L. (2003). The status of method: Flexibility, consistency and coherence. *Qualitative Research, 3,* 345–57.

Hollyn, N. (2014, March 11). A message from UFVA president Norman Hollyn. *UFVA.org.* Retrieved from http://www.ufva.org/news/message-ufva-president-norman-hollyn-7.

Kemmis, S., & McTaggart, R. (2009). Participatory action research. In N. K. Denzin & Y. S. Lincoln (Eds.), *Strategies of qualitative inquiry* (pp. 271–330). Thousand Oaks, CA: Sage Publications.

Krikelas, J. (1983). Information-seeking behavior: Patterns and concepts. *Drexel Library Quarterly, 19*(2), 5–20.

Patton, M. Q. (2007). *Qualitative research & evaluation methods* (3rd ed.). Thousand Oaks, CA: SAGE Publications.

Petersen, M. G., Madsen, K. H., & Kjaer, A. (2002). The usability of everyday technology: Emerging and fading opportunities. *ACM Transactions on Computer-Human Interaction, 9*(2), 74–105. doi:10.1145/513665.513667

Reber, A. S. (2004). Implicit learning and tacit knowledge. *Journal of Experimental Psychology, 118*(3), 219–35.

Savolainen, R. (1995). Everyday life information seeking: Approaching information seeking in the context of "way of life." *Library and Information Science Research, 17,* 259–94.

Silverman, K. (1983). *The subject of semiotics.* New York: Oxford University Press.

Wiedenbeck, S., & Zila, P. L. (1997). Hands-on practice in learning to use software: A comparison of exercise, exploration, and combined formats. *ACM Transactions on Computer-Human Interaction, 4*(2), 169–96. doi:10.1145/254945.254967

Wilson, T. D. (1997). Information behaviour: An interdisciplinary perspective. *Information Processing & Management, 33*(4), 551–72.

4

Cultural Heritage Informatics and Intellectual Property Rights

Dick Kawooya and Tucky Taylor

ABSTRACT

Cultural heritage informatics as a field of study and practice deals almost exclusively with cultural artifacts and resources in digital form. Many resources are born digital, meaning they are created exclusively in digital form. However, others already exist in nondigital format, requiring digitization in order to be part of the digital cultural heritage. Cultural heritage informatics offers opportunities to widen and ease access to digital cultural resources. Use of cultural resources is enhanced once digitized. However, digital resources present significant legal challenges in the sense that ease of access and use, moreover on a global scale, potentially subjects digital resources to misappropriation. Using technological protection measures of different kinds, we have come to a point where it is possible to securely and irrevocably fence off digital cultural resources that previously existed in the public domain. In this chapter, we examine the legal opportunities and challenges presented by digital cultural resources through the narrow lens of intellectual property law, copyright in particular. We examine legal issues as they apply to different cultural institutions including, but not limited to, libraries, archives, museums, and historical societies. The choice of institutions reflects those whose primary function is the storage, preservation, and dissemination of cultural information.

INTRODUCTION

The Cultural Heritage Informatics Initiative at Michigan State University defines *cultural heritage informatics* as the "creative application of information and computing technology to (and in) the domain of cultural heritage" (Cultural Heritage Informatics Initiative, n.d., para 2). Evidentially, cultural heritage informatics involves cultural resources in digital forms otherwise known as digital cultural resources. The primary focus of cultural heritage informatics, as an emerging field of research and practice, is on developing innovative technology tools for creating, preserving, conserving, and facilitating access to and use of digital cultural resources (Arnold, 2008). Some in fields like computer science see a role of promoting "basic research both to increase the understanding of basic research issues in ICTs (Information and Communication Technologies) and to develop improved technology to meet specific needs of Cultural Heritage" (Arnold, 2008, p. 2188). Other disciplines have come to cultural heritage informatics with similar objectives of finding tools to address challenges presented by cultural resources. However, the legal questions relating to digital cultural resources and tools, and how they are created, used, or applied, are only beginning to gain the attention of cultural heritage informatics researchers. While some cultural institutions or domains like libraries have done extensive work on the legal issues pertaining to the preservation of and access to digital cultural resources, the same cannot be said of other cultural institutions and domains (Striphas & McLeod, 2006).

This chapter is an attempt to address some of the pressing legal issues relating to the core objectives and activities of the cultural heritage informatics discipline. The chapter is necessarily limited to certain cultural institutions and the intellectual property area of law with specific reference to copyright. Emphasis on copyright is based on the fact that the majority of cultural institutions and the resources in their collections deal with copyright issues more than other areas of intellectual property law. That said, we are aware of other areas of law such as trademark, contract law, and patents, that impact on digitization, access, or use of digital cultural resources (Corbett, 2007). Yet copyright presents the most serious challenge to digital cultural resources today.

We approach cultural heritage informatics as the unifying discipline under which legal challenges and issues that cut across different cultural institutions should be examined among those institutions. Arguably, some are more pronounced in certain institutions than others. Yet a piecemeal approach to issues like ownership of digital cultural resources undermines the ability to find legal solutions across cultural institutions. Only when practices shared among cultural institutions are examined, and related copyright implications analyzed, can we begin to understand how these institutions and cultural heritage informatics can collectively address the legal barriers likely to threaten the discipline and accessibility of digital cultural resources in general.

To understand some of the copyright challenges faced by cultural heritage informatics and cultural institutions in general, we are examining the questions below:

1. Who owns cultural resources held by cultural institutions?
2. Is it fair for cultural institutions to massively digitize orphaned and/or donated works in their collections?
3. Is copyright in derivative works drawn from the public domain valid?
4. Does the right to display within the institution extend to the web?

CULTURAL HERITAGE INFORMATICS AND DIGITAL CULTURAL HERITAGE PRESERVATION

The definition of *cultural heritage informatics* by Michigan State University implies the discipline deals primarily with digital resources or digitization of the same in specific institutional contexts. However, given the diversity of institutional missions and activities, there are differences in the nature and scope of digital resources or digitization activities. Archives, for instance, grapple with the digitization of collections donated in nondigital formats to make such collections accessible to a wider audience beyond individual users that visit the brick-and-mortar archive (Lukasik, 2013). Likewise, some museums scan and make available 2D or 3D versions of physical artifacts in their collection in order to reach more web or social network-oriented users. Yet the simple and, oftentimes noble, act of digitizing to preserve and widen access raises legal questions for museums and other cultural institutions. As noted later in the chapter, some digitization activities can attract copyright in the new digital copy, especially if there is modest contribution in the digitization process. Hence, the copyright problem in the process of mass digitization involves not only copyright restrictions on the nondigital work due to be digitized but also copyright restrictions that arise as a result of digitization (Rahmatian, 2010). The latter situation can potentially put public domain works under copyright protection simply because they have been digitized.

The cultural heritage informatics community of scholars is developing tools for digital curation, documentation, standards for digital preservation, handling of digital objects, and digital asset management systems, among others. While cultural heritage informatics scholars (Cultural Heritage Informatics Initiative, n.d.) have dealt with the technical aspects of digitizing the artifacts, the legal questions, specifically copyright, remain unanswered (Frankel, 2010; McKeough, 2012). Moreover, for cultural institutions, the primary purpose of digitization, which is widening access, is not consistent with the current legal and policy goals of copyright laws, which is preservation (Corbett, 2011). Indeed, most copyright exceptions for libraries, archives, and other cultural institutions may not provide legal cover for the kind of mass digitization and global access most cultural institutions undertake today. Copyright law, in this case, is out of step with current digitization trends and practices—a problem that requires a unified voice from the cultural heritage informatics community of scholars.

Digital cultural heritage, like its nondigital form, is an important aspect of any given culture or people. Increasingly, digital cultural heritage is the best way to preserve a people's culture. Derclaye (2010) succinctly enumerates reasons for the preservation of cultures:

> It [culture] reflects the country's intellectual and economic wealth. It ensures that a people's memory is kept alive and thus preserves a country's history, which in turn helps to ensure avoidance of past mistakes and unnecessary duplications, the progress of

> education, of science and knowledge, the maintenance of cultural diversity, the mutual understanding between peoples and, hopefully, peace. It also helps increase personal and sustainable development, all sorts of benefits to humankind but also to all living beings and the planet. (p. viii)

Preservation and access to cultural heritage are increasingly more important in the digital realm since less and less of these resources are accessible in nondigital formats. However, legal barriers to access abound, in some cases hindering even the creation of digital cultural heritage in the first place. While the innovative technical work of cultural heritage informatics is appreciated, without favorable legal framework, the products of cultural heritage informatics will not have the widespread impact that field envisions.

The key question we tackle is how can copyright ensure the preservation of and access to digital cultural heritage? While that question seems simplistic, and some would argue has been addressed by existing copyright laws such as § 108 of the U.S. Copyright Act,[1] the more cultural institutions develop cultural resources in digital form, the more complex the legal questions become. For that matter, while § 108 somewhat addresses the preservation function and roles of cultural institutions, it doesn't sufficiently address the access objectives of users who are increasingly expecting unfettered access to cultural resources in digital form. The second reason why that question is complex is because except for a few cultural institutions, libraries in particular, legal issues and particularly copyright have not been sufficiently addressed in relation to preservation and access to digital cultural heritage. Libraries and librarians have been actively involved in copyright issues, but other cultural institutions are only now coming to the conversation. That necessarily limits the discourse surrounding copyright issues to libraries, although some of the issues affect other cultural institutions more than they do libraries. Archives, for instance, face a far more daunting challenge with orphaned works, an issue we explain and return to later. All institutions face problems of making available digital resources, whose creation was made possible by the preservation provision of the copyright law. The rest of the chapter is dedicated to these legal issues, starting off with a brief introduction to copyright law followed by an examination of the legal issues faced by some or all of the cultural institutions. Finally, we look at possible legal remedies all cultural institutions must advocate for if preservation and access to digitized cultural resources is to be truly achieved across these institutions.

INTELLECTUAL PROPERTY RIGHTS SIMPLIFIED

Intellectual property (IP) is intangible property resulting from creative minds or innovation. Without the idea of creations of the mind, intangible property like IP would not exist. Nonetheless, the idea of IP remains a controversial proposition because unlike physical property, IP entails a wide range of information-related goods and services or "kinds of property." Due to the differences in IP, the laws and regulations designed to create, regulate, and/or protect this kind of property are numerous and varied. Collectively, the laws are referred to as the Intellectual Property Rights (IPRs). In this chapter, we focus on the copyright law, which has the most direct impact on cultural institutions and, specifically, digital cultural resources. That is not to suggest that other areas of IP do not affect culture.

Copyright is a form of legal protection. It provides creators with broad exclusive rights in their works with the intention of motivating them to continue creating. Thus, copyright helps us advance cultural resources. The exclusive rights include the right to control copies and works that are derived from the original creation, as well as the right to control where the work is publicly displayed or broadcasted, including the web. Copyright can be sold or inherited, just like other forms of property. Not much is required for copyrights to be attached to a work or creation. Any work that is created independently with a modicum of creativity will do. Novels, sculpture, paintings, and songs are all commonly understood to enjoy these rights. However, letters written to a friend, family photographs, speeches, and many other types of works can also be covered under copyright law. Creative arrangement of data or other elements can be covered by copyright law, even if the elements of the work themselves do not have protection.

When copyright was written into the U.S. Constitution, the rights lasted only fourteen years. What was covered under this law was narrowly construed. Creators had to register and publish their works, as well as deposit a copy with the Library of Congress (LOC). Foreign works have not always enjoyed copyrights, nor have advertisements or translations. Throughout the years, copyright law has dramatically expanded in scope, strength, and duration.

These changes did not occur all at once. Some aspects of copyright law were retroactive and some were not, creating a complex tangle of rules. Unpublished works prior to 1898 and published works prior to 1923 are now part of the public domain, a commons of information that may be freely used by all. However, not all works that were created after these dates are covered by copyright laws. All works created prior to 1978 were covered under the 1909 copyright statute. This statute, although changed several times over the years, included several conditions that those who sought to enjoy these rights had to meet. These conditions included registration, publishing with the copyright notice, renewal of copyrights, and deposit of the work with the LOC. If the owner of the rights did not meet these conditions, then the work would become part of the public domain. Again, these conditions were not static, and this moving target of requirements changed several times between 1898 and 1978, when the current 1976 law took effect.

For works created after 1978, copyright now extends to 70 years upon the death of the creator, or up to 120 years for a work created as a "work for hire." There are no longer any formalities. Once the creator puts the work into a fixed, tangible form, it is automatically covered by copyright law. There are no registrations, no notice, and no obligation to deposit the work with the LOC or anywhere else. Copyright law originally did not cover much more than the order of the words themselves or extend to commercial works such as advertisements. The line dividing what is "inspired by" versus "derived from" has been pushed far toward the rights holder. Today, any work created with the original work in mind that bears substantial similarity to the original may be considered a copy of original work, even if the creator is unaware of the influence of the original.

The capacious rights afforded to copyright owners are tempered with many limitations and exceptions. The current U.S. Copyright Act was written in 1976, although sections have been amended or added over time. Section 108 of Title 17 covers exceptions for libraries and archives, demonstrating the value that Congress placed on the importance of these cultural institutions. Section 108 gives a laundry list of specific exceptions granted to libraries and similar cultural institutions, and offers definitive, specific rules on the conditions of their application. Unfortunately, many of these exceptions are out of date. Section 108 is hopelessly inadequate for covering the preservation needs of libraries and archives today, let alone their digitization needs. As Corbett (2011) rightly points out, "The exemptions [like §108] provided in copyright law for cultural heritage institutions have been drafted from the view that the sole purpose of digitization is to preserve copies of those items in collections that are in danger of deterioration" (p. 188). Corbett argues that "cultural heritage institutions digitize their collections because they wish to provide accessibility to a wider audience" (p. 188). Although § 108 allows for several uses such as preservation, interlibrary loan, and personal research, it prohibits access to digital copies outside of the library premises. Although some have made the argument that "the premises of the library or archive" should be construed broadly to include e-access, the answer is far from clear. Section 108 does not come close to approaching an adequate safe harbor for those wishing to digitize collections with the goal of providing broad access for users, a task that most users now expect libraries and archives to perform with their rare and archival collections.

Another exception to the exclusive rights granted to copyright holders is "fair use," found in § 107. Unlike the specific list with clear conditions, fair use is a broad doctrine found in the copyright statute that not only applies to libraries but to almost any type of uses (Fisher, 2014). Fair use is a defense that allows the user of the copyrighted work to contend that although she infringed, that her use was "fair," and thus excused. Fair use is a safety valve that allows culture to progress despite technological changes. Fair use has many applications. It allows for parody, criticism, and many other culturally important uses. According to Fisher (2014), without fair use, copyright law could well run afoul of the First Amendment rights enshrined in the U.S. Constitution.

Fair use determinations are based on four factors. The first factor examines how the copyrighted work has been used. Nonprofit, educational uses are highly favored, which covers many aspects of uses by cultural institutions. The second factor considers the work itself. Works that are more creative are more protected, as are works that have not been published before. Factual works have less protection. The third factor looks at how much of the copyrighted work has been taken or used. This factor is misleading, as it suggests that the less the copyrighted work is taken, the more likely the use will be found to be fair use. A more accurate measure of this rule is "was the amount taken the appropriate amount for the use?" In some instances, a few sentences of an entire book can be too much, if these sentences represent the heart of the work. In other instances, the entire work can be taken if it is the amount of the work that was necessary, as in the case of parody. One cannot parody a work without taking a substantial portion of it. The fourth factor is the effect of the use on the market or the potential market. Just because the rights holder has not exploited a particular market, such as selling rights to digitally transmit their work over the Internet, does not mean that others have the right to usurp their place in that market.

The factors are not a concrete set of rules but a guideline set forth by Congress in the 1976 law. They were not meant to be static, but instead to be flexible and bend with the changing needs of our culture in the face of rapid technological change. The factors are all weighed, but they do not have to be considered equally. Until recently, the fourth factor, market effect, has been weighed heavily by the courts in fair use determinations. This trend changed in 1994 with a Supreme Court case, *Campbell v. Acuff-Rose Music, Inc.*,[2] that determined that parody was a strongly favored, transformative use. Transformative use has since colored many fair use determinations. Transformative use is generally considered to be an aspect of the first factor, the nature of the use. If a use is deemed to be transformative, the other factors may be weighed less, although not completely discounted. Although parody is firmly determined to be a type of transformative use, several other uses of copyrighted materials have also been proffered as transformative, to include criticism, physical modification of the work, using the work for a different purpose, creative uses, and socially beneficial uses. For digitization initiatives in cultural institutions, the key question is whether digitization, for whatever purpose, constitutes or involves transformativeness that meets the fair use test. We return to this question in the next section.

CASE STUDIES OF CULTURAL INSTITUTIONS

In this section, we examine specific functions, services, or practices in cultural institutions relating to digitization or digital resources and how they are affected by copyright or the unintended consequences of the copyright law.

Ownership of Cultural Resources and Orphaned Works

Most cultural institutions face the daunting task of identifying authors of works whose ownership or authorship is unknown, commonly known as orphaned works (van Gompel & Hugenholtz, 2010). Orphaned works are a major stumbling block to the digitization efforts many archival and other cultural institutions are engaged in to make cultural resources accessible on the web and other digital platforms. The orphan works problem, as van Gompel & Hugenholtz (2010) refer to it, is particularly acute today as the digitization trend has moved from an atypical occurrence to an almost expected service in the minds of the public. There are many reasons that digital collections are valuable additions to cultural institutions and their users. For the caretakers of these objects, it is of great value to have the items subjected to less wear and tear as users no longer need access to the original artifact. If the item is text based, searching electronic databases is possible using keywords if the full text has been documented. Users from all over the world can access the works, at any time, without assistance from curators. The works can be discovered and used by a much wider audience, and with considerably less effort. In addition, viewing the works as a whole as they relate to each other in a collection can add value to the research. A user would not be able to explore as many items in person as they can online. All of these reasons have placed great pressure on cultural institutions to make their collections available online. Cultural heritage informatics has made tremendous contributions to providing the tools that make these and more digital resources possible. Yet copyright presents some limited possibilities to facilitate access to the digital cultural resources. It presents even more constraints on digitizing and making available these resources.

The first constraint is the ability to determine if the work is indeed covered by copyright law, or if instead it has risen into the public domain. In the United States, any work published after 1923 is potentially protected by the Copyright Act. Works that are not published, as is the case for many works in archives and other cultural institutions, are potentially covered by copyright law if they were created in 1894 or after. The works could be covered for the life of the author plus seventy years. Only the works of people who died in 1944 or before are part of the public domain as of 2014. If the work was created as a "work for hire," usually a copyrighted work made by an employee in the course of their job duties, these works could be covered for 120 years. This renders most current and twentieth-century collections encumbered by copyright law. Since copyright law no longer requires formalities, all works, including unpublished works, are potentially covered by these laws (Cornell University, 2014).

Most cultural institutions have agreements with the donors of the collections that they receive. The agreements give the institutions the ability to do certain things with the collections they receive. If the agreements were written before the advent of digital collections initiatives, it is often the case that the agreements did not have the forethought to allow for the scanning and making available digital versions of the resources. Sometimes the original donors have died, and if they died after 1944, their works might still be covered by copyright. Since copyrights are inherited just like other types of property, the beneficiaries of the often unknown-to-them rights must be tracked down and new agreements negotiated. Even more problematic, the beneficiaries are often unknown or unknowable to the cultural institution hosting the collection. Determining ownership involving scenarios like this one are often cumbersome and time wasting for most resource-poor or constrained cultural institutions.

Breakdown in the system for tracking ownership of copyright works occurs because of the lack of formalities such as mandatory registration of copyrighted works.

If the date of death cannot be determined, there will be difficulty knowing for certain that the work is within or out of copyright. Likewise, the authors of works are sometimes difficult to determine. For example, the copyrights for photographs often rest with the photographer. For most nonprofessional photography, it is next to impossible to determine definitively who took the photograph. Many archival collections often contain letters written to their donors. The institution physically owns these letters, but the copyright rests with the person who wrote the letter, not the recipient, and subsequently, the institution to which the collection was donated (Dickson, 2010). Circumstances like this require tracking down the author of the letter as well as determining if the letter was written by a person as an individual or a person who created the letter under the work-for-hire doctrine, as the dates of coverage for these two types of copyright are different. The cost of this work can be prohibitive. Often it is impossible to determine from whom the letter originated. These works of undetermined authorship are termed *orphaned works*. Orphaned works represent a serious roadblock to many cultural institutions, as they add to the level of uncertainty. Unfortunately, many cultural institutions have no specific safe harbor exception as can be found in § 108 for some other library and archive uses. Even if there were exceptions, they would only cover libraries and archives for certain. Fortunately, cultural institutions can still avail themselves of the broad exception found in § 107, the fair use doctrine.

The fair use doctrine examines four factors to determine if a use can be deemed fair: the nature of the use, the nature of the work, the amount of the work used, and the effect on the market or potential market. The factors are not weighed formulaically, but instead considered as a whole. Fortunately for cultural institutions, most of the uses fall under the nonprofit educational category, which are highly favored under the first factor. In addition, the uses can often be considered transformative, as the case might be if digitization makes the collection more accessible to users with disabilities or the works can be used as a whole instead of as individual pieces (Dickson, 2010). Transformative works are highly favored, thus increasing the chances of prevailing.

The nature of the work would prove less favorable in most instances, as creative and unpublished works generally enjoy a greater level of protection. However, it is not necessary to win on every factor to prevail in a fair use analysis. The amount taken would also be less favorable than the first factor in most cases, although it could be argued that the amount necessary for the use would be the entire amount. The fourth factor, the effect on the market for the work, would generally be very limited, although perhaps not always.

That said, misconceptions abound on the scope of fair use, such as the belief that it is acceptable to post copyrighted works on the web for noncommercial purposes or by nonprofit entities such as cultural institutions. Other misconceptions include, but are not limited to, the idea that owning physical copies of donated letters in a collection means owing copyrights in the works and, therefore, the institution can digitize and display the digital copy at will. Finally, relating to the orphaned works, there is a misconception that if you cannot find the owner, the institution is allowed to make and post a digital copy.

Most cultural institutions are risk averse. However, it is arguable that in instances where the consequences of adherence to a strict interpretation of copyright law could be contrary to the primary mission of these organizations, it would be appropriate to evaluate the risk and consider all options. Statutory damages can be high, up to $150,000 for willful infringement. For works that are not registered, however, the damages are limited to actual or potential damages. Even if works are registered, § 504(c)(2) provides that statutory damages be remitted for some fair use arguments, even if the argument does not prevail, if the infringer were "an employee or agent of a nonprofit educational institution, library, or archives acting within the scope of his or her employment who, or such institution, library, or archives itself, which infringed by reproducing the work in copies or phonorecords." Additionally, many cultural institutions are state, federal, or tribal institutions that possibly have "sovereign immunity," allowing them to escape all relief except for injunctions, greatly lessening the chances of a frivolous lawsuit. Other reasonable risk management measures, such as controls over downloads or easily available takedown request forms, could also prove useful by limiting the potential for offending the copyright owners.

Right to Display of Digitized Works

Displaying of digitized works, especially those digitized under preservation copyright provisions, presents serious legal challenges. It is closely related but not entirely connected to the orphaned works problem above. Some donors of works to cultural institutions prefer or insist not to make available their works beyond the confines of the institution, as the case would be if digitized. In this case, even if the owner of the work is known, the institution may not transfer that work for any purpose other than preservation. It certainly cannot make it available to the user public without serious legal consequences.

Public Domain Derivative Works

Cultural heritage institutions have historically relied on public donations, user access fees, and, most recently, the sale of souvenirs to support their work. Increasingly, many rely on copyrighted souvenirs in the form of calendars, caps, T-shirts, cups, and the like to generate revenue for supporting activities and functioning of the institutions. The souvenirs are often made using public domain resources such as images or illustrations. Some souvenirs are made using or based on resources donated to the institution. Digitization provides another avenue for cultural institutions like museums to create derivative works of all kinds in digital format based on public domain resources and beyond. As variously noted above, digitization is a noble and welcome action, especially to the extent that it widens access and ensures long-term preservation. However, digitization resulting in copyrightable derivative works, especially those based upon or drawing from the public domain, achieves the opposite goal. The resultant cultural products are the property of the cultural institution, which limits what the user public, particularly those involved in creative endeavors, can do with the derivative works. While most of the derivative works are often interpreted as the intellectual property of the institution, the fact that some are drawn from public domain resources raises serious legal and ethical questions. In a landmark case, *Bridgeman Art Library v. Corel Corporation*,[3] the Southern District of New York ruled that museums and related cultural institutions could not claim copyright in derivative works drawn from the public domain where little to no creative effort went into making the derivative work. While that case seemingly protected misappropriation and enclosure of the public domain, it left open the possibility of cultural institutions using new digital tools to make derivative works that meet the low originality test required for copyrightable materials. Some legal scholars such as Allan (2007) have argued that *Bridgeman Art Library v. Corel Corporation* was badly decided; that the court erred in not granting cultural institutions the right to claim copyright in derivative works drawing from the public domain. With increasingly sophisticated digital tools, granting cultural institutions the right to enclose the public domain would be counterproductive in the sense that soon there would be less public domain works in the digital environment. Cultural institutions hold cultural resources in digital or other forms in the public trust to ensure posterity (Prott, 2002). That basic function is more critical in the digital environment than before.

Conclusion and Recommendations

Orphan works were identified as the most pressing problem for cultural institutions involved in digital resources. The solution to orphaned works can be found in the Canadian approach to orphaned works. According to van Gompel and Hugenholtz (2010), the Canadian approach centers on the Canadian Copyright Board, established to grant licenses to users if they can prove that a reasonable search was conducted but did not result in discovery of the owner of a work. Van Gompel and Hugenholtz (2010) note that a reasonable search requires "the applicant to contact different collecting societies and publishing houses; to consult indexes of national libraries, universities, and museums; to check registration systems of copyright offices; to investigate inheritance records; and to simply search the Internet" (p. 67). Van Gompel and Hugenholtz are clearly satisfied with the Canadian solution to the orphaned works issue, noting that:

> [The] Canadian system . . . provides the user with adequate legal certainty about being able to use an orphan work. Where a user is granted a license, he is authorized to use an orphan work without the risk of an infringement claim should the rights owner come forward. At the same time, the legitimate interests of the rights owners concerned are not unnecessarily compromised. First, a verification of the good faith of a user is performed by an independent public body, which serves the needs of prospective users while taking due account of the legitimate interests of the rights owners concerned. Second, exceptions

> to the rights of the rights owner are made on a case-to-case basis, thereby avoiding disproportional prejudice to the principle of exclusive rights that is inherent to the copyright system. Third, the license issued is not all-inclusive, but granted to a particular user for a specific kind of use only. Finally, the system does not result in a loss of income for rights holders. If a rights holder eventually shows up, he is compensated. (p. 68)

While the Canadian legal and practical solution is far from perfect for cultural institutions whose resources may not permit securing licenses for orphan works, it remains the most reasonable remedy in practice at the moment. Most importantly, it gives the institutions legal certainty once the license for a work or collection has been secured. To make it workable, we suggest a tiered approach where nonprofit cultural institutions involved in mass digitization for purposes of public access and posterity pay lower license fees than for-profit entities or private users.

Other options have been proposed as solutions for the orphaned works problem, such as a return to formalities, opt-out systems, or the creation of an exception similar to those found in § 108 to allow such projects. These solutions would be complicated to craft, as well as difficult to navigate through the political process as it stands today. Film, publishing, and recording industries exercise enormous influence over copyright legislation and treaties, as well as frequently mount well-funded litigation. Cultural institutions' needs have become collateral damage in the crossfire as these powerful industries fight to guard their financial interests. Compulsory licenses have been successfully used for other types of works in the United States, specifically musical compositions. A compulsory license system seems to be the most reasonable solution, although there is no obvious perfect solution yet (Fisher, 2004).

Besides orphaned works, we identified the problem of digitization of public works, which at times could result in copyrighting of resultant or derivative works. Some cultural institutions, museums in particular, rely on this to generate revenue that keeps institutional services and activities running. It is critical that cultural institutions are not denied these revenue streams. However, such activities must not result in the enclosure of works previously in the public domain simply because the cultural institution has created a derivative work through digitization or other means. As a principle, no one, not even cultural institutions, should be able to claim copyright in an analog work in the public domain that is marginally transformed in the digital environment (Deazley, 2010). Likewise, there ought to be no copyright infringement on restored public domain derivative works (Rahmatian, 2010).

The foregoing discussion demonstrates some of the legal challenges cultural heritage informatics faces above and beyond developing innovative tools for digitizing cultural heritage. It is our hope that bringing this debate within cultural heritage informatics, and more specifically, addressing the issues across cultural institutions, will draw the attention of cultural heritage informatics practitioners and hopefully join others that have worked on these issues outside the context of digital cultural heritage.

NOTES

1. 17 U.S.C. § 108—Limitations on exclusive rights: Reproduction by libraries and archives.
2. See *Campbell v. Acuff-Rose Music, Inc.*, 510 U.S. 569 (1994).
3. *Bridgeman Art Library, Ltd. v. Corel Corp.* [Bridgeman I], 25 F. Supp. 2d 421 (S.D.N.Y. 1998); *Bridgeman Art Library, Ltd. v. Corel Corp.* [Bridgeman II], 36 F. Supp. 2d 191 (S.D.N.Y. 1999).

REFERENCES

Allan, R. J. (2007). After *Bridgeman:* Copyright, museums, and public domain works of art. *University of Pennsylvania Law Review, 155*, 961–89.

Arnold, D. (2008). Cultural heritage as a vehicle for basic research in computing science: Pasteur's quadrant and a use-inspired basic research agenda. *Computer Graphics Forum, 27*, 2188–96. doi:10.1111/j.1467-8659.2008.01195.x

Corbett, S. (2007). Digital heritage: Legal barriers to conserving New Zealand's early video games. *New Zealand Business Law Quarterly, 13*(5), 48–71.

Corbett, S. (2011). Copyright and cultural heritage: Preservation and access to works in a digital world [Review of the book *Copyright and cultural heritage: preservation and access to works in a digital world*, edited by E. Derclaye]. *Prometheus, 29*(2), 188–94. doi:10.1080/08109028.2011.616027

Cornell University. (2014). *Copyright term and the public domain in the United States.* Retrieved from http://copyright.cornell.edu/resources/publicdomain.cfm.

Cultural Heritage Informatics Initiative. (n.d.). *About the Cultural Heritage Informatics Initiative.* Retrieved from http://chi.anthropology.msu.edu/program/.

Deazley, R. (2010). Photography, copyright and the South Kensington experiment. In E. Derclaye (Ed.), *Copyright and cultural heritage preservation and access to works in a digital world* (pp. 77–110). Cheltenham, UK: Edward Elgar.

Derclaye, E. (2010). Introduction. In W. Derclaye (Ed.), *Copyright and cultural heritage preservation and access to works in a digital world* (pp. viii–xvii). Cheltenham, UK: Edward Elgar.

Dickson, M. (2010). Due diligence, futile effort: Copyright and the digitization of the Thomas E. Watson papers. *American Archivist, 73*, 626–36.

Fisher, W. (2004). *Promises to keep: Technology, law and the future of entertainment.* Stanford, CA: Stanford University Press.

Fisher, W. (2014, February 18). *CopyrightX: Lecture 9.2, fair use: Fair use today* [Video file]. Retrieved from https://www.youtube.com/watch?v=hN5KEQb-nTw.

Frankel, S. (2010). Digital copyright and culture. *Journal of Arts Management, Law & Society, 40*(2), 140–56. doi:10.1080/10632921.2010.486294

Lukasik, C. J. (2013). Breaking and entering: Reflections on the archive. *Western Humanities Review, 67*(2), 36–41.

McKeough, J. (2012). Copyright review: Issues for cultural practice. *Deakin Law Review, 17*, 309–19.

Prott, L. L. (2002). Individual or collective rights for cultural heritage in the information society? *Museum International, 54*(4), 7–12.

Rahmatian, A. (2010). Copyright protection for the restoration, reconstruction and digitisation of public domain works. In E. Derclaye (Ed.), *Copyright and cultural heritage preservation and access to works in a digital world* (pp. 51–76). Cheltenham, UK: Edward Elgar.

Striphas, T., & McLeod, K. (2006). Strategic improprieties: Cultural studies, the everyday, and the politics of intellectual properties. *Cultural Studies, 20*(2/3), 119–44.

van Gompel, S., & Hugenholtz, P. (2010). The orphan works problem: The copyright conundrum of digitizing large-scale audiovisual archives, and how to solve it. *Popular Communication, 8*(1), 61–71. doi:10.1080/15405700903502361

II

PARTICIPATORY CULTURE

5

"Knit and the World Knits with You"

Studying Participatory Culture in U.S. Newspapers through World War I[1]

Jennifer Burek Pierce

ABSTRACT

Participatory culture, per Henry Jenkins and allied theorists, is often regarded as a relatively recent phenomenon facilitated by new social media. However, U.S. newspapers' cultivation of their readers' contributions at the turn of the previous century represents a prototype for what Jenkins has labeled participatory culture. Newspaper knitting columns, where publishers encouraged individuals to interact and form a sense of community, provide one instance of participatory culture. The aim of this chapter is to assess archival media to understand more about how knitters learned from one another when print was the only alternative to face-to-face communication. A nineteenth-century knitter's notebook reveals knitting information in the mainstream periodical literature, and digitized newspaper articles preserve discourse and link knitting with the formation of various kinds of communities and affinity groups. By juxtaposing these hitherto separate histories and using conventional and digital archives in tandem, a sense of the past is contextualized and connected. Online media archives illuminate the ways knitters throughout the nation sought and shared information long before the creation of social media platforms, challenging stereotypes about the cultural resonances of handcrafts and women's work.

INTRODUCTION

As articulated by Henry Jenkins, the participatory culture theory holds that disruptive technology and distinctive social change factor in creating connection among dispersed individuals who want to share their expertise in areas of mutual interest. These contentions about the nature of communities created by affinity rather than proximity are more often endorsed than critically examined, but the practices U.S. newspapers adopted at the turn of the previous century provide perspective on these claims about how individuals come together around common interests. Beginning in the late nineteenth century, newspapers sought to secure readers' engagement with their print products by encouraging interaction and a sense of community. Their efforts to attract a demonstrable and committed readership centered on elements other than what we now think of as front-page news: photography contests and lifestyle stories represented opportunities for readers to reveal their skills. Knitting was among the subjects that received this sort of treatment. If participatory culture is "one in which members believe their contributions matter . . . [or] care about what other people think about what they have created," U.S. newspapers' cultivation of their readers' contributions at the turn of the previous century represents a prototype for what Jenkins has labeled participatory culture (Jenkins, Clinton, Purushotma, Robison, & Weigel, 2006, p. 3).

In this same era, knitting remained a common and even necessary hand skill. Although knitting machinery existed, its commercial utility was not fully exploited until well into the twentieth century. Not only was machine knitting a relatively new phenomenon, so were indexing and other techniques that would facilitate information access. Unless a knitter possessed one of a relatively small number of treatises on techniques and patterns, she or he would learn more about working with fiber from another knitter. While some discussion of a knitter's needs might have taken place in person, the resources of which that individual might avail himself or herself expanded significantly as newspapers endeavored to change the reach and responses of their readership.

My aim in this chapter is to assess archival media that allow us to understand more about how knitters learned from one another when print was the only alternative to face-to-face communication. Two sets of documents are essential to the analysis, as a nineteenth-century knitters' notebook calls attention to its creator's documentation of her handcraft skills and to the existence of knitting information in mainstream periodical literature. I evaluate a selection of the numerous newspaper articles on knitting from this earlier era with two central, related purposes in mind: to identify publishing trends on needlecraft and ways that journalistic practices fostered early iterations of the phenomena now recognized as participatory culture. Through this assessment, we can see two scholarly assumptions modified, if not dispelled. Not only do versions of participatory culture emerge well in advance of recent social media technologies, but knitting, typically characterized as a skill learned face to face, has long had a presence in print culture. The material conditions associated with both phenomena, then, seem, in fundamental ways, to differ from prevailing theory. Further, the newspaper articles that preserve discourse on an otherwise ephemeral subject links knitting with recent scholarly interest in the conditions that lead to the formation of various kinds of communities and affinity groups.

Simultaneously, this chapter illustrates an iterative research process for the study of material culture, in which traditional archival material and resources conserved as online media are interdependent. Adam Kirsch has recently raised questions about whether the findings resulting from tools and methods associated with the digital humanities are in fact distinct from those resulting from long-established scholarly practices; I would revise his argument to suggest that research is strengthened by using conventional and digital archives in tandem (Kirsch, 2014). Material archival media would focus attention on the activities of a singular individual; drawing on digitized historical media would demonstrate an enduring and popular preoccupation with knitting, without as strong a sense of what the myriad articles might have meant in a reader's daily life. By seeing these resources as interrelated and essential to informing our understanding of the cultural activity they depict, we arrive at a sense of the past that is contextualized and connected. Online media archives can be used to illuminate the ways knitters throughout the nation sought and shared information long before the creation of blogs, YouTube videos, and platforms such as Ravelry. In this, they also challenge stereotypes about the cultural resonances of handcrafts and women's work.

PARTICIPATORY CULTURE AND DISPERSED COMMUNITIES

Several scholars have turned their attention to the construction and conventions of participatory culture, a notion loosely synonymous with some theoretical delineations of community because of similar attentions to the formation of relationships among individuals whose communications are primarily mediated ones. While some researchers use these concepts to anchor historical study, others seem more interested in them as a means of critiquing or valuing recent media use. The defining characteristics, then, often have to do with the communicative mechanisms used. According to Jenkins, who links the rise of participatory culture to fans' relationships to science fiction on screens small and large, features of participatory culture include interactivity, blurring of lines between media production and consumption, and activism. While these traits are not inherently the result of contemporary media, Jenkins nonetheless attributes their origins to "specific historical conditions . . . the development of feminism, the development of new technologies, the atomization and alienation of contemporary American culture" (Jenkins, 2013, p. 3). It is worth noting that Benedict Anderson's invocation of the imagined community, an entity whose members "will never know most of their fellow-members . . . yet in the minds of each lives the image of their communion," is linked to the formation of nations in the eighteenth century (Anderson, 1983, p. 49). This effort to understand how a group of geographically dispersed individuals form bonds, signals that these communities need not be conceptualized with reference to technologies that have flourished in the twenty-first century.

Beyond the impetus of the particular historical moment, Jenkins et al. list affiliations, whether through formal or informal membership in groups; expression, or the production of media; collaboration, particularly with an intention of developing "new knowledge"; and circulation, or the "flow of media," as the outgrowth of cultural changes (Jenkins, et al., 2006, p. 3). Such changes, in turn, Jenkins has argued, foster textual poaching as a social group attempts "to define its own culture and to construct its own community" and strives to craft "meaning from materials others have characterized as trivial and worthless" (Jenkins, 2013, p. 3). Again, Anderson's study of nations as "cultural artifacts" capable of creating "deep attachments" with implications for self-governance, interpretation of texts, and market forces seems to anticipate particular dimensions of Jenkins's interest in shared cultural activities (Anderson, 1983, pp. 48, 52–53).

The idea of poaching as an approach to media use, initially articulated by Michel de Certeau, has been characterized as appropriative, neglectful of intellectual property rights, and even of meaning. Such concepts are engaged by the work of Ellen Gruber Garvey (2013) on scrapbooks as a once standard way of reading and writing. Garvey, along with Chasar (2012) and Rubin (2007), have advanced the idea that readers' experiences of popular texts may function in ways that diverge sharply from authorial intent, while still being honest and emotionally significant. The archival media with which this research began illustrates a private manifestation of these entwined approaches to understanding media use as a facet of a particular community's development.

THE CLUE IN THE SCRAPBOOK, THE SEARCH IN CYBERSPACE

The archives at Winterthur Museum, Library, and Gardens contain an undated swatch book of knitted lace from the late 1800s. Its compiler and creator is unidentified, but its mode of construction is evident. Dozens of newspaper clippings of directions for knitting lace are pinned to the lined pages of a small notebook, followed by samples of lacework that model many of the printed patterns (Lace instruction, undated). The reverse sides of these clippings, as well as the newsprint on which they were published, indicate their source: stories about temperance, farming, and contemporary political issues suggest that these snippets of needlework instruction were published in general interest newspapers. Drawing in part on material from newspapers and in part of her own efforts with needles and fiber, someone created a booklet to which multiple labels might be applied. It could be called a scrapbook, because of its assembly, per Garvey's (2013) research. Because of its content, it could be referred to as a stitch dictionary, a self-generated one that predates volumes such as Barbara Walker's *Treasury of Knitting Patterns* (1998) or Vogue Knitting's *Stitchionary* series (2005, 2006a, 2006b, 2007, 2010, 2011), which provide knitters with directions and images for executing different types of stitches, including lace and cable patterns. Regardless of the label one applies to it, it is a curiosity.

Most histories of needlework assert its transmission through personal instruction, individuals sitting side-by-side with their needles and wool, yet this notebook shows that some knitters advanced their skills with information gleaned from print sources. While these self-made guides to knitting are not abundant, the Winterthur swatch book is not an isolated phenomenon. Searches of historical newspaper databases such as *Chronicling America: Historic American Newspapers* via the Library of Congress reveal that the creator of this swatch book was one of many readers of a prolific area of news publishing: the knitting column. The circulation statistics for any given newspaper mean the potential readership of such content is significant. Publishing knitting patterns and related information in the newspaper was standard by the late nineteenth century, and the popularity of this content grew as the United States became cognizant of the hardships caused by the international conflict known then as the Great War. Further, the specific information in these articles from a time referred to as the Long Nineteenth Century or the Progressive Era evince a participatory print culture that developed around knitting.

The publication of columns on knitting represents a demonstrable instance of a participatory, if readerly, community. Although news coverage of knitting originated in conjunction with the women's page, after the United States entered World War I, readers of either sex, and of all ages, participated in knitting. Their efforts were reflected by a print culture that supported the enterprise, once knitting became synonymous with patriotism. As the *Ogden Standard* advised its readers in July 1917, "Knit and the World Knits with You" (Winthrop, 1917). The *Ogden Standard*'s article was one of thousands of articles on knitting published by U.S. newspapers between the late 1800s and the end of World War I. This proliferation both makes possible, and makes difficult, the determination of the nature of information sharing among knitters around the turn of the previous century.

Libraries' efforts to preserve U.S. newspapers reveal myriad matches for material like that collected in the Winterthur notebook, confirming that knitting was featured in many general interest papers, rather than in specialized outlets focused on craft. The *New York Tribune*, for example, published patterns for Shell-Edged Lace (1881) and an Olive Leaf Pattern (1880) suited to numerous decorative purposes. Patterns for everything from neckties (Tunisian lace necktie, 1881) to curtains (Knitted curtains, 1881) also appeared in the *Tribune*. Because search queries in *Chronicling America: Historic American Newspapers* indicate that the word *knit* appears, in some context, more than seven thousand times in the *New York Tribune* alone, the examples discussed here, drawn from two New York papers with expansive readerships, are selective, rather than exhaustive. I would note further that the availability of other online repositories of historic newspapers, including amateur efforts such as the Old Fulton New York Post Cards site (http://www.fultonhistory.com/fulton.html) that claims to contain nearly twenty-seven million pages of content from old newspapers in the New York region, indicate the possibility of adding material that could enhance this sort of study.

From the 1880s and into the twentieth century, the *New York Tribune* encouraged knitters to share their own patterns and seek help from other knitters via a "Scrap Bag" column in the paper's women's pages. In these outlets, knitters became writers as they exchanged information. Accordingly, in 1880, Mrs. G. M. M. contributed "A Pretty Edging," while C. M. B. sought a pattern for a knitted hood for a three-year-old, and Mrs. Diana Millspane "asks for directions for knitting gentlemen's silk mittens—knit round and round" (Scrap-bag, 1880). To these calls for information, the section editor promised that new patterns would be made available soon (Scrap-bag, 1880). The kinds of answers these requests received is demonstrated by Miss E. Allen, a Manhattan knitter, who provided another knitter with "directions . . . for a golf vest, without collar or sleeves" (Golf vest, 1903). At other times, knitters offered stitch-by-stitch modifications of existing patterns (Insertion to match child's collar, 1881). Knitters apparently found such contributions useful, if we accept the testimonial of C. F. G. that "the Tribune knitting patterns are much superior to those printed elsewhere, in that they come out right" (Scrap-bag, 1880).

The editors also noted distinctive needlework in other contexts, such as a 1900 charity drive that saw the donation of mittens by Mrs. A. Holcomb of Connecticut, who "though more than fourscore years of age, is ever busy preparing sunshine for someone." It was not just her age that deserved note, but her technique, as editors apprised readers that her knitting was not "the ordinary kind" but used "two colors in fancy stitches almost unknown at the present day" (Contribution received, 1900). In these and other issues, the paper's editors mediated and moderated exchange among knitters who aspired not simply to recognition in print, but to discuss craft.

The valence of these conversations began to shift as World War I began to occupy the nation's attention. Newspapers connected knitting and the war effort before the United States entered the conflict. A 1916 photo spread in the *New York Tribune* that called readers' attention to the way Germany "[remembered] the birthday of the Prince of Peace" began with an image of "Berlin school girls" who knitted "Christmas gifts for their fathers and brothers in the trenches" (The *Tribune* graphic, 1916). Although these young women knitted for individual family members, they gathered together to do so—an informal group aligned for the common purpose of wartime knitting.

Once the United States declared war against Germany and other Central powers, the Red Cross and other organizations launched knitting drives to benefit troops and refugees, the best known of which was the "Knit Your Bit" campaign. Strawn (2007, p.107), for example, has noted the prevalence of a sock pattern that was promoted by the Red Cross and republished by many outlets. These activities saw group efforts like the one modeled in the Berlin photo enacted on U.S. soil. Newspapers supported the endeavors with publicity, placing a new importance on the knitting column established in the previous century. The new tenor could be seen in a 1918 photo page in the New York *Sun* that celebrated the knitting drive with images of a Red Cross parade. Images included "Red Cross knitters on a float equipped with knitting machines" that celebrated their efficiency, boasting that a sweater could be completed in as little as eight minutes and socks in fifteen. The symbolism of hand knitting, as well as the pragmatism of machinery, was noted. "Socks have a new meaning nowadays," readers were told in a caption that highlighted Red Cross nurses' socks as "a novel and conspicuous feature" of the nation's patriotism (*Pictorial Magazine*, 1918). Knitters also aligned under other banners to support the war effort and express their collective creativity.

The *Sun* regularly published readers' verses about wartime knitting, which the paper called Sock Songs, a weekly feature that began in May 1918 (Sock singer in south registers protest, 1918; Write a prize sock song, 1918) and was touted on the paper's masthead (see, e.g., *Pictorial Magazine*, 1918). As the editors explained later in the summer of 1918, "the idea of a Sock Song, you know, is a bit of verse that could appropriately be tucked in with the socks sent off to France" (Sock song singers from Pennsylvania, 1918). While a "quartermaster sergeant in one of our coast defenses" paid tribute to the "good women folk who had worked so diligently with their needles" (Sock song singers from Pennsylvania, 1918), contributors were male and female, and wrote from as near as Atlantic City and as far away as Texas (Sock singer in south registers protest, 1918). As a verse by H. S. Wyllie testified, "For Liberty our young men die,/For Liberty, with many a sigh;/Both sexes, juvenile and old,/To ward our fighters' feet from cold,/Aid in the fight by knitting" (Sock song writers swamp judges, 1918). The hundreds of verses that vied for the weekly prize of wool varied between adaptations of popular music and more original content, but were limited to ten lines or less (Sing a sock song, 1918). Editors claimed that paper rationing also factored in these restrictions (Sock song writers swamp judges, 1918).

Collectively, newspapers' publication of knitting-related information encouraged knitters to see themselves as part of a community. Knitters were linked by common purpose, whether care of family at home or of those who had gone to fight in faraway battles. The practice of printing information made this community visible and encouraged its loose membership to contribute their voices, whether for recognition of their expertise or to help others. Artifacts may be the principal product of a knitter's activity, but it would be much more difficult to assess historical knitting without the print culture that documents the creation of all those socks, scarves, and sweaters.

KNIT AND THE WORLD KNITS WITH YOU: NOTES FOR FURTHER RESEARCH

The curious knitter of Winterthur, who created her own scrapbook from the kinds of information found in the *Sun* and the *Tribune*, then, was not simply an isolated individual making what is now known as a stitch dictionary before they were commonly and commercially available. While her clippings and knitted swatches no doubt helped her practice of craft, these materials also aligned her with a dispersed community of knitters who communicated through print venues where they could respond to other knitters' questions with their own knowledge and design innovations. The notebook calls our attention to nineteenth-century instances of "peer-to-peer learning" and "the emergence of a cultural context" that facilitated "widespread participation in the production and distribution of media" (Jenkins et al., 2006, pp. 3, 6). Admittedly, the knitting writers of this earlier era differed from her notebook documents in the use of information that developed and flourished because of its presence in newspapers at significant moments in the nation's history.

Much as Jenkins sees feminism as a cause for participatory culture and textual poaching, most extant research on newspapers and women focuses on the female writers who broke with restrictive conventions and became well-known reporters. Yet this robust publishing on knitting suggests an attentive and engaged readership for more traditional content (Chamber, Steiner, & Fleming, 2004; Mills, 1988; Conboy, 2002; Whitt, 2008). Much research on the history of knitting neglects the print culture that surrounds the craft, looking for documentation of its past primarily in the few textiles that have survived and been preserved in institutional settings (Strawn, 2012). While exemplary scholarship is based on the use of textiles as primary sources, it is unnecessarily limiting as a means of understanding knitting as a cultural phenomenon. This chapter juxtaposes these hitherto separate histories by focusing on newspapers as sources of perspective on the early participatory culture of knitting. The burgeoning print culture surrounding craft offers a new perspective on established wisdom, as well as documentation of these aspects of cultural heritage.

As the Winterthur notebook is undated, it is difficult to locate its compiler at an exact moment with respect to the shifting culture that surrounded knitting during the era under study. The content on the reverse of the knitting instructions clipped from newspapers guides us to a range of dates, rather than specific years. The mention of temperance, for example, locates the media within a span of some eighty years, from the beginnings of the temperance movement in the 1830s to the passage of Prohibition in 1917 (see *Roots of Prohibition*, 2011). The language of the undated, sometimes partial articles, however, would suggest a time frame somewhat earlier than the later Anti-Saloon League language associated with the German war enemy and the language of the constitutional amendment. Vocabulary as well as topic, then, tells us something about when the Winterthur knitter clipped articles. Less an effort at matching, verbatim, the text of the clippings with content found in online newspaper archives, this manifestation of participation in a community of knitters made possible by print media remains the artifact of an era, rather than of a particular date.

Additional tools and technologies might make it possible to extend the number of articles used to develop this chapter. Barring a more computational approach, the scale of such a study poses challenges, and the value of further examples would have to exceed simple aggregation. Much of what might be learned from such material would seem to require extensive reading and analysis. For example, while many of these newspapers seem, by title or other descriptive matter, to be regional ones, the information in each column indicates that the readership might be geographically diverse. Further, a researcher confronts the problem of false drops; because most of these sites prioritize the digitization of media, the search mechanisms might not be as sophisticated as is technically possible. The difficulty of distinguishing between a column on how to knit and an advertisement for knitted garments, however, would remain, as overlapping contextual words would make it exceptionally difficult to rule out related terms without losing a fair amount of relevant material. Thus, while digitization makes content easily available to researchers, long-standing analytical approaches remain essential to these texts.

Further, though we label this time period with terminology intended to reflect continuity—the Long Nineteenth Century, the Progressive Era—knitting activities during this same time period could be divided into two stages. First, there was the entwining of need for and interest in fiber goods for home and family; this was succeeded, gradually, by a commitment to knitting for the war effort. While it was not unheard of for men to knit during the first stage, their efforts were more publicized during the second.

Additional differences characterize wartime knitting as a sort of social movement. It has been argued that World War I, which was declared in 1914 in Britain, witnessed a dynamic willingness to knit in support of the troops (Carron, 2007; see also Strawn, 2007). It is not surprising that British knitters preceded their American counterparts in this endeavor, given the disparity in the dates at which their nations entered the war. What is unexpected, though, lies in the contentions of one writer about the nature of this wartime knitting:

> American expatriates in London began to urge women stateside to take up their needles as well, which they did, but serious effort on the American side didn't really begin until the United States declared war in April 1917. Surprisingly, American governmental officials tried to thwart the women's efforts. (Carron, 2007, p. 18)

It seems significant that the writer represents knitters as female, rather than male, despite other primary and secondary sources that indicate men as well as women knitted (Rutt, 1989). Particularly because these characterizations of wartime knitting are not cited to sources, they represent a potential avenue for research.

More interesting than the suggestion that the U.S. government was not eager for hand knitters to provide men in the trenches with woolen garments, though, is the passing mention of communication between knitters in England and in the United States. Implicit in this brief assessment of the historic situation, then, is a sort of validation of the newspaper headline with its grand claim, "Knit and the World Knits With You." If documented, these exchanges could reveal that the network of knitterly information sharing was transnational. As many histories of knitting claim that it is impossible to date connections and transfer of knowledge among national groups of knitters, this further and separate aim would begin to repair the often-acknowledged holes in the extant histories of hand knitting (see e.g., Netto, 1802). As such, attention to the print, and subsequently digitized, culture surrounding knitting augments our knowledge of the role of information exchange in heritage handcrafts.

NOTE

1. The author wishes to acknowledge that the development of this chapter was supported in part by a research fellowship at Winterthur Museum, Library, and Gardens.

REFERENCES

(1918, June 2). The *Sun*, section 3, p. 1. Retrieved from http://chroniclingamerica.loc.gov/lccn/sn83030431/1918-06-02/ed-1/seq-25/.

A pretty edging. (1880, June 20). *New York Tribune*, p. 9. Retrieved from http://chroniclingamerica.loc.gov/lccn/sn83030214/1880-06-20/ed-1/seq-9/.

Anderson, B. (1983). *Imagined communities: Reflections on the origin and spread of nationalism.* London, UK: Verso. Retrieved from https://www2.bc.edu/marian-simion/th406/readings/0420anderson.pdf.

Carron, C. (2007). Socks in wartime. In Vogue Knitting, *The ultimate sock book: History, technique, design* (pp. 18–23). New York: Sixth & Spring Books.

Chamber, D., Steiner, L., & Fleming, C. (2004). *Women and journalism.* London, UK: Routledge.

Chasar, M. (2012). *Everyday reading: Poetry and popular culture in America.* New York: Columbia University Press.

Conboy, M. (2002). *The press and popular culture.* London, UK: Sage Publications.

Contribution received. (1900, March 20). *New York Tribune*, p. 5. Retrieved from http://chroniclingamerica.loc.gov/lccn/sn83030214/1900-03-20/ed-1/seq-5/.

Garvey, E. G. (2013). *Writing with scissors: American scrapbooks from the Civil War to the Harlem Renaissance.* New York: Oxford University Press.

Golf vest. (1903, February 14). *New York Tribune*, p. 7. Retrieved from http://chronicling america.loc.gov/lccn/sn83030214/1903-02-14/ed-1/seq-7/.

Insertion to match child's collar. (1881, January 9). *New York Tribune*, p. 9. Retrieved from http://chroniclingamerica.loc.gov/lccn/sn83030214/1881-01-09/ed-1/seq-9/.

Jenkins, H. (2013). *Textual poachers: Television fans and participatory culture.* (Updated Twentieth Anniversary ed.) New York: Routledge.

Jenkins, H., Clinton, K., Purushotma, R., Robison, A. J., & Weigel, M. (2006). *Confronting the challenges of participatory culture: Media education for the 21st century.* Chicago, IL: MacArthur Foundation. Retrieved from http://www.macfound.org/media/article_pdfs/JENKINS_WHITE_PAPER.PDF.

Kirsch, A. (2014, May 2). Technology is taking over English departments: The false promise of the digital humanities. *The New Republic.* Retrieved from http://www.newrepublic.com/article/117428/limits-digital-humanities-adam-kirsch.

Knitted curtains. (1881, June 12). *New York Tribune*, p. 9. Retrieved from http://chroniclingamerica.loc.gov/lccn/sn83030214/1881-06-12/ed-1/seq-9/.

Lace instruction. (undated). [A small notebook containing newspaper clippings of directions for knitting lace, as well as samples of lacework that model many of the printed patterns]. (Col. 50, 78x100, T-7784). Winterthur Museum, Garden and Library.

Mills, K. (1988). *A place in the news: From the women's pages to the front page.* New York: Dodd, Mead, & Company.

Netto, J. F. (1802). *L'art de tricoter.* Leipzig, Germany: Chez Vosset et Compagnie.

Olive leaf pattern. (1880, June 20). *New York Tribune*, p. 9. Retrieved from http://chroniclin gamerica.loc.gov/lccn/sn83030214/1880-06-20/ed-1/seq-9/.

Pictorial Magazine. (1918, May 26). *The Sun*, section 4. Retrieved from http://chroniclingamerica.loc.gov/lccn/sn83030431/1918-05-26/ed-1/seq-33/.

Roots of Prohibition. (2011). Retrieved from PBS: http://www.pbs.org/kenburns/prohibition/roots-of-prohibition/.

Rubin, J. S. (2007). *Songs of ourselves: The uses of poetry in America.* Cambridge, MA: Belknap Press.

Rutt, R. (1989). *A history of hand knitting.* Loveland, CO: Interweave Press.

Scrap-bag. (1880, June 20). *New York Tribune*, p. 9. Retrieved from http://chroniclingamerica.loc.gov/lccn/sn83030214/1880-06-20/ed-1/seq-9/.

Scrap-bag. (1880, August 22). *New York Tribune*, p. 9. Retrieved from http://chroniclingamerica.loc.gov/lccn/sn83030214/1880-08-22/ed-1/seq-9/.

Shell-edged lace. (1881, May 8). *New York Tribune*, p. 9. Retrieved from http://chroniclingamerica.loc.gov/lccn/sn83030214/1881-05-08/ed-1/seq-9/.

Sing a sock song. (1918, May 25). The *Sun*, p. 10. Retrieved from http://chroniclingamerica.loc.gov/lccn/sn83030431/1918-05-25/ed-1/seq-10/.

Sock singer in south registers protest. (1918, October 6). The *Sun*, section 6, p. 10. Retrieved from http://chroniclingamerica.loc.gov/lccn/sn83030431/1918-10-06/ed-1/seq-66/.

Sock song singers from Pennsylvania get two prizes. (1918, July 21). The *Sun*, section 3, p. 7. Retrieved from http://chroniclingamerica.loc.gov/lccn/sn83030431/1918-07-21/ed-1/seq-27/.

Sock song writers swamp judges with clever jingles. (1918, September 8). The *Sun*, section 6, p. 9. Retrieved from http://chroniclingamerica.loc.gov/lccn/sn83030431/1918-09-08/ed-1/seq-61/.

Strawn, S. M. (2007). *Knitting America: A glorious heritage from warm socks to high art.* Minneapolis, MN: Voyageur Press.

Strawn, S. M. (2012, September). Knitting as scholarship. In *Textiles and politics.* Textile Society of America 13th Biennial Symposium Proceedings, Washington, DC. Retrieved from http://digitalcommons.unl.edu/tsaconf/747/.

The *Tribune* graphic. (1916, December 3). *New York Tribune*, section 2. Retrieved from http://chroniclingamerica.loc.gov/lccn/sn83030214/1916-12-03/ed-1/seq-55/.

Tunisian lace necktie with Normandy edge. (1881, July 31). *New York Tribune*, p. 9. Retrieved from http://chroniclingamerica.loc.gov/lccn/sn83030214/1881-07-31/ed-1/seq-9/.

Vogue Knitting. (2005). *Stitchionary volume one: Knit & purl.* New York: Sixth & Spring Books.

Vogue Knitting. (2006a). *Stitchionary volume two: Cables.* New York: Sixth & Spring Books.

Vogue Knitting. (2006b). *Stitchionary volume three: Color knitting.* New York: Sixth & Spring Books.

Vogue Knitting. (2007). *Stitchionary volume four: Crochet.* New York: Sixth & Spring Books.

Vogue Knitting. (2010). *Stitchionary volume five: Lace knitting.* New York: Sixth & Spring Books.

Vogue Knitting. (2011). *Stitchionary volume six: Edgings.* New York: Sixth & Spring Books.

Walker, B. (1998). *A treasury of knitting patterns.* Pittsville, WI: Schoolhouse Press.

Whitt, J. (2008). *Women in American journalism: A new history.* Urbana: University of Illinois Press.

Winthrop, H. (1917, July 28). Knit and the world knits with you. *The Ogden Standard.* Retrieved from http://chroniclingamerica.loc.gov/lccn/sn85058396/1917-07-28/ed-1/seq-24/.

Write a prize sock song, get $5 worth of wool. (1918, May 12). The *Sun*, section 3, p. 9. Retrieved from http://chroniclingamerica.loc.gov/lccn/sn83030431/1918-05-12/ed-1/seq-37/.

6

Community Archives

Andrea J. Copeland

ABSTRACT

Many underrepresented communities have created archives for use by their members to advocate for their current and historical representation in society. In this way, community archives fill gaps left by traditional formal archives while supporting access to and preservation of community records. The goal of this chapter is to present the current research and discussion on community archives in the context of archival science and community informatics, beginning with a brief overview of the themes, concepts, case studies, and community informatics research relating to community archives for the years 2013 to 2014. Using the framework of six emergent questions raised during Anne Gilliland's and Andrew Flinn's 2013 keynote address, "Community Archives: What Are We Really Talking About?" from the Nexus, Confluence, and Difference: Community Archives Meets Community Informatics: Prato CIRN Conference, the themes and concepts will be unpacked and illustrated using case studies and other research from recent community archive literature. Conclusions drawn include the suggestion that, collectively, archivists, librarians, and informatics researchers can create community-inclusive collections and archives that will remain relevant and accessible over the long term.

INTRODUCTION

In the broadest sense, community archives support access to and preservation of records of the community they are intended to document. Many underrepresented communities have created archives for use by their members to advocate for their current and historical representation in society. In this way, community archives fill gaps left by traditional formal archives that are usually a function of the state and of the dominant social narrative. The goal of this chapter is to present the current research and discussion on community archives in the context of archival science and community informatics.

This chapter will start with a brief overview of the themes, concepts, case studies, and community informatics research identified on community archives for the years 2013 to 2014. Anne Gilliland and Andrew Flinn's (2013) keynote address, "Community Archives: What Are We Really Talking About?" from the Nexus, Confluence, and Difference: Community Archives Meets Community Informatics: Prato CIRN Conference will provide a framework for unpacking the themes, concepts, and case studies using the six emergent questions they have raised about the study of community archives.

OVERVIEW: THEMES, CONCEPTS, CASE STUDIES, AND COMMUNITY INFORMATICS RESEARCH

Themes

Several themes emerged throughout the readings as important to our understanding of what makes an archive a community archive. Community archives use records beyond their traditional purpose, require control and participation by community members, are driven by context rather than neutrality, support activism and advocacy for the community, prioritize the use of records to support current community information needs rather than long-term preservation, contain nontraditional acquisitions generated through community member donations, develop collections dictated by community members, and are challenged by sustainability as they are often founded by one or two passionate individuals and are maintained by volunteers. Relationships between community and traditional archives will best be developed through shared stewardship and reflective practice.

Concepts

Three concepts relevant to community archives emerged: collective memory, pluralism, and social justice. While the following authors did not specifically mention community archives, the ideas inherent to their discussions relate directly to the need and motivation for the development of community archives. Trond Jacobsen, Ricardo L. Punzalan, and Margaret L. Hedstrom (2013) mapped the emergence of the concept of collective memory in the archival literature. They identified four major threads that relate directly to the developing significance of community archives. Michelle Caswell (2013) provides insightful connections between religious pluralism and the future of archival pluralism. The lack of plurality within the formal archival narrative is a driving motivator of community archive creation.

Social justice is often the end goal of community archivists; it is a goal that community members do not believe can be met through traditional state-supported archives. Mark A. Greene (2013) and Randall C. Jimerson (2013) debate the role that social justice should play in professional ethics. Duff, Flinn, Suurtamm, and Wallace (2013) discuss the impact social justice is having on the archives profession.

Case Studies

Several authors present case studies from diverse geographic areas. Michelle Caswell (2014) applies a community archive perspective in her development of a survivor-centered approach to the documentation of human rights abuses, citing cases in Rwanda, Guantanamo Bay, and Cambodia. Tracy B. Grimm and Chon A. Noriega (2013) describe a community-oriented approach to documenting Latino arts and culture within the context of stand-alone university libraries dedicated to these areas of study: Chicano Studies Research Center at the University of California, Los Angeles, and the Institute for Latino Studies at the University of Notre Dame. Two different articles talk about the importance of activism in the historical development of three distinct queer community archives in California. Diana K. Wakimoto, Christine Bruce, and Helen Partridge (2013) examine the Gay, Lesbian, Bisexual, and Transgendered Historical Archives; the Lavender Library, Archives, and Cultural Exchange of Sacramento, Inc. (LLACE); and the ONE National Gay & Lesbian Archives. Wakimoto, Hensen, and Bruce (2013) expound on the LLACE archive development as it relates to professional practice.

Three additional case studies highlight the connection to digital information, social media, and a community informatics context. Sian Evans, Anna Perricci, and Amy Roberts (2014) describe the challenges and the motivations of a community with little organization and a great deal of diversity in documenting their experience of Occupy Wall Street. Patrick Lo (2013) discusses the process of building an online crowd-sourced community archive of Hong Kong's history and culture. Elizabeth Tait et al. (2013) describe the Hebridean Connections—a community-managed online historical resource for the local place-based community heritage of the Outer Hebrides of Scotland.

Community Informatics Research

The final three case studies mentioned above provide context-based examples of how community informatics tools and analyses have been applied to specific archives. The following three articles examine community archives generally, using social media as a venue for documenting cultural heritage. Jonathan S. Hare et al. (2014) and others from the European Union Archiving Community Memories project provide an overview of techniques used for the capture, analysis, and documentation of multimedia web content relevant to communities of interest formed around social events and phenomena. Andrea Copeland (2014) explores the use of personal value estimations to determine which content shared through social media represents community heritage and therefore could potentially be preserved in public library digital collections. Noah Lenstra (2014) explores the provision of heritage information by public libraries and the use of social media to cyberorganize everyday community heritage at the local community level.

WHAT ARE COMMUNITY ARCHIVES?

Gilliland and Flinn (2013) note that over the past ten years, some regions of the world have experienced increasing development of community archiving, while others have not. During this time, varying definitions of what a community archive is have emerged, and the authors question if it is possible or desirable to develop a formal definition of community archiving given the inherent fluidity of communities and their archives. The multifarious nature of community archives motivates their second question, which asks: "What distinguishes community archives from other community-based heritage activities?" These and four other questions asked by them are addressed in varying degrees throughout the aforementioned articles. The questions address the extent to which technology has driven the social purposes and agendas of community archives; how community archives and their priorities evolve over time; the relationships that form around community archives and the equity and mutuality of these relationships; and finally, how community archiving and community informatics can benefit from each other.

Gilliland and Flinn (2013) offer the Community Archives and Heritage Group's definition of community archives: the subject matter is the people of the community, be it a community of place or of interest. Further, the process has to involve the community; typically this means that volunteers have played a role. They identified key elements: the archives must have actual collections, the subject matter should be about a particular community, and archive creation should involve the participation of community members. The last element is flexible. The collection could primarily belong to one person but is openly shared with the community.[1]

Further, the authors offer the following four characteristics as a way of describing community archives:

1. The *collections* are comprised of diverse materials not usually found in traditional archives.
2. The *form* of the collections is increasingly both physical and digital and often begins with one or two personal collections.
3. The *aims and objectives* focus on living archives with emphasis placed on use over preservation. Contributors to community archives seek to reappropriate or control their own story and how their memories are preserved. Building the archive is a form of activism intended to influence the current political and social status of the community. The archive provides a space for community identity and a place in which to work from to prioritize community goals and decide how best to accomplish them.

4. The *structure and governance* helps to define the archive in terms of who founded the archive, the motivation for creation, degree of flexibility and inclusivity, and the degree of independence from the state. Priorities formed within these structures are not fixed, and eventually some custodial relationship with a formal archive may be needed.

Community Archives' Impact on Formal Archives

Gilliland and Flinn (2013) observed that the professional archival community has contrasting views on the impact of the growth of community archiving, with some viewing this as a timely opening up of archives to greater diversity while others find it a worrisome and threatening development. These contrasting views are probably best understood by reading the two papers debating the role of social justice in archival work, with Jimerson (2013) taking the former view and Greene (2013) the latter. Community archives are often based in activism and a passion for justice, whereas traditionally, archives strive for objectivity and neutrality. The very existence of community archives illuminates the real or perceived failing of mainstream, formal, and institutional archival policies and collections to be inclusive of the full human experience.

It is asserted that the ideas of otherness and separateness from society help to define a community in many cases, but in other cases it is geographic location or area of interest. In any case, community archives place emphasis on the community, not the archive. In the United Kingdom and the United States, the development of the community archives movement involved members of the working class, ethnic groups, and the queer community. Their involvement stemmed from the belief that the mainstream archives had no interest in their stories. Further, there is mistrust between these communities and archival institutions because of past interactions and documented misrepresentations. Caswell's (2013) discussion on the tenets of religious pluralism provides much insight toward the development of an archival pluralism.

Relationships develop around community archives among people, other community organizations, and with agencies of the state. These relationships raise the question for some: "Can the state represent anything but its own agenda?" Communities have the right to their own memories and attempt to control those memories by participating in the creation of their own archives. Jacobsen's (2013) and others' discussion on the impact of the symbolism and the power associated with the archival record on the collective memory is relevant to the social archives movement.

THE SIX EMERGENT QUESTIONS

Question One: Is It Possible for a Formal Definition of Community Archiving to be Developed, or Is Its Conceptual Fluidity Part of Its Appeal and Strength?

The fluidity of the conceptualization of community archiving adds to the difficulty in defining community and archive. In her analysis of survivor-centered approaches to archiving, Caswell (2014) suggests five guiding principles to be used for community archiving to promote localized approaches to understanding and documenting the past: participation, shared stewardship, multiplicity, archival activism, and reflexivity. Different types of communities will have different experiences and issues to resolve. She provides the contrasting examples of the transgendered community in Los Angeles, California, and the survivors of state-led violence in Syria—different communities and experiences, indeed.

To add to this comparison, Hare et al. (2014) propose intelligent web harvesting tools that would illuminate and allow for the archiving of a community's response to specific entities, topics, and events on the social web. This is community archiving as well, but only the first of Caswell's five principles can be applied to this type of archiving. Perhaps a continuum of community archiving could be devised based on the degree to which certain principles are met—not necessarily those suggested by Caswell, but they could certainly be a start. Such a framework continuum would help develop a shared research agenda between community informatics and community archives.

Question 2: What Distinguishes Community Archives and Archiving from Other Kinds of Archives and Archival Activities? And Indeed, What if Anything Distinguishes Community Archives from Other Kinds of Community-Based Heritage Activities, Museums, and Resource Centers?

There is much discussion in the case studies related to both questions. The guiding principles identified by Caswell (2013) and the four characteristics described by Gilliland and Flinn (2013) go a long way to describe what distinguishes the community archives from other archival activities. The themes identified earlier and discussed throughout serve to do that as well. The first part of this question is more easily addressed than the second.

As for the second part of the question, a clearer answer does not emerge. In the article about LLACE, the authors (Wakimoto, Hansen, and Bruce, 2013) liken the kinds of acquisitions made by their community archive to the kinds made through GLAM (galleries, libraries, archives, and museums) initiatives. These initiatives strive to create connections among cultural institutions in order to create holistic educational and research centers. Community archives provide the opportunity to question the need for distinctions among cultural institutions. Together, the democratization of information and the rise of the community archives movement may serve to liberate the functionality of cultural institutions based on distinctions alone.

Question Three: To What Extent Has the Use of Technology Driven the Social Purposes and Agendas of Community Archives?

The articles on the crowd-source community archive of Hong Kong, the Hebridean Connections of Scotland, and the Occupy Wall Street archive best demonstrate that technology is having some influence over the social purposes and agendas of community archives. Interestingly, issues around control within communities are heightened by the use of technology.

Hebridean Connections is an online collection of cultural heritage resources representing local heritage associations, or Comainn Eachdraidh, from the Outer Hebrides of Scotland (see Tait et al., 2013). The website has two functions: maintain records for the Comainn Eachdraidh and broaden the audience of the Hebridean diaspora to the wider world. The first function is primary as the communities (represented by the Comainn Eachdraidh) are faced with a knowledge management problem, as many of the older community members are dying off, and with them knowledge valuable to preserving local heritage and to the tourist industry that seeks to maintain the cultural landscape of old. The website allowed for cocreation contributions from the member communities. Linkages between objects from different communities allowed for understanding heritage across their communities that was not possible before the use of databases and descriptive metadata. The technology allowed them to recognize and embrace similarities in the development of their communities' cultures.

Initially, several of the local communities did not want to participate, for members were worried about losing control of the resources and their story through the collaboration. Once the site was functioning, however, their attitudes changed. Unfortunately, due to the lack of resources, the website is in abeyance. Based on lessons learned from the Hebridean Connections, Tait et al. (2013) are currently building a toolkit to address the sustainability and organizational issues of online community archives.

The Occupy Wall Street archive provides an example of a modern movement that is the mix of born digital and paper-based articles and artifacts (see Evans, Perricci, & Roberts, 2014). The archive includes the signs made of cardboard that surrounded the Occupy Wall Street compound and jewelry that was made from police tape used at the protest site. This movement produced records that blurred the lines between art, archives, and innovation. They created technology innovations, including apps like "I'm getting arrested," and the Freedom Tower—a robust mobile hotspot.

This movement was highly visible in the mainstream media, with many from outside of the movement documenting its progress. This archive is recognized by the New York City General Assembly of Occupy Wall Street, and it is needed to record and to preserve their stories about the experience so that the mainstream media's record is not the only one that survives. This is not a homogenous group, as is true with most communities. The members hold differing views on the movement as well as expertise related to archives and preservation. Some members did not want certain documents stored on the web privately or publicly for reasons of privacy and general distrust of the existing power structure. Other members did not want their contributions to the movement included in the archives; rather, they desired nonparticipation.

A British ex-patriot is the founder and developer of the online crowd-sourced archive called Gwulo.com (see Lo, 2013). The community is comprised of those individuals who are living in Hong Kong or abroad who are interested in the history and current affairs of Hong Kong. This example is significant because of its unique political and social history; the archive has an international community base, and the online format allows this community to form. The founder is aware of the formal archives that exist documenting the history of Hong Kong but believes that Gwulo.com allows for a natural voice to emerge. The archive is comprised primarily of photographs to which the community members then attach narratives explaining the images. Community members make edits to the narrative without conflict, as the authority is shared. The main purpose is for people to connect with each other around a heritage they share. The emphasis on shared heritage over historical evidence perhaps makes the need for control less imperative.

Question Four: How Do Community Archives and Their Priorities Evolve over Time?

Every case study discussed here has sustainability issues. In most cases, one or two volunteers started the archives and dedicated their personal resources to sustain it. Over time, several archives have had to partner with universities for their survival.

Currently, the Occupy Wall Street archive is trying to find a home, and in doing so is dealing with issues around aggregation and distribution of the archive's content. The Occupy Wall Street archival group is trying to negotiate a deal with the Tamiment Library and Robert F. Wagner Labor Archives housed at New York University (NYU). While the Tamiment Library is supportive of unions and Occupy Wall Street, several occupiers protested NYU's lack of recognition of the graduate students' union. Political conflicts such as this illustrate the difficulties of partnering with formal institutions.

The specific community context and member resources influence the long-term sustainability of any given community archive. For example, two of the aforementioned queer archives have experienced different fates. In 2010, the ONE Archives, perhaps the largest and oldest queer archive in the world, became part of the University of Southern California Libraries systems in order to sustain its development. Conversely, the GLBT Historical Society, founded in 1985, has grown to include collaboration with the San Francisco Public Library Hormel Gay and Lesbian Center to provide greater access to its most used collections. Further, in 2011, the Society added the GLBT History Museum, providing a space to exhibit the archive's permanent collections. This is another example of how the lines of community-based heritage activities blur.

The Hong Kong crowd-sourced archive started out as hobby; its founder began collecting photos and sharing stories about the city. Over time it has become an archival resource to scholars and genealogists. The archive now includes diaries of individuals interned at the Stanley Internment Camp during the Japanese occupation in World War II, with transcriptions of the diaries taking place over time. Further, the founder hopes to make accessible through the site the early jury lists from the 1800s to 1940 during the British colonial period. The jury lists included names, occupation, company, and addresses of the jurors. Already a resource for sharing cultural heritage memories, the online archive is evolving to include a documentary role as well.

Question Five: What Kinds of Community, Institutional, and Professional Relationships Form around Community Archiving, and to What Extent and When Are They Based in Mutuality and Equity or Formed out of Necessity?

The need for community archives to form relationships with other agencies emerges when sustainability issues arise. Over time, relying on volunteers and limited or sporadic financial resources threatens their long-term existence. The desire for formal or mainstream archives to form relationships with community archives stems from a professional responsibility to build more inclusive and culturally relevant collections. In creating these relationships, community archivists are concerned with retaining control of the archive and maintaining participation of the community members. The most productive relationship becomes one based on joint stewardship rather than one based on custodial transference of ownership to the institutional archive.

Caswell's (2014) approach of taking a survivor-centered perspective in building government archives reflects the goals of community archives—community-member controlled and created through their participation. Caswell poses the question: "Who better to record the memories of genocide than the survivors or the family members of the victims?" Grimm and Noriega (2013) discuss the importance of involving community members in the creation of formal archives documenting Latino culture in the United States. Currently, most Latino archives reside in private collections, and for institutional archives to create collections that illuminate Latino art and culture, relationships with members of the Latino arts community must be ongoing in order to build trust and maintain authenticity.

The concepts of social justice, collective memory, and pluralism come to bear on these types of relationships. Duff, Flinn, Suurtamm, and Wallace (2013) explore the impact of social justice on professional archival endeavors. The challenge for the professional archivist is figuring out how to simultaneously take the long historical view and engage in present social justice issues. Also, the democratization of information has had its influence on archival selection as expertise and power have been decentralized in the process. The effect of this is seen as community members are increasingly viewed as experts in the collections unique to their communities (Shilton & Srinivasan, 2007).

Duff et al. (2013) offer an archival social justice framework that also supports the mission of many community archives, which is to use information documenting the past to change the present by taking action. This action involves the participation of and control by the communities seeking justice as well as other individuals taking personal responsibility for effectuating change. The authors suggest the use of Brophy's model, a model used to assess whether or not archival services result in a change in personal behaviors that then bring about social change. Social justice provides a mechanism for archivists to reflect on the importance of acknowledging and remedying the historical inequalities in their collections.

The debate between Greene and Jimerson provides a great deal of reflection on the extent to which archivists should be engaged with social justice in a professional capacity. Put dichotomously, Greene (2013) cautions against the social justice imperative for fear of politicizing the profession and greatly limiting the objectivity of archival evidence. On the other hand, Jimerson (2013) argues that archives have always been entities in service to those in positions of power; to not realize this is to ignore the responsibility of archivists to be inclusive and to document fully the collective human experience.

Greene (2013) provides the example of the DOVE (Desegregation of Virginia Education) archive at Old Dominion University. According to Greene's archival perspective, it is better not to promote its use as an educational advocacy tool because to do so could alienate segregationists and greatly limit any hope of them volunteering their records for inclusion in the same university archive. But one begins to wonder about the purpose of this collection—is it not to be used to advocate change? Perhaps this an area for collaboration with those interested in the application of cultural informatics research to community and social heritage projects. Often informatics research, particularly community informatics, uses a social science approach and, therefore, is in a better position than archival science to embrace value-laden research.

Caswell's (2013) discussion relating the principles of religious pluralism to the potential development of an archival pluralism has much insight to offer. The basic principles are energetic engagement, understanding, strengthened commitment, and dialog. These principles are designed to help mitigate the major tensions inherent in religiously diverse cultures: claims of universality, inattention to power, silencing dissent, and collapsing difference. The application of these principles sheds light on how archives can begin to move from an archival universe dominated by one cultural paradigm to an archival multiverse, one that includes community archives. From her initial exploration, we can begin to think about how one archive containing divergent views can contain multiple truths.

Jacobsen, Punzalan, and Hedstrom (2013) mapped the emergence of the concept of collective memory in archival science. They identified four trends around the use of the concept of collective memory that relate to the rise of the community archives movement. First, archives provide a symbolic foundation for collective memory. If one's community was never written into collective archives, one will not be part of the collective memory. Next, the discussion on collective memory offers a critique of the role of archival records in the creation and construction of social memory, as well as an exploration of the relationships among archives, memory, and power. Both trends relate to the social justice issues inherent in the creation of many community archives and the lack of plurality in institutional archives. Lastly, discussions on collective memory are used to propose new ways of thinking about the nature of records as evidence of the past, including the notion of an archival memory.

While the authors do not mention community archives specifically, the last trend identified is an attempt to understand the archive beyond its traditional function and, in doing so, links archives with local heritage and the collective memory. They assert that the relationship between archives and memory forces one to look at the spatial boundaries between the two, which leads back to the boundaries between mainstream archives and diverse communities of memory. We are reminded that archives are not memories in themselves but rather function as touchstones to memories. To have meaning, archives must be used, which leads to the contextual connections to pluralism and social justice. The primary lesson to be learned from community archives is that institutional archival endeavors need to continue opening the framework to include the collective human experience if they wish to remain relevant to the collective memory and heritage enterprise.

Question Six: How Might a Closer Proximity between Community Informatics and Community Archiving Benefit Each Field?

In mapping the concept of collective memory in archival science, Jacobsen, Punzalan, and Hedstrom (2013) found that those in the field working on this concept are insular in that they talk only to each other; no one outside of the field is citing them, and they are citing very few outside disciplines. Through *Web of Science* and Google Scholar analyses, they discovered that there is an emerging field of memory studies that archives are not a part of. This perhaps is an opportunity for those interested in cultural informatics, including community informatics, to bridge this connection as informatics research is less theoretical. Through applied research, one can make connections to the context in which community archives function.

Using the specific context of the challenges faced by the Hebridean Connections, Tate et al. (2013) are building a toolkit aimed at assisting online community archives to move beyond the challenges related to technical organization and sustainability to encourage their future development as a cultural heritage resource. This is the type of partnership or interaction between the fields that can be beneficial to both.

Hare, et al. (2014), Lenstra (2014), and Copeland (2014) examine the role social media could play in developing or augmenting community archives. The research of Hare et al. (2014), from the Arching Community Memories project, begins to look at ways to make sense out of the billions of data points shared through social media in a diversity of contexts. They are developing practical applications of multimedia analytics for web archiving and web archive analysis. The emphasis of informatics research on using technologies to create tools that benefit human interactions with information is an area of applied research that could greatly benefit the appraisal, collection, arrangement, and description of born digital materials for inclusion in archives. Greene and Meissner's (2005) now frequently invoked article, "More Product, Less Process," articulates the problems associated with traditional approaches to processing archives and the backlog that has resulted. This backlog refers to physical items for processing; when adding the digital to traditional approaches, the backlog becomes infinite without the intervention of data mining applications.

Lenstra (2014) uses the term *cyberorganizing*, from the community informatics lexicon, which means to embed digital technologies in community organizing so that local individuals and groups can use digital tools for their own purposes. He found that public libraries are using social media, particularly Facebook, to augment heritage information services they already provide. Cyberorganizing through Facebook allows the everyday local heritage of community members to be shared, thereby building a more inclusive community in the present and, at the same time, documenting today's events for tomorrow's digital archive. Facebook permits the official records provided by the library to be presented side by side with unofficial memories of all groups within a community.

Copeland (2014) explores the values associated with photographs shared through social media as they relate to community heritage and preservation. In doing so, she explores the potential for public libraries to assume the role of community digital repositories. Thirty public library users and thirty librarians were solicited from the Indianapolis metropolitan area to evaluate five images selected from Flickr in terms of their value to public library digital collections and their worthiness of long-term preservation. Public library users and librarians had similar value estimations of the images in the study. This is perhaps the most significant finding of the study, given the importance of collaboration and forming partnerships for building and sustaining community collections and archives.

Lenstra (2014) and Copeland (2014) both see a role for public libraries in community informatics and archives research. Public libraries have evolved to become a function of the communities they serve, and as such may become part of the solution to sustaining community archives. It has often been said that the digital information revolution has made the archivist more concerned about providing community access than ever before, and the librarian more concerned about preservation and long-term access issues. Hopefully these concerns will bring archivists, librarians, and informatics researchers together to create community-inclusive collections and archives that will remain relevant and accessible over the long term.

NOTE

1. The Ten Years project of photographer Zoe Strauss. From 2001 to 2010 Strauss documented lives and landscapes within her own community in South Philadelphia. This project documents a community through snapshots of street life from the perspective of one individual. Her photos were shared with the community under an Interstate 95 overpass for $5 a photo, in city museums, and on billboards around Philadelphia.

REFERENCES

Caswell, M. (2013). On archival pluralism: What religious pluralism (and its critics) can teach us about archives. *Archival Science, 13*, 273–92.

Caswell, M. (2014, April 30). Toward a survivor-centered approach to records documenting human rights abuse: Lessons from community archives. *Archival Science*, 1–16. doi: 10.1007/s10502-014-9220-6

Copeland, A. (2014). The use of personal value estimations to select images for preservation in public library digital community collections. *Future Internet, 6*(2), 359–77.

Duff, W. M., Flinn, A., Suurtamm, K. E., & Wallace, D. A. (2013). Social justice impact of archives: A preliminary investigation. *Archival Science, 13*, 317–48.

Evans, S., Perricci, A., & Roberts, A. (2014). "Why archive?" and other important questions asked by occupiers. In M. Morrone (Ed.), *Informed agitation: Library and information skills in social justice movements and beyond.* Sacramento, CA: Library Juice Press.

Gilliland, A., & Flinn, A. (2013). Community archives: What are we really talking about? Keynote address. *Nexus, Confluence, and Difference: Community Archives Meets Community Informatics, CIRN Conference, October 28–30, 2013, Prato, Italy.*

Greene, M. A. (2013). A critique of social justice as an archival imperative: What *is* it we're doing that's all that important? *American Archivist, 76*(3), 302–34.

Greene, M. A., & Meissner, D. (2005). More product, less process: Revamping the traditional archiving processing. *American Archivist, 68*, 208–63.

Grimm, T. B., & Noriega, C. A. (2013). Documenting regional Latino arts and culture: Case studies for a collaborative, community-oriented approach. *American Archivist, 76*(1), 95–112.

Hare, J. S., Dupplaw, D. P., Lewis, P. H., Hall, W., & Martinez, K. (2014). Exploiting multimedia in creating and analyzing multimedia web archives. *Future Internet, 6*(2), 242–60.

Jacobsen, T., Punzalan, R. L., & Hedstrom, M. L. (2013). Invoking "collective memory": Mapping the emergence of a concept in archival science. *Archival Science, 13*, 217–51. doi: 10.1007/s10502-013-9199-4

Jimerson, R. C. (2013). Archivists and social responsibility: A response to Mark Greene. *American Archivist, 76*(2), 335–45.

Lenstra, N. (2014). Cyberorganizing everyday heritage in and around public libraries: An exploratory study. *Public Library Quarterly, 33*(1), 1–22.

Lo, P. (2013). Building a crowd-sourced community archive in Hong Kong: The challenges and rewards—An information interview with David Bellis, founder of Gwulo.com. *Journal of East Asian Libraries, 157*, 102–18.

Shilton, K., & Srinivasan, R. (2007). Participatory appraisal and arrangement for multicultural archival collections. *Archivaria, 63*, 87–101.

Tait, E., MacLeod, M., Beel, D., Wallace, C., Mellish, C., & Taylor, S. (2013). Linking to the past: An analysis of community digital heritage initiatives. *Aslib Proceedings, 65*(6), 564–80. doi: 10.1108/AP-05-2013-0039

Wakimoto, D. K., Bruce, C., & Partridge, H. (2013). Archivist as activist: Lessons from three queer community archives in California. *Archival Science, 13*, 293–316.

Wakimoto, D. K., Hansen, D. L., & Bruce, C. (2013). The case of LLACE: Challenges, triumphs, and lessons of a community archives. *Society of American Archivists, 76*(2), 438–57.

7

Social Media and Participatory Culture

Opportunities and Challenges for Reforming the Contemporary Museum

Stan A. Trembach and Liya Deng

ABSTRACT

The purpose of this chapter is to explore social media as a cultural phenomenon that has revolutionized the relationship between contemporary museums and their users. The authors draw on a variety of scholarly sources to conduct a critical analysis of the advantages and disadvantages of various social media platforms for museum audience development and engagement. It is argued that by establishing a presence in this growing universe, museums can build a more robust marketing strategy and capitalize on social media's untapped potential for creating participatory learning environments. However, the use of social media in museum practice also raises concerns about user privacy, identity, and accountability, along with issues of cultural authority and the authenticity of museum objects. Through an examination of the current cultural scholarship, the chapter demonstrates how a thoughtful approach to the use of social media tools may position museums for long-term sustainability and success during the current economic recession and beyond.

INTRODUCTION

In recent decades, the nature of communication has evolved dramatically due in large measure to the indelible impact of information and communication technologies (ICTs), particularly social media, on every aspect of human existence. Social media have been immersed in our lives by gradually being introduced into a range of professional and cultural fields. Museums are also starting to come to the forefront of the media revolution by enthusiastically embracing new formats of user-to-user and user-to-all interaction afforded by social media. In light of the fact that the impact of social media on socioeconomic and political structures has long been in the spotlight of scholarly attention, the role of social media in the intellectual and cultural spheres is worthy of an equally scrupulous examination. There are both philosophical and practical considerations for why these technologies are winning over the museum world. It may have been a painstaking process, but museums are finally talking about social media, albeit sometimes with mixed feelings of love, hate, curiosity, or indifference (Wong, 2012). No matter the attitude, such a wide range of emotions shows genuine interest on museums' part in the promise of social media, which is a positive sign for the future.

Given that possible applications of media technologies have already generated considerable conversation in the cultural arena, this chapter intends to extend the discussion even further based on the premise that the impact of technology goes beyond transforming the algorithms of information exchange. Our thought process and the way we perceive communication as a daily activity have also changed as a result. As more and more people turn to the Internet for professional and social purposes, we are witnessing a revolutionary growth of new places for communication to transpire and new avenues for users to interact. Therefore, it is hardly surprising that social media have by now paved their way into the mainstream of innovative communication means. Due to their ubiquity and increasing accessibility, particularly with the younger generations, social media have left an imprint on practically every walk of life. They are used by contemporary museums as a vehicle to address issues of marketing, promotion, and audience engagement, as well as broader questions of museum roles and relevance in the digital age (Wong, 2012).

Today, interactions facilitated by social media exemplify the aforementioned paradigmatic shift in communication practices that now tend to emphasize spontaneity, informality, and active participation. The pervasiveness of social media in the cultural domain is a globally recognized phenomenon (Simon, 2010; Giaccardi, 2012). In this spirit, cultural institutions worldwide are acknowledging the power of ICTs to bring the user and the content together, urging heritage organizations and practitioners to use social media on a larger scale in order to encourage visitors to interact with cultural materials and establish steady social connections with one another (Simon, 2010). Despite these new expectations placed on the cultural sector, the problem is that this somewhat indiscriminate fascination with the promise of ICTs for en masse cultural education and exchange may lead to a skewed perception of social media applicability in the context of day-to-day museum practice. Indeed, little emphasis has been given in professional literature to the need to critically analyze both the advantages and disadvantages of using various types of social media for audience development and engagement in contemporary museums. In other words, there has been insufficient attention paid to, and little understanding of the fact that, the ability of social media to affect cultural experience is still complex, ambiguous, and in need of further scrutiny.

This chapter aims to narrow the above-mentioned void in the museum literature by attempting to delve into particular obstacles and opportunities social media present to cultural institutions and individual users. Through an extensive review of the current cultural scholarship, the authors demonstrate how social media have for a number of years been used in the museum world to provide a shared platform through which diverse and technology-savvy museum visitors can look for a common identity, explore a variety of social connections, and establish the basis for creating communities of their own. Since "going virtual" is becoming a commonly accepted practice in cultural institutions, social media carry an important mission of taking the world to the world; that is, creating a global awareness of the wealth of cultural resources available to visitors both physically and virtually. This research then seeks to position the museum in relation to the current trends in social media development and explore the relevance and implications of these trends as museums are actively responding to the new agenda.

Social media are also viewed in the cultural heritage scholarship as significant means of promoting cultural organizations to wider audiences than have ever been reached before. An increasing number of museums are developing a profile on social media sites to post news, advertise exhibitions, or disseminate information in other ways. A recent study involving in-depth interviews with staff members of twelve art museums in the midwestern region of the United States revealed that the use of social network sites was effective for building visitor awareness of the diverse museum activities, providing behind-the-scenes tours, and serving as "a memory-keeping device for past events" (Chung, Marcketti, & Fiore, 2014, p. 196). The emergent participatory culture fostered by social media offers numerous benefits for peer-to-peer learning, collaborative problem solving, and the development of a more empowered sense of citizenship, as well as skills vital in modern academic settings and the workplace.

At the same time, excessive reliance on social media and other forms of online representation has brought to the forefront of the academic discourse the danger of detachment from the roots, or losing the authenticity of the museum physical experience. Other pressing issues include the widening participation gap and significant changes in socialization patterns, particularly affecting younger museum visitors and their perception of themselves as community participants. In the digital age, there is a pronounced need for museums to offer new ways of sustaining their cultural authority, reemphasize the value of the conventional museum experience, and create a balanced mix of digital and physical offerings.

This chapter is written with the intent to contribute to the ongoing discussion about the potential of social media to provide a wide-open forum for communication and cultural exchange. Through an intensive review of professional literature, including journal articles, agency papers, reports, and current research, the authors attempt to identify what is already known about the ways in which interactive technologies alter the relationships between museums and their visitors. This review draws on the evidence from scholarly sources to take a closer look at the benefits and challenges related to the integration of social media and their ability to enrich museum visitor experiences. The insights gained from this analysis will be useful for understanding the role of social media in addressing the most common reasons for public dissatisfaction with museums, including their inclusiveness and relevance to diverse audiences. It is hoped that the findings will suggest areas for further research and lead to improved services to museum visitors across the board.

THE RISE OF INFORMATION AND COMMUNICATION TECHNOLOGIES

The Internet has revolutionized many aspects of human behavior, including the way individuals communicate and interact with one another. As the overall pace of life became more and more frenetic, so did the speed of transmitting information—between people, nonprofit organizations, businesses, cultural institutions, and entire states. The very term *information society* implies that information has become the sought-after commodity and the dominant factor that determines the course of many social, political, and economic processes taking place in the contemporary world. Information deluge is no longer a gaudy metaphor; it is the reality and the norm. To cope with the imminent data flood, communication, or exchange of information, has become increasingly spontaneous, terse, and informal. Above all, information exchange has become technology mediated, meaning that it can happen any time and virtually anywhere, regardless of the geographical boundaries that may exist between the sender and the receiver.

Another connotation that the term *information society* carries is that of a social and largely communal structure. The need to communicate is indeed inherent in human nature, and the help from ICTs could not have come at a more opportune time. Technological innovation gave birth to devices used to expedite not only the delivery and dissemination but also the exchange of information. With ICTs making human interaction progressively faster and easier, users thrive in the environment where instant sharing of one's personal successes, failures, political views, research agenda, or cultural preferences has become as common as penmanship was centuries ago.

In the frenzy of the twenty-first-century world, critics say, information users tend to be more pragmatic and individualistic than ever before. There are reasons to believe otherwise, though. New broadcast outlets created by the Internet, such as Facebook, Twitter, or YouTube, bring in hundreds, thousands, sometimes millions of followers who join a network of like-minded individuals united by a civic cause or a shared interest. Fueled by the steady infusion of Web 2.0 into the world's digital fabric, a plethora of social networks have emerged as platforms where people communicate, collaborate, create, and disseminate various types of information. Due to their overwhelming diversity, multifunctional nature, and enormous communicative capacity, social networks formed and maintained on various social media sites signify profound changes in human communication patterns aimed to make peer-to-peer interactions more extemporaneous and global.

DEFINING SOCIAL MEDIA

In its broadest sense, the term *social media* has been used in reference to designated Internet sites designed to provide opportunities for interaction, information sharing, and discourse with the help of a multimedia mix of text, pictures, videos, and audio files. Experts from the Smithsonian Institution put it best when they defined social media as "an umbrella term that encompasses websites that integrate technology, social interaction and content creation and dissemination" (Smithsonian, 2011). Over the years, social media have evolved into many different formats, including blogs, wikis, forums, message boards, social networks, social bookmarking tools, photo and video sharing, and many more. There exists a rich and diverse ecology of social media sites, which vary in terms of their scope and functionality, such as Facebook, Twitter, YouTube, Pinterest, Flickr, LinkedIn, WordPress, Blogger, LiveJournal, Wikipedia, Wetpaint, Wikidot, Second Life, Del.icio.us, Digg, Reddit, and so on.

It is virtually impossible to speak with certainty about the total number of social media outlets available on the Internet. Suffice to say, social media usage has grown to constitute a significant portion of all user activity online. In 2013, the Pew Research Internet Project reported that fully 71 percent of online adults used Facebook, and usage among seniors had increased significantly in just one year, with Facebook being the platform of choice (Duggan & Smith, 2014, p. 4). According to a recent report by Nielsen, a leading global information and measurement company, the time spent by consumers on social networks is greater than the time they spend on any other category of sites, and the gap continues to widen (Nielsen, 2012). The research conducted by the Nielsen experts combines two segments of the consumer population—those using personal computers and those using mobile devices. It concludes that the total time spent by users on browsing or interacting through social media in the United States increased by 37 percent to 121 billion minutes in July 2012, compared to 88 billion in July 2011 (Nielsen, 2012).

While social media are typically associated with a certain format, such as a blog, a file-sharing site, or a career network, in actuality they have become a cultural phenomenon that profoundly impacts the information flow in contemporary society. To explain what attracts users to various social media communication channels, Kaplan and Haenlein (2010) offer a more user-focused definition of this notion, whereby all social media are viewed as "a group of Internet-based applications that build on the ideological and technological foundations of Web 2.0, and that allow the creation and exchange of user-generated content" (p. 61). In a rapidly changing technological climate, learners are not satisfied with passive consumption of online content, whether of an educational or entertainment nature. Rather, they aspire to be creators, disseminators, and critics of information, making their voices heard across a broad spectrum of audiences and online communities of interest. Such a high degree of involvement is observed not only on the individual but also on the institutional level, particularly in the remit of cultural heritage where opportunities to think, talk about, assess, and augment content is galore. In the dynamic twenty-first-century world, the culture fostered by social media provides an appropriate response to the need for more dynamic methods of presenting knowledge (Wong, 2012).

SOCIAL MEDIA AND MUSEUM VISITOR ENGAGEMENT

The ubiquity of the Internet has ensured expanding connections to the totality of its users and has thus affected the operations of contemporary museums (Stein, 2012). Arguably, the interactive nature of social media technologies has played a significant role in the rise of participatory culture within the museum world. Long known as educational and cultural hubs, museums of today invite participation, and their ambience speaks of a learning environment in which members believe their contributions matter and feel some degree of social connection with one another (Jenkins, 2006). The tenets of participatory culture are closely aligned with the core values of the current generation of learners; namely, unimpeded access to a range of information sources and cultural perspectives, and low barriers to self-expression, along with emphasis on creativity and civic engagement (Giaccardi, 2012).

Granted that social media embody a powerful construct with which to advance audience participation, it seems inevitable that museums should establish a firm presence on various social media portals. In doing so, museums have simply been going to where the users already are. And simply put, museums must increase and engage their audiences in order to overcome the repercussions of the lingering economic downturn (Johnson, Witchey, Smith, Levine, & Haywood, 2010). At present, hard decisions have to be made across all levels about the funding and maintenance of museums. Such issues invoke hard questions about the justification of museums, their general functions and potential, as well as about their role in the community. These discussions are necessary because if the perceptions of value remain low, museums may run the risk of staff dismissals, collection weeding, or even building closures (Hooper-Greenhill, 1995). Today, the educational role of museums appears to be one of the major justifications for their existence because knowledge and the opportunity for interpretation and further creation are viewed as key commodities museums offer to their service communities. Therefore, audience engagement is especially relevant in an era of burgeoning participation opportunities present on the social Web.

The trend for greater community engagement represents a marked shift from past practices that emphasized a division between the "collection" space where the curator produced expert knowledge and the "public" space where visitors consumed cultural products made available to them through museum exhibits or displays. Presently, we are witnessing a convergence of the two spaces, so that exhibitions and even collections are increasingly becoming the product of a joint effort between audiences and museum curatorial staff. Museums of all types are concerned with projecting an image of institutions that are open to the public, responsive to visitor needs, and welcoming feedback in order to be more competitive in the entertainment marketplace. The idea of the museum as a "total destination" is not new, for scholars have been tracing its evolution for nearly twenty years (Hooper-Greenhill, 1995). This notion illustrates the reconceptualization of what a visit to a museum means now. Besides the cultural experience with the artifacts delivered either onsite or remotely, a museum visit may come along with a family outing, a dinner at a local restaurant, or attending a sports event or other notable attractions. Striving to find their niche in the entertainment industry, museums of today agree on the need to create offerings that would not only appeal to a wide range of audiences but also fit into the mainstream of conventional leisure activities. Social media help museums achieve this goal by reinforcing the notions of openness and connectedness in the public mind.

Growing visitor diversity represents a serious concern for contemporary museums as they strive to ensure a rewarding and fulfilling cultural experience "for all." Although almost every museum has conducted visitor studies based on popular demographics categories such as age, gender, race, ethnicity, income, education, and occupation, taken in isolation these criteria provide only a very blunt instrument for understanding museum visitors, their motivations, experiences, and reactions to both physical and virtual museum offerings (Falk, 2009). What the statistics accomplish is a rather incomplete explanation of who the visitors are. The general picture demographics data depict the average visitor as "better educated, older, and wealthier than the public as a whole, and also white and female" (Falk, 2009, p. 30). The problem with this collective persona is that demographic statistics cannot express the totality of individual visitor experiences. Although variables such as age, race, or education and income levels do tell us some facts about a segment of the museum population, these variables can hardly explain how these visitors relate to museums, what they draw out of their visits, and what museums may have to do to serve their users better.

Clearly, the only way to decipher the enigma of the visitors' experience is to get into their world and hear firsthand about their feelings and emotions induced by the interaction with culturally valuable artifacts. It follows, then, that besides quantifiable, easily measured demographic data, museums need another vantage point from which to gather insights into what value the audiences derive from their visit, and where the emphasis lies—on the content, the services, or the sociocultural milieu. Social media offer an attractive option in this regard due to their ability to facilitate audience feedback and bring the people into museum practice. Thinking about museum visitors through the lens of their contributions on social media can help all parties offset the all–too-common proclivity to focus on either the museum or the visitor side. The reality is that the completeness of a museum experience can only be achieved when the user and the content come together and form a unique, inseparable entity.

ADVANTAGES OF SOCIAL MEDIA FOR MODERN MUSEUMS

Unquestionably, social media figure prominently in today's life. They are instantaneous and powerful as they carry messages that can profoundly impact the social, political, and cultural landscape. It will not be an overstatement to claim that social media are transforming the way that people communicate, create, and disseminate information, and form relationships in modern society. A relatively short time ago, it was almost unimaginable that a scientific breakthrough, a social event, or a political uprising would be broadcast in real time by those actually experiencing it so that millions of others around the globe could learn, think, and participate. Although in most cases the messages transmitted through social media are not so momentous, the very fact that they are sent and received through such a potent, omnipresent venue has far-reaching consequences that we are only beginning to comprehend. No matter how unremarkable the communication on social media may be, it is changing how the world is seen and experienced, how fast the information flows, and how users react to the influx of new data. Social media have become one of the characteristics by which twenty-first-century society is defined. As everything else powered by technology, social media are a constantly evolving phenomenon, but one that will most likely remain part of the world in which we live for the foreseeable future.

By definition, social media embody freedom, including freedom to engage in conversation about any topic (Lipscomb, 2010). The ability to offer innovative, participative channels of communication is perhaps one of the greatest benefits of social media that can be advantageous for both the user and the museum. Considering that the Internet has emerged as the primary gateway to an array of social spaces for work, research, and entertainment, networking sites such as Facebook, Twitter, or Instagram attract users as a space to interact on public message boards, in private chats, and also through a variety of other visual means, such as a user profile, an avatar, or both.

In general, social media are an important factor in forming among their users a sense of togetherness or a common identity. There are many social media resources built around identity that require users to set up profiles and disclose a certain amount of information that portrays them in highly distinctive ways, such as name, age, gender, profession, location, favorite food, and so on. For museums, monitoring their virtual users' identities is essential because, according to Kaplan and Haenlein (2010), the presentation of a user's identity can often happen through the conscious or unconscious self-disclosure of subjective information such as thoughts, feelings, likes, and dislikes. Greater awareness of visitor preferences and frustrations factors in the decision-making process on the part of museum administrators and curatorial staff, whether they implement short-term initiatives or establish long-term strategic priorities.

The use of social media is advantageous for contemporary museums in many other respects, particularly for knowledge exchange, content sharing, and content creation (Russo, Watkins, Kelly, & Chan, 2007). Besides, when used correctly, social media open new ways to arrange and present content that arise from more opportunities to display the scope and variety of museum collections. Additionally, social networks afford museums ample space for the effective marketing of new services, promoting websites and blogs, along with spreading the word about ongoing and future professional development initiatives. Furthermore, a study conducted in 2008 about how young people were engaging with technology in the United States put forth an argument that the high level of interactivity and engagement users enjoy on social media is conducive to developing in them a sense of camaraderie, rethinking social norms, and experimenting with new forms of critical expression in the course of self-directed learning (Ito, 2008).

Therefore, within the museum community, social media seem to be the natural extension of the work that is done onsite and, most recently, online. The challenge is facilitating an overall experience that works both online and off to ensure that visitors consistently participate in meaningful ways (Bernstein, 2011). According to the 2010 Horizon Report Museum Edition, even if a museum does not yet maintain an active presence in any of the major social media spaces, its users are already there—talking about their museum-related experiences (Johnson et al., 2010). This is hardly surprising because of how prevalent social media are today and how rapidly the number of people using them has been growing (Fitch, 2012). A 2010 Pew research report indicates that 93 percent of American teens, aged thirteen to eighteen, have access to the Internet, and 73 percent of those regularly use a social networking site (Lenhart, Purcell, Smith, & Zickuhr, 2010, pp. 2, 4). For this reason, by establishing a firm presence within the social media universe, museums can reach out and get connected to their target audiences in noticeably efficient ways that are not always attainable by any other outreach activities. In this sense, social media play the role of a marketing tool where the museum provides an initial impulse and users do most of the marketing themselves, sometimes as a byproduct of interactions involving other topics.

Another area of the cultural realm where social media have found a practical application is education and interpretation. Similar to their strictly marketing efforts, heritage institutions, particularly art museums, can take advantage of various social media utilities and create conversations around posted videos, photographs, 3D objects, entire collections, and other aspects of museum business. YouTube and Flickr are especially potent methods for displaying and curating culturally meaningful video content, while Twitter offers an equally tremendous opportunity. In the process, users find it easy to interact not only with their peers but also with institutions that have produced the content. Interestingly enough, the immense educational potential of social media is globally recognized. For example, in the United Kingdom, the Tate Museum has proudly featured the John Martin's *Underworld* exhibit enhanced with an interactive story that is taking place on Twitter. It is Twitter users who make the art of John Martin live and breathe by following the main character, Elena Batham, on their accounts and supplying advice about her journey through the strange and daunting underworld. Twitter allows visitors to feel part of the story themselves as their thoughts and responses help Elena make it back to reality.

The Tate success story speaks to an important benefit museums derive from being present on social media—diversifying and enlarging their audiences. Indeed, in the case of *Underworld*, everybody is welcomed to participate. Virtual visitors do not need to be experts on the subject for their opinion to matter in the game and be respected. Participants do not need to know about art, or John Martin, to play this game. Google, the Great British Art Debate website, and Tate's online collection provide all the necessary information that makes it easier to participate. The audience can influence the outcome by simply asking the right or timely questions. It is a classic example of education through participation as contributors are presented with a free interpretation of the life, times, art, and influence of the artist John Martin. The interaction between Tate and Twitter users is not limited to *Underworld* alone. Visitors are strongly encouraged to leave their requests to collaborate with other readers on the choices in the game or share non-story-related comments on anything pertinent to Tate's operations.

With the rise of social media, communication between people and institutions has been greatly democratized. Control over the media domain has shifted from agencies and their marketing departments to individuals and communities that create, share, and consume blogs, tweets, Facebook entries, movies, pictures, and so forth. This is why it is safe to say that social media hold significant promise in securing the engagement of museum visitors and society at large by providing interactive and networking opportunities when and where users want. This openness and flexibility puts museums in a position to "demonstrate their continued importance for people's understanding of themselves and the world and thereby strengthen their public connections and enduring social relevance" (Drotner & Schroder, 2013, p. 6). Through social media, museums are also able to project an evolving image of themselves as institutions for somebody rather than merely historical sites about something.

In an era when learning is firmly embedded in people's daily activities and routines, the rapid spread of social media enables museums to redefine their relationship with learners by providing opportunities for bidirectional communication about the cultural experience induced by museum objects. Relationship marketing, a concept that has recently grown in popularity in museum circles, emphasizes fostering long-term relationships with visitors built on mutually beneficial partnerships and trust (Chung, Marcketti, & Fiore, 2014). Since social media provide for an increased presence of the Internet in the lives of millions of users, museums are now in a position to capitalize on their online presence and engage in relationship marketing in more innovative and cost-effective ways. The push for a more customer-centric museum illustrates the importance of cultural heritage for performing three primary educative functions of museums; namely, the increase of visitors' cultural competencies, the diffusion of new knowledge, and ultimately learning through interpretation (Kelly, 2013). A critical issue about the integration of social media into museum practice is that cultural enlightenment takes place on social networks where users can enrich their museum learning experience by sharing ideas and seeking peer input through a range of social media tools.

One of the biggest innovations on the Internet, social media make museums more fairly representative of increasingly diverse populations by supporting communication across a plethora of applications. The term *social media outreach* has been used in the professional discourse to describe museums' response to the pressure of diversifying their user population (Wong, 2012). What other means, if not social media, is better suited to make museums regularly present in everyday life? Contrary to a popular stereotype that social media are a pastime of the young, studies by the Pew Research Center indicate that the fastest growing Facebook audience worldwide is adults over fifty-five years old (Zickuhr & Madden, 2012). What it means for museums is that in order to enlarge their audiences, they must not only think about the types of physical experiences provided to visitors but also keep in mind the variety of their online audiences accustomed to participatory activities in their virtual social lives.

Fletcher and Lee (2012) stress such features of social media as speed and the capacity for customization in terms of increasing an organization's use of two-way and multiway communication that centers on active participation from both the institution and its constituencies. In a similar fashion, Wright and Hinson (2009) characterize the ongoing tendencies in the museum-visitor dynamics as a change from unidirectional to bidirectional dialog, in which the public can exercise much more control over what information is taken in as important versus messages that can be ignored. Following these trends, museums have moved from their historical function as social and cultural entities to an experience-based modus operandi involving active circulation of knowledge during visitors' participation.

Mnemonically, the benefits of social media can be summed up as leading to a museum that *CARES* about its users (Figure 7.1). We followed Fletcher and Lee's (2012) analysis in breaking down the acronym into cost (C), access (A), reach (R),

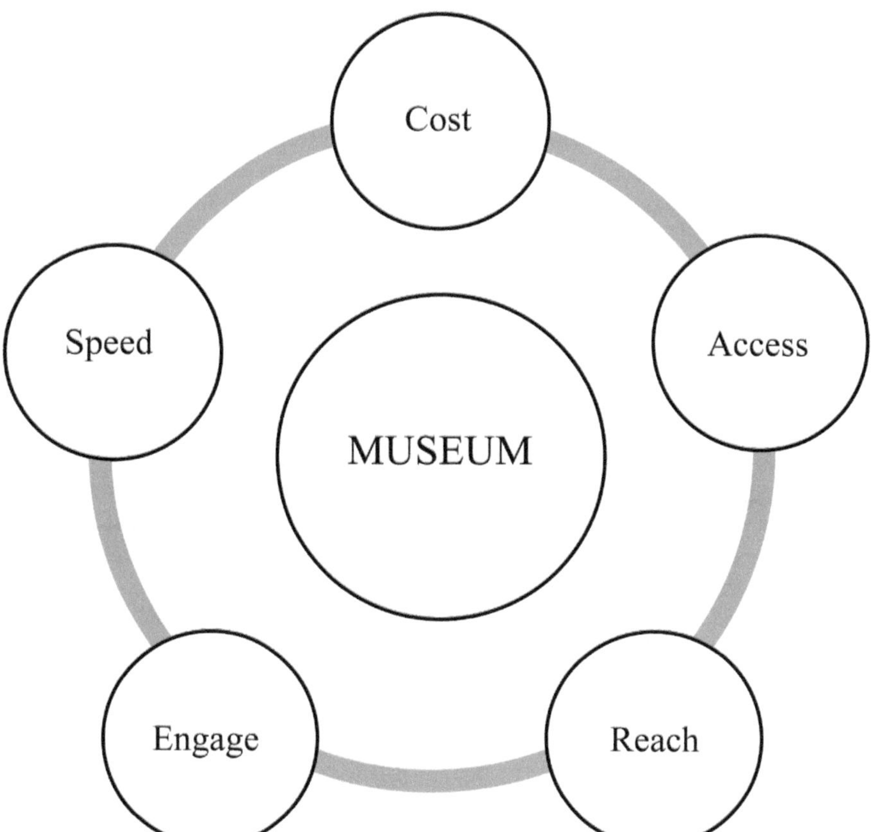

Figure 7.1. Benefits of social media use in contemporary museums.

engagement (E), and speed (S). Indeed, there is no membership fee required to join most of the social networks, and they provide worldwide access to the content, thus helping to expand the reach of an organization to larger or newer target populations. Social media also allow museums to sustain and reinforce their relevance to those audiences by allowing an unprecedented degree of learners' engagement in content production and speedy dissemination. Taken together, these benefits allow museums to perform a more efficient monitoring and a faster collection of strategically vital user opinions about programs and services that may need improvement, along with those initiatives that evoke positive reactions from the public.

CHALLENGES OF SOCIAL MEDIA USE

Despite the fact that social media can be advantageous for both the institutions and the communities they serve, their implementation in museums has come along with multiple challenges as well. Some of those problems are not new, but they have been intensified through the use of social media. One of the biggest hurdles is managing the enormity of user-generated content and incorporating it into current museum databases (Marselis & Schutze, 2013). Museums are challenged by the sheer amount of information circulating through social media, as well as by the fact that this information is often produced in different languages on a variety of social media platforms. Consequently, not all of this information can be taken at face value, so it becomes an added responsibility for museums to sort through and pick the content that is reliable and useful.

The large amount of user output and the variety of experiences enjoyed by members of networked communities add to the complexity of the social media environment. These factors challenge museums to develop their online user services in ways that can satisfy growing user expectations without jeopardizing the museum reputation and authority in the visitors' eyes. Social media make for a decentralized museum, and decentralization inevitably comes with the delegation of authority. Russo (2012) depicts the process in detail when she explains that the roots of the museum cultural authority lie in the ability to control the scope and variety of collections, as well as influence the collective interpretation of meaning by the audience. However, once physical collections are digitized and/or discussed on social media, at least part of the content no longer falls within the remit of the museum, as it is now being managed by the visitors. Key to understanding the current role of museums in delivering demand-driven cultural product is the realization that the growing visitor engagement through social media is changing public perception of museum authority. The skepticism about the absolute invincibility of the museum intellectual stance is rooted in the maturation of visitors' independent judgment stemming from the proliferation of social media in the cultural heritage domain. The irony of the situation is that by resorting to social media to uphold their relevance in the digital age, museums are voluntarily surrendering part of the grandeur they have so carefully nurtured throughout their existence. As a result, museums' cultural assertiveness is undermined, and they are ill suited to act as dominant mediators of the visitor cultural experience (Russo, Watkins, Kelly, & Chan, 2007).

They are acting as partners instead. So, in the long run, sharing authority on social media seems to be the right choice most museums will have to make. Distancing from the social media movement, museums would only do themselves a disservice by overlooking a potent mechanism with which to observe and participate in the virtual life of their visitors. In the digital age, museums simply cannot afford such nonchalance if they want to retain their social relevance. In the end, engaging and sharing authority with social media users ensures for museums fuller control over their image in the public eye. To act differently is to let others decide "how their content is presented and discussed in the vast archive of networked digital media" (Wong, 2011, p. 108). It is only through being active across numerous social media resources that museums can impact the culture and ethics of these spaces, thereby commanding the respect of the audiences.

For museums, acknowledging the power of engagement means taking a more proactive approach to understanding their visitors. It is a worthwhile tactic in light of perennial discussions about museums' roles in society. Now that social media have forayed into the current cultural landscape, the fact that heritage information can be reproduced and made globally available in a blink of an eye raises concerns about the authenticity of museum objects. With Facebook and Twitter, YouTube, and Flickr available on personal computers and mobile electronic devices, users enjoy hundreds of options with which to remix and disperse digital information, threatening to undermine the position of museums as the sole determinants of the content (and context) of cultural heritage collections.

As has been argued throughout this chapter, the use of social media has exploded in the last several years, so much so that it now touches almost every facet of our lives, including the cultural sphere. For all their undeniable contributions to diversifying and enriching museum visitor experiences, the influx of social media presents significant challenges from the standpoint of assailing the historical authority of museums as the primary stewards of human cultural heritage. Social media present challenges to users as well, from the standpoint of their privacy and information security. In a networked world, the line between private and public is thinning when personal information and opinions enter the public domain. Therefore, the use of social media has invariably been linked to the persistent tensions between creativity and security, protecting one's personal and professional identity, and privacy and openness (Nathan, MacGougan, & Schaffer, 2014).

Privacy, identity, and compliance have been singled out as the more pressing challenges facing museums in relation to the use of social media for marketing and audience engagement. These problems arise from the fact that a significant number of social media platforms, for example, Facebook, YouTube, and Twitter, are owned by third parties, thus making it difficult to control how user-generated content is disseminated and used. In particular, since user information is housed on servers outside museums' purview, concerns abound regarding the protection of privacy, information retention, information security, and access. Therefore, rigid safeguards, such as terms of service, are implemented to impose on users a variety of requirements in order to fully engage with social media applications. The downside of these policies is associated with the risks of fraud and identity theft that are heightened when user personal information is revealed, including their names, email addresses, and consent to have the information they post on a social media publicly shared and used to endorse products and services (see Facebook, *Statement of Rights and Responsibilities*, 2013). The high level of trust museums enjoy in their relationship with visitors calls for high standards of transparency and accountability that should regulate institutional approaches to the collection and use of personal data. Concerns over the appropriation of personal information are valid today and may have ethical standing in the future, presenting "a whole new area of sensitivity for museums to navigate" (American Alliance of Museums, 2014).

Predicated on the collective creation and sharing of user-generated content, social media open the doors to increasingly complex legal, intellectual property, and information ownership issues. Apart from those, proper management of media communication channels requires a substantial investment of time and other resources that neither the institutions nor the users can easily allocate (Russo et al., 2014). As a result, content on some of the more popular social media outlets is not updated as frequently as visitors may desire. When social media are used in museums, they provide an information space that is structurally ambiguous (Russo et al., 2007). In a situation when virtually anyone with access is able to copy and transmit information, museums cannot predict the ways in which that information, and social media themselves, might be used. They also can hardly predict the number of people who might participate or the length and the duration of such participation.

These challenges are compounded by the barriers museums encounter when attempting to control the quality of information published on social media. Given the unheard-of diversity of social media audiences, the interaction occurring in the networked domain is still in the realm of the amateur, regardless of how much it is guided by museum professionals or by the theoretical underpinnings of the current museum scholarship. While cultural institutions clearly benefit from the breadth of experiences that audiences bring with them, preserving the accuracy of information surrounding cultural content is one of the toughest obstacles museums have to overcome in an "unplanned" social media environment.

These risks and uncertainties warrant the development of sound social media use policies as the foundation for any social media governance model. The purpose of a social media policy is twofold. On the one hand, it is to guide users within the "general rules of respectful civil discourse" (Institute of Museum and Library Services, 2014). On the other hand, a well-designed policy will protect both an organization and its users from the hazards of the open-ended social media realm. Besides, social media policies implemented by cultural heritage organizations can serve as educational tools to explain why the institution or organization uses social media in the first place (Cadell, 2013).

There is no universal model or format for a social media policy. However, these documents serve a common purpose—to deliver a message outlining the points that are central to the institutional use of social media. The Smithsonian Institution's social media policy (2011) is a good example in this regard. It is direct and to the point, succinctly highlighting the purpose of the policy, along with the roles and responsibilities of those using social media within the institution. The Smithsonian document illustrates that, if crafted with the attention to organizational goals, as well as to the needs of its target audiences, a comprehensive social media use policy is the starting point for an organization's social media risk management. In their governing roles, social media use policies are wedded to the notion of museum visitor engagement as they deliver clarity of perspective, inspire confidence, and encourage social media use for the benefit of both the museum and its visitors.

CONCLUSION

Since the emergence of the Internet in the mid-1990s, museums have been quick to set their feet on the new platform of communicating with visitors. From the very onset, earlier social media formats acted as the harbinger of more substantial and pervasive changes to communication between organizations, communities, and individuals. They presented an enormous opportunity and also a challenge for cultural institutions, including museums, as many established communication methods and marketing techniques are ill suited to deal with customers who are no longer satisfied with the passive reception of information. Instead, visitors want museums to listen, appropriately engage, and respond. Social media have become effective competitors in delivering traditional museum missions. Emerging media technologies hold enormous promise for evaluating and fine-tuning what museums do, and for meeting the rising demands of the public, along with further personalizing visitor experiences. Thus, museums face the need to develop a congruent social media strategy based on the appropriate balance of education, interpretation, social interaction, and entertainment for their service communities.

This chapter has been written to inform the thinking of the museum and scholarly community about how social media will continue to shape the world, what it would be like to live in the world they may create, and how museums as cultural organizations might respond. Further, to what extent should the emergence of social media platforms require a new approach by museums, and in what ways can they solidify their position at the core of participative global exchange about individuals, culture, and society? Social media are envisioned in this chapter as a crucial resource for museums and the profession. It is a viable mechanism of promoting innovative and future-oriented thinking among museum visitors who will help position museums for long-term sustainability and success at the time of the economic recession and beyond. Clearly, the use of social media in museums requires striking a delicate balance between inevitable risks and exciting opportunities (Livingstone, 2010). This chapter concludes that the risks are worth taking because of the new horizons social media can open in the relationship between the museum and the learner. Social media activities vary in terms of their function and impact. Hence, for museums, the value of social media has not always been easily identifiable and acceptable. However, museums interested in getting seriously involved in the social media remit find themselves in urgent need of understanding and embracing this value. Arguably, it lies in the ability of social media to provoke culturally significant conversations, build rapport with visitors from various strata of the community, and provide a forum for progressive thinkers from all sectors to share ideas and explore joint solutions to the challenges currently facing cultural institutions and society at large.

REFERENCES

American Alliance of Museums. (2014). *Trendswatch 2014*. Washington, DC: American Alliance of Museums. Retrieved from http://www.aam-us.org/docs/default-source/center-for-the-future-of-museums/2014_trendswatch_lores-with-tracking-chip.pdf?sfvrsn=0.

Bernstein, S. (2011, October 11). Comment. In R. Stein, Please chime in: The challenges and opportunities of participatory culture [Indianapolis Museum of Art web log comment]. Retrieved from http://www.imamuseum.org/blog/2011/10/11/please-chime-in-the-challenges-and-opportunities-of-participatory-culture/.

Cadell, L. (2013). Socially practical or practically unsociable? A study into the use of social media policy within the State cultural heritage institutions in Queensland. *Australian Academic & Research Libraries, 44*(1), 3–13.

Chung, T. L., Marcketti, S., & Fiore, A. M. (2014). Use of social networking services for marketing art museums. *Museum Management and Curatorship, 29*(2), 188–205.

Drotner, K., & Schroder, K. C. (Eds.). (2013). *Museum communication and social media: The connected museum*. New York: Routledge.

Duggan, M., & Smith, A. (2014, January). *Social media update 2013*. Washington, DC: Pew Research Center. Retrieved from http://www.pewinternet.org/files/2013/12/PIP_Social-Networking-2013.pdf.

Facebook. (2013). *Statement of rights and responsibilities*. Retrieved from https://www.facebook.com/legal/terms.

Falk, J. H. (2009). *Identity and the museum visitor experience*. Walnut Creek, CA: Left Coast Press, Inc.

Fitch, D. (2012). Youth in foster care and social media: A framework for developing privacy guidelines. *Journal of Technology in Human Services, 30*(2), 94–108.

Fletcher, A., & Lee, M. J. (2012). Current social media uses and evaluations in American museums. *Museum Management and Curatorship, 27*(5), 505–21.

Giaccardi, E. (Ed.). (2012). *Heritage and social media: Understanding heritage in a participatory culture*. New York: Routledge.

Hooper-Greenhill, E. (1995). *Museums and the shaping of knowledge*. New York: Routledge.

Institute of Museum and Library Services. (2014). *IMLS commenting and posting policy*. Retrieved from http://www.imls.gov/news/imls_commenting_policy.aspx.

Ito, M., Horst, H., Bittanti, M., Boyd, D., Herr-Stephenson, B., Lange, P. G et al. (2008). *Living and learning with new media: Summary of findings from the digital youth project*. Chicago: The MacArthur Foundation. Retrieved from http://digitalyouth.ischool.berkeley.edu/files/report/digitalyouth-WhitePaper.pdf

Jenkins, H. (2006). *Confronting the challenges of participatory culture: Media education for the twenty-first century.* Chicago, IL: MacArthur Foundation.

Johnson, L., Witchey, H., Smith, R., Levine, A., & Haywood, K. (2010). *The 2010 horizon report: Museum edition.* Austin, TX: The New Media Consortium.

Kaplan, A. M., & Haenlein, M. (2010). Users of the world, unite! The challenges and opportunities of social media. *Business Horizons, 53*(1), 59–68.

Kelly, L. (2013). The connected museum in the world of social media. In K. Drotner & K. C. Schroder (Eds.), *Museum communication and social media: The connected museum* (pp. 54–71). New York: Routledge.

Lenhart, A., Purcell, K., Smith, A., & Zickuhr, K. (2010, February 3). *Social media & mobile Internet use among teens and young adults.* Washington, DC: Pew Research Center. Retrieved from http://pewinternet.org/Reports/2010/Social-Media-and-Young-Adults.aspx.

Lipscomb, J. (2010). What is social media? *Dental Economics, 100*(4), 6–7.

Livingstone, S. (2010). *E-Youth: (Future) policy implications. Reflections on online risk, harm, and vulnerability.* Paper presented at the E-Youth: Balancing between Opportunities and Risks Conference, University of Antwerp, Belgium, May 27–28, 2010. Retrieved from http://eprints.lse.ac.uk/27849.

Marselis, R., & Schutze, L. M. (2013). "One way to Holland": Migrant heritage and social media. In K. Drotner & K. C. Schrøder (Eds.), *Museum communication and social media: The connected museum* (pp. 75–92). New York: Routledge.

Nathan, L. P., MacGougan, A., & Schaffer, E. (2014). If not us, who? Social media policy and the iSchool classroom. *Journal of Education for Library and Information Science, 55*(2), 112–32.

Nielsen. (2012). *State of the media—The social media report 2012.* Retrieved from http://www.nielsen.com/us/en/insights/reports/2012/state-of-the-media-the-social-media-report-2012.html.

Russo, A. (2012). The rise of the media museum. In E. Giaccardi (Ed.), *Heritage and social media: Understanding heritage in a participatory culture* (pp. 145–57). New York: Routledge.

Russo, A., Watkins, J., Kelly, L., & Chan, S. (2007). Social media and cultural interactive experiences in museums. *Nordisk Museologi, 1*, 19–29.

Russo, A., Watkins, J., Kelly, L., & Chan, S. (2008). Participatory communication with social media. *Curator: The Museum Journal, 51*(1), 21–31.

Simon, N. (2010). *The participatory museum.* Santa Cruz, CA: Museum 2.0.

Smithsonian Institution. (2011). *Social media policy.* Retrieved from http://www.si.edu/content/pdf/about/sd/SD-814.pdf.

Stein, R. (2012). Chiming in on museums and participatory culture. *Curator: The Museum Journal, 55*(2), 215–26.

Wong, A. (2011). Ethical issues of social media in museums: A case study. *Museum Management and Curatorship, 26*(2), 97–112.

Wong, A. (2012). Social media towards social change. In R. Sandell & E. Nightingale (Eds.), *Museums, equality, and social justice* (pp. 281–293). New York: Routledge.

Wright, D. K., & Hinson, M. D. (2009). An analysis of the increasing impact of social and other new media on public relations practice. In K. Yamamura (Ed.), *Proceedings of the 12th Annual International Public Relations Research Conference* (pp. 718–36). Miami, FL: IPRRC.

Zickuhr, K., & Madden, M. (2012, June 6). *Older adults and Internet use.* Washington, DC: Pew Research Center. Retrieved from http://www.pewinternet.org/files/old-media/Files/Reports/2012/PIP_Older_adults_and_internet_use.pdf.

III

EDUCATION

8

HHA

Using Handheld Technology to Foster Interdisciplinary Learning between Art and the Humanities

Karen Heid and Jessica Dame

ABSTRACT

Given the almost universal presence of mobile devices in the learners' world, the research team set out to find a way to help teachers use art, mobile technologies, and integrative learning to enhance instructional practice. The Handheld Art (HHA) project encourages the interdisciplinary study of art and the humanities by accessing art collections by means of handheld devices such as tablets and smartphones. Initially using digitized images from the Columbia Museum of Art collections in Columbia, South Carolina, HHA encourages students to go beyond the acquisition of facts and skills to focus on Enduring Ideas—larger concepts that dwell in the nature of human experience, cross all disciplines, and stand the test of time. Instead of acquiring discipline-specific knowledge, students using HHA explore Enduring Ideas such as Power, Meaning and Objects, and Alienation in depth across multiple disciplines. Following a discussion of HHA methodology, project organization, website content, and results of initial assessments from the field, the future directions for the project are highlighted, including the development of a Handheld Art Tool expected to become an essential means for introducing learners to the interdisciplinary reality of arts, humanities, and a life well lived.

INTRODUCTION

> Mobile phones and handheld devices are not ever going to go away. Somehow we need to figure out how to make these devices work for us in the classroom, rather than against us. There is a way to do this, and we need to figure it out. (Taylor, Ballengee-Morris, & Carpenter, 2008)

Sitting at a presentation at a National Art Education Association Convention in New Orleans, the speaker suggested the above words. And indeed, mobile phones and handheld devices seem to be even more ubiquitous than ever. Out of seven school districts that surround Columbia, South Carolina, five have made significant financial investments in handheld technology for middle and high school students so that their students could begin replacing textbooks and three-ring binders with electronic tablets. There are rumors of more tablets coming to more districts (conversation with art teachers, 2013). Given the almost universal presence of these devices in the learners' world, the research team set out to find a way to help teachers use art, mobile technologies, and integrative learning to enhance instructional practice.

The stated mission of the Handheld Art (HHA) project is to encourage an interdisciplinary study of art and the humanities by accessing the collections of the Columbia Museum of Art (CMA) by means of handheld devices such as tablets and smartphones. As art museums and libraries continue to bring rich content, collections, and programming to learners and the public, new technologies for teaching and learning may make collections easier for teachers and students to access. One might imagine that with a click of the download button in iTunes or the Android Store, many institutions might be able share their content through mobile apps and handheld devices. Similarly, through the HHA application, K–12 teachers and university professors who are interested in interdisciplinary methods for teaching and learning can virtually visit the CMA collections without needing to visit in person. Through HHA, methods of teaching and learning and the pedagogy and practice of using art to strengthen interdisciplinary methods of teaching may be greatly influenced. Of most importance for the purposes of this investigation, the innovative platform that provides the capability of using handheld devices may serve as a model for other collections that would like to present their images to the public for integrative study.

THEORETICAL FRAMEWORK

Extending the Repository Website

In preparation for the launch of this study, our initial steps included reviewing methods of teaching art history to K–12 students. That effort revealed that art history continues to be integrated through a timeline or linear narrative (Stewart & Walker, 2005). As the Common Core State Standards for K–12 teaching emphasize thematic understanding and depth of knowledge as opposed to focusing on rote coverage of material, we began thinking about interdisciplinary approaches for teaching and learning. Similarly, colleges and universities have also implemented interdisciplinary methodologies in higher education courses. In fact, in submitting its accreditation report to the Southern Association of Colleges and Schools, the University of South Carolina launched an initiative that had at its core an interdisciplinary curriculum approach that embraced learning that moved beyond single disciplines or classrooms into the real world in which students lived (i.e., USC Connect). We began searching for an approach that would allow art to be the cohesive agent that could hold disciplines together through common themes. Such an approach might be identified as interdisciplinary. *Interdisciplinary* refers to the explicit recognition and subsequent connection of content and instruction across more than one subject of academic discipline in the teaching and learning experience. Contrary to interdisciplinary philosophy, a traditional and subject-rooted curriculum would require subject areas to remain distinct. Within this traditional approach, teachers plan for the delivery of content by giving primacy to a subject-based, content-specific classroom, and less about overarching or thematic ideas that might more easily emerge in interdisciplinary pedagogy.

But cross-disciplinary instruction does not have a presence in the tradition of American schooling. Based on efficiency and ease of collecting data, schools during the Industrial Revolution (i.e., late nineteenth to mid-twentieth century) moved away from the one-room schoolhouse and one-room teacher and started hiring teachers who only teach one subject—a disciplined-based approach. Kelehear and Heid (2002) argue a contrary view, consistent with theorist and researchers from the progressive school, that disciplined-based instruction constricts learning and artificially isolates student learning into fields of study as opposed to what they claim are more nearly holistic and thus authentic learning settings.

Taylor, Carpenter, Ballengee-Morris, and Sessions (2006) suggest if an art teacher is only discussing Raphael's *The School of Athens*, he/she might be contributing to an inadequate education especially if he/she were not to include a discussion of linear perspective and go even further by discussing the golden mean, the Pythagorean Theorem, and other rules of geometry. Essentially, the art teacher is not only teaching math but also math connections. Similarly, a math teacher might incorporate *The School of Athens* using a handheld device to support teaching the Pythagorean Theorem. And if the math teacher were to tell the story of Pythagoras, his contribution to history, religion, ancient Greece, Freemasons, and the impact this had on our developing new nation, she/he might be also teaching social studies.

The use of Enduring Ideas helped this research team bring cohesiveness to the project and allowed integrative approaches for classroom use. An Enduring Idea is larger than a theme. It dwells in the nature of human experience, crosses all disciplines, and stands the test of time (Stewart & Walker, 2005). Enduring Ideas such as Power, Meaning and Objects, and Alienation are broad, encompassing, and integrate easily into multiple disciplines. The Enduring Idea is the intellectual linchpin that holds essential understanding that focuses on making knowledge more easily transferred across disciplines with lasting value instead of fragments of discipline-specific knowledge. In this Enduring Ideas approach, it is intended that students learn to go beyond the acquisition of facts and skills to focus on larger concepts and in greater depth. Those notions or concepts then become transferrable to new situations and disciplines. They provide an enlarged purpose for learning the content and answering the question, Why is this topic worth studying? Under each Enduring Idea, there is the potential for hundreds of instructional units to be written. We chose thirty Enduring Ideas for our project and began aligning the images from the CMA to art units of instruction that were connected to state-adopted standards.

HHA creates an intersection of technology and the arts by combining the digitization and documentation of images from the CMA into a website. Also, HHA integrates computer technology into an interactive and dynamic tool for teaching and learning. Because of its reliance on a philosophy of interdisciplinary understanding, HHA benefits a host of humanities disciplines and fields involved in K–12 education as well as the students and researchers in higher education. Additionally, by using Enduring Ideas rather than a linear narrative, HHA has become an innovative approach for the way art teachers and students approach the study of art. HHA has contributed to the humanities by allowing students to see the elegant fit between visual art and performing art, history, religion, philosophy, literature, languages, or many other subjects.

Using images for teaching and learning can be an important resource for understanding history and culture (Taylor et al., 2006). Images as a primary source for teaching and learning are complex, and must be read with attention to descriptive information, historical context, interpretive meanings, and evaluation. HHA offers teachers a collection of ideas and examples of meaningful interdisciplinary approaches for teaching. These contemporary approaches position visual art as both a subject for study and a vehicle for inquiry. This dual purpose may challenge traditional and standards-based approaches to curriculum.

Columbia Museum of Art Partnership

The CMA is centrally located in the heart of downtown Columbia, South Carolina, just three blocks from the state capitol building and the main University of South Carolina (USC) campus. The collection ranges from antiquity to the present day with a focus on European, American, modern and contemporary, and Asian art. A large gift from the Samuel H. Kress Foundation formed the nucleus of an important permanent collection of more than seven thousand objects of fine and decorative arts across a broad range of centuries and media. HHA was able to draw from notable works as well as lesser-known works. Highlights from the museum include a Botticelli *Nativity*, the only Botticelli fresco outside of Italy; Canaletto's *View of the Molo*; Hans Burkhardt, an influential artist at the genesis of the American Abstract Expressionist movement; and an important early drawing by Ilya Bolotowsky, a leading artist of Geometric Abstraction. The CMA was an ideal museum to partner with HHA due to the large and varied collection of art for teaching and learning through digital media.

Technology

Art museums both large and small have made inroads into technology by digitizing objects and placing them in online repositories such as the Google Art

Project for the purpose of education. Using a handheld device for research or viewing images while one is in the museum benefits educational museum goals, such as the ability to explore additional information on an artwork they are viewing or being linked to additional artworks by an artist. In a persistent and now somewhat anachronistic approach to maintaining discipline, teachers and administrators, on the other hand, have spent years combating the use of cell phones and similar devices in classrooms. They have been considered disruptive of instruction. With the educational potential of handheld technologies now recognized, schools across the country are incorporating iPads and tablets into their curricula. This transition to the acceptance of technology in schools may be becoming the norm in South Carolina as iPads are distributed to students in both middle and high schools instead of textbooks. It is clear, however, that merely placing a tablet in every student's hand does not in itself make students more capable, teachers more effective, or test scores higher. Such devices must deliver content in a manner that engages learning, and instructional practices and educational attitudes must change to make use of them.

Art museums and libraries have a long history of investing in the development of citizens by encouraging their contemplation of artworks. If the artworks are significant and/or rare, patrons are unlikely to be allowed to handle them. The needs of preservation require cultural heritage institutions to curtail what might be a natural impulse to touch that which compels our attention. By means of digital copies, HHA encourages that impulse—not that it urges investigators to confuse the copy with the material object, but it lends itself to the tactile curiosity other modes of engagement necessarily thwart. These other modes include now commonplace web interfaces, where interaction with art takes the form of clicking links, enlarging or minimizing views, and reading textual descriptions. HHA augments this approach by encouraging a qualitatively different form of exploration, one in which the student encounters the artwork as a manipulable, tactile surface. This interface itself is significant to humanistic exploration, which favors intuition, imagination, and interpretation over the methodical trial-and-error of experimental science.

HHA draws on the growth of handheld platforms to achieve transformational participatory learning in humanities through art. Three key features of the handheld technology capture its unique capability as a platform for educational computing: its ubiquity, portability, and intimacy. First, handheld devices are ubiquitous. A 2013 Pew Report asserts market saturation for mobile phones as ownership rates among late teens approach 100 percent, representing a greater popularity than either the desktop computer or cable television (Rainie, 2013). For teachers and administrators who have spent years addressing the issues of having cell phones in their classrooms, the problem has moved from ringing phones or texting in class to how we can turn the ubiquitous into an educational advantage.

Secondly, handhelds are extremely portable. This portability, both in terms of battery life and physical size/weight, means that students carry these devices with them and use them almost constantly. For teachers and administrators interested in uniting students' learning across multiple social spaces, both within and beyond the classroom, handheld devices represent the best chance to facilitate asynchronous participation for students who have learned to adapt to an ever-growing array of learning approaches.

Thirdly, handhelds are a curiously personal device. For reasons and in ways that researchers have only just begun to study, individuals experience an intimate relationship with the mobile phone (Cooley, 2008). Mobile phones become an extension of self. It is in our hands, internalizing and sublimating its interface as a natural extension of self-expression.

Technology Applied

HHA can be accessed online (handheldart.org) and by an app available for iOS and Android devices (Figure 8.1). Using Omeka, an open-source content management system, provided a focus of exhibiting cultural heritage objects and extended its functionality through themes and plug-ins. The front-end results in Omeka required an individual with programming and design experience, while the backend content management for loading content and managing metadata was easy to follow due to its template system and use of Dublin Core standards. Partnering with the University of South Carolina's Center for Digital Humanities (CDH), a graduate student information specialist, an undergraduate student programmer, and the aid of a full-time graphic designer contributed to the project. Choosing to use one of Omeka's default themes, the student programmer (with the aid of the graphic designer) built in the added features such as the scrolling images on the homepage and browsing features under the tabs Enduring Ideas, Unit Plans, and Browse.

The iOS application was programmed using XCode, an integrated development environment with software development tools for the creation of software for OS X and iOS. Coding was done by a CDH programmer, with the assistance of the graphic designer on visual aspects such as icons. The CDH team created a frame that is fully intractable and scales HHA website's content into a size appropriate for mobile view (Figure 8.2). When a change is made to the HHA website, it is reflected in the app without the need to update. Currently, the iOS app was updated and supports iOS 7. The Android app, however, is awaiting licensing clearance before being released.

METHODOLOGY

Organizing a Web Project

Creating the content for the website and app required many discussions with the directors at the CMA. The creation of a new website that would essentially act as an open sourced repository of the CMA's images required a good deal of convincing the

Figure 8.1. Screenshot of Handheld Art homepage.

directors that they had not lost control over access to the museum holdings. Up until the summer of 2013, when the Getty Museum of Art decided to make all their images open source, most art museums held control of who would be allowed to download or copy their images (Getty Museum of Art, 2013). CMA opened their vault to the research team fully two years before the Getty Museum, and we expect that many other museums will follow in their path. Once the permission to access the CMA vault was granted we were well on our way to allowing content to be uploaded.

With internal funding from USC and external funding from the National Art Education Association, the project director secured the CDH to help with digital programming. The CDH led the team of technologists in the design and development of a prototype while the project director guided the prototype's construction in order to ensure pedagogical efficiency and conformity to existing standards of education. The server was purchased with grant funding and is housed and monitored at USC in fireproof rooms. Our plan included working with museum curators

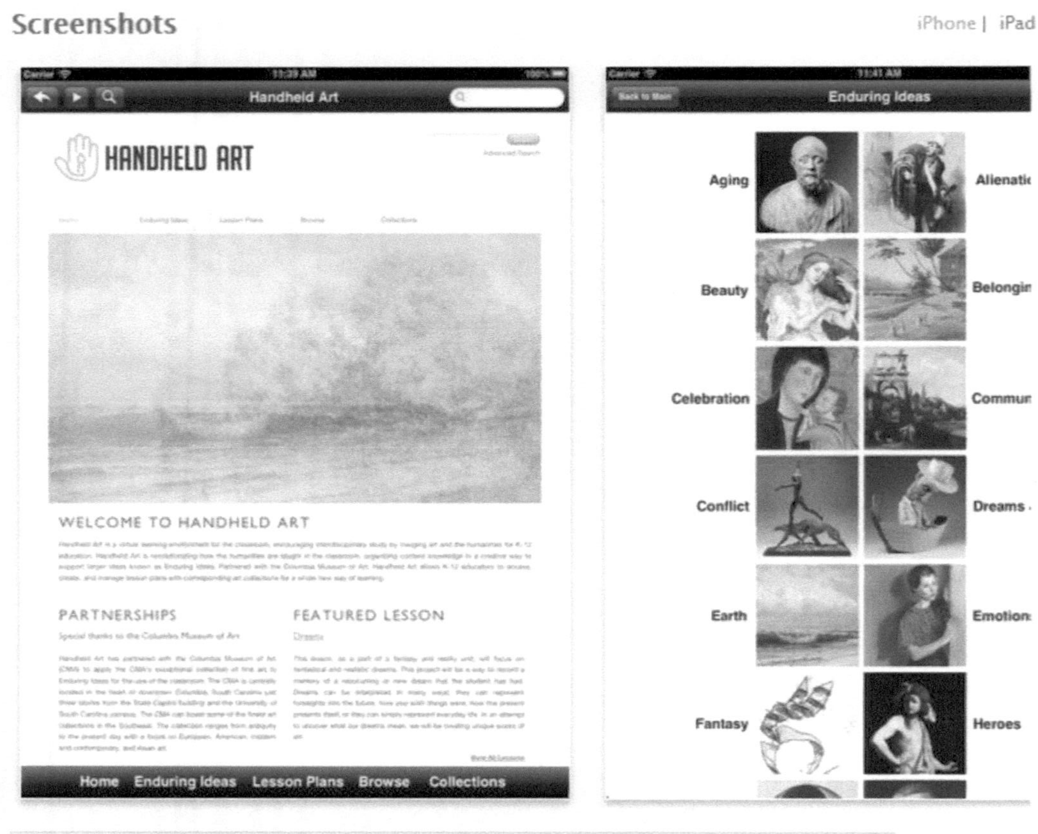

Figure 8.2. Screenshots of the mobile app as it would appear on an iPad.

and accessing the underlying data—the same images, the same metadata, the same descriptions—using server-side transforms to present the information to mobile devices in a tidy browser environment. Using Omeka, we are able to deliver the same image, metadata, curriculum, and descriptive content to iPhone, iPad, Android, and tablet-based platforms. In effect, we cross-populate these platforms with the exact same content, but customized to the particularities of a handheld technology. Servers housed at USC provide the connections between the remote repositories at the CMA and cellular networks. The prototype launched on the Internet with limited content in January 2012.

Once a working model was in place and a few images from the CMA were uploaded, we were ready to hire independent reviewers to assess the use of the technology and units of instruction. As part of our assessment, five secondary education experts and two professors, experts in visual literacy education, were brought to Columbia to provide feedback of the prototype solution. The results of the assessment indicated that the HHA prototype was a platform that awaited content creators and more images, but they also suggested that it would be necessary to partner with museum educator experts, classroom teachers, and university faculty to create the content that drives the interaction. Using their suggestions, we were able to bring together stakeholders to create the content that would help propel the project to excellence. As HHA expands, we anticipate that our design will serve as a model that may be used by other art museums and educators throughout the United States that may be interested in teaching through art, Enduring Ideas, and integrative means.

Organizing a Website and Content

The early development of the HHA prototype focused on testing out organization and display options while gathering the first round of images from the CMA. The earliest round of content included five Enduring Ideas, fifty images, and fewer than ten unit plans. In the year following the prototype, CDH's staff grew to include more student assistants and full-time staff, expanded the scope of technologies they designed, and moved their offices to a centralized location on campus. This growth fostered the expansion of HHA through the image collection and creation of the mobile application. Simultaneously, educators from the 2013 workshop were producing unique unit plans, writing up Enduring Ideas, and adding to the overall content. During this period of growth, HHA was able to grow to thirty Enduring Ideas, three hundred images, and eighty unit plans.

Organization of the website was achieved through the organic process of building the prototype and finding what worked best for the content over time. HHA is divided into Enduring Ideas, Unit Plans, Browse (by images or tags), and Collections. A search box and advanced search are included, and appear on every page for quick searching. Additionally, each page is sharable across Facebook and Twitter through an Omeka plug-in.

Enduring Ideas is the largest section comprised of the thirty ideas, each including an Introduction, Rationale for Teaching, Key Concepts, Essential Questions, links to the current standards, and links to corresponding unit plans, artists, and artworks. Using the example of Belonging, the Enduring Idea Introduction introduces the big idea to set the stage for concepts to follow. Rationale for Teaching narrows in on how this big idea relates to the student. For example:

> Learners from an early age become aware of how they belong in their family, school/peers, and community. Belonging is a crucial aspect of identity, exploring how to "fit in" with the desired group is a constant and lifelong struggle. By exploring how we belong, learners can better understand their environment, culture, and self.

The big idea is then broken down into key concepts, usually a group of three, that highlight major themes to be explored. For example:

- Belongingness, by developing social bond, is a basic human need.
- The need to belong can affect our daily choices and identity.
- Everyone belongs to numerous complex groups, which can generate either positive or negative psychological outcomes.

Essential Questions highlight a few general questions to be explored and discussed. All of these components come together and relate to the unit plans. Additionally, these components can be discussed as a stand-alone with the tagged artworks.

Other search options include Unit Plans and Browse. Dublin Core metadata is used to describe unit plans and images with the most basic information, such as: title, creator, date, and rights (Figure 8.3). Unit plans include the unique metadata: description, duration, standards, objectives, and materials. Each unit plan is accessible through PDF format. Images include the unique metadata: identifier, coverage, original format, and physical dimensions. Both are tagged with Enduring Ideas and can be searched using a tag cloud (Figure 8.4).

In preparation for more content, our team established a HHA Review Board. Made up of fifteen practicing teachers and education scholars, the board will solicit for peer-reviewed instructional units. Accepted units will be published to the website.

Organizing a Workshop

During the summer of 2013, the project directors organized a two-week workshop so that units of instruction could be written for the website. The project director put out a call for teachers who are interested in integrative teaching and writing to participate in the HHA summer workshop. With nine teachers, one social media relations person, two graduate students, and the project director, we set out to have a dynamic and productive workshop.

Dublin Core

Title
Portland Vase

Creator
Josiah Wedgwood & Sons (manufacturer)

Date
designed 1789 ; this example c. 1820-1840

Rights
All rights reserved by the Columbia Museum of Art.

Identifier
CMA accession number: 1997.16.2

Coverage
English (Etruria Staffordshire)
1759-present

Still Image Item Type Metadata

Original Format
Jasperware

Physical Dimensions
10 x 7 1/2 in. dia.

Files

Tags
Earth, Materialism, meaning and objects, Nature

Citation
Josiah Wedgwood & Sons (manufacturer), "Portland Vase," *Handheld Art*, accessed November 12, 2014, http://handheldart.cas.sc.edu/items/show/506.

Social Bookmarking

Figure 8.3. Screenshot of image metadata (handheldart.org).

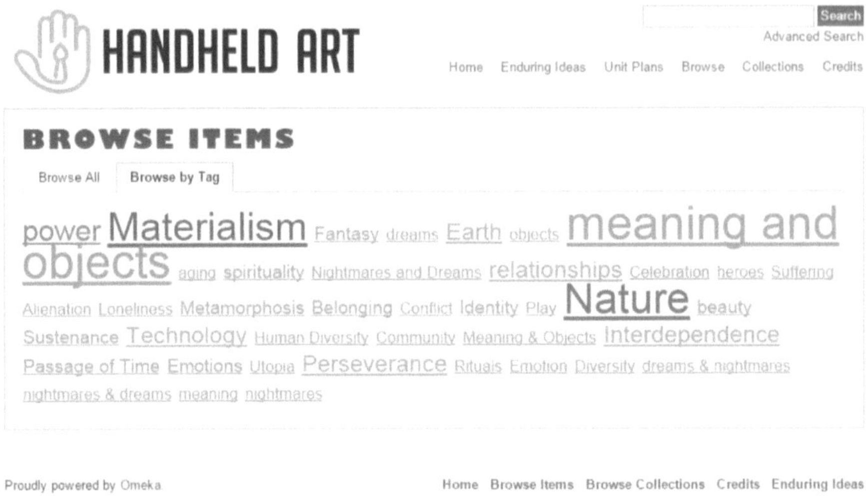

Figure 8.4. Screenshot of tag cloud under browse by tag (handheldart.org).

The aim of employing these particular workshop participants was the hope that they would be part of a pedagogical change in their districts and schools. We prepared the workshop participants to work as catalysts of change within their departments, schools, and districts, informed by the recent visual culture and visual literacy movement in arts education. Our interdisciplinary approach, where students engage in art production, art history, aesthetics, and art criticism within their own subjects, was implemented with readings and discussion. Additionally, the workshop prepared the participants with new readings on mobile devices—its ubiquity, its portability, and its intimate connection with the individual as a means for developing pedagogy for the HHA website.

Workshop participants took an active role in the website content. Excitement about the project permeated the participants, and new ideas were pitched, batted about, and mulled over during the seminar atmosphere. Thirty Enduring Ideas were chosen, over three hundred images were added, and nearly eighty unit plans were added to the website. A highlight of the workshop included several visits to the CMA vault to determine images that would be useful for their interdisciplinary units of instruction. At the end of the two weeks, the website had changed drastically. The website was full, exciting, and amazingly beautiful. By now, our project team had greatly expanded, and it seemed that every day more people liked us on Twitter and Facebook.

EARLY FINDINGS

Practicing Teacher's Assessment

In academic year 2013 to 2014, five practicing teachers actively used HHA in their classrooms in fulfillment of a grant from the National Art Education Foundation. Their preliminary reports indicate that the project successfully allowed them to use open source visual materials to bridge two or more disciplines according to the Enduring Ideas paradigm. Blogs from the teachers describe their students' excitement about being able to access, download, and interact with artworks. For example, one teacher explains, "Students can carry the images around with them on their tablets, thinking all the while about aspects of that image." The teacher continues, "One of the things they like to do the most is to seek out other apps on their own that will allow them to import the image for making mash-ups and other aspects of study" (high school teacher blog comment, retrieved November 16, 2013).

While statistics quantifying the success of HHA have yet to be compiled and interpreted, informal feedback suggests that K–12 educators are eager to move forward with the next iteration of HHA. The HHA project demonstrated that a relatively small selection of artworks from the collections of the CMA could inspire K–12 educators and students. It also revealed that a much larger selection of materials would be needed to integrate this approach with K–12 curricula more broadly. Ideally, educators would have at their disposal a collection of materials as large and diverse as the Internet would allow.

Of particular note for this stage of the investigation is the need for both qualitative and quantitative assessments from stakeholders to affirm HHA's impact. Anecdotal and suggestive evidence are positive thus far.

CONCLUSION

Based on the HHA preliminary findings and assessment with five practicing art teachers, several researchers, museum curators, and classroom teachers have approached our team about extending the HHA brand into other realms—specifically, other collections. Although the HHA website and app has been successfully used in K–12 classrooms, teachers suggested that HHA would be a wonderful asset to the classroom if it included a tool where students could download collection images and manipulate it on the tablet screen. Shortly after thinking about this new idea, the director of the Irvin Department of Rare Books and Special Collections at USC approached us about including the Arader Collection, a recently donated collection, into the Handheld Art Project.

Handheld Art Tool (HAT)

W. Graham Arader, III, recently donated a $30 million collection of 8,500 natural history watercolors, woodcuts, engravings, lithographs, chromolithographs, and maps from the sixteenth to nineteenth centuries to the University of South Carolina. The collection illuminates the historical conditions of possibility for the American experiment and cultivates an appreciation for the natural world and the manner of its representation. Thus, the collection lends itself to examination of the values encouraged by European representations of the natural world during a period of amazing scientific discovery and of colonial expansion. Known as the Arader Collection, his intention for the donated collection was for teachers to use the images for teaching and learning in interdisciplinary methods.

Capitalizing on using HHA as a brand, our project team has set sights on including a tool that will extend the digital humanities pilot project, HHA, to the next implementation phase. The HAT will take full advantage of the touchscreen interface to engage learners in a range of disciplines. It will leverage a parallel project at USC to digitize a large and diverse collection of visual materials and will expand dramatically the resources available to educators. Through collaborative efforts with technologists and scholars at affiliated universities, HAT will use the power of the semantic web to incorporate materials from any number of repositories and to integrate with other open source scholarly research, teaching, and publication platforms. Additionally, the project will train a group of primary and secondary school teachers in the use of the tool, develop portable instructional units suitable for integration with Common Core State Standards curricula, and encourage adoption of the tool nationwide. This project will allow students of all ages to interact with visually rich archival materials by means of touch. Rather than the point-and-click of a mouse, students will pursue close and integrative examination of content by means of their hands: learning will be quite literally *hands-on.*

HAT will allow learners and educators to access, explore, annotate, manipulate, write about, and curate digitized archival materials from the Web, beginning with the Arader Collection. Using the touchscreen interface, they will be able to move around within the field of a selected image, using their fingers to zoom in on any detail (e.g., to consider brushstrokes) and to return the image to its original dimensions. They will be able to select whole images or image details and annotate them using their own terms or a provided controlled vocabulary. With a swipe of the fingers, they will able to view selected annotated images and/or image details in other facets of the tool as examples of particular terms or commentaries on particular concepts. They will be able to share their notes and collections with their teachers for evaluation, and might chose to publish them.

With the implementation of this new tool, the HHA project will make major strides toward moving our original mission to a realized tradition: that museums and collections across the world will find the Handheld Art brand essential as a means for introducing learners to the interdisciplinary reality of arts, humanities, and a life well lived.

REFERENCES

Cooley, H. (2008, December). Ecologies of practice. *Journal of Visual Culture*, *7*(3), 267–76. doi: 10.1177/1470412908096336

Getty Museum of Art. (2013, August). Getty announces new program lifting restrictions on use of digital images. Retrieved from http://news.getty.edu/press_materials.cfm#2-3-5812.

Kelehear, Z., & Heid, K. A. (2002). Mentoring in the art classroom. *Studies in Art Education, 44*(1), 67–78.

Rainie, L. (2013, June 6). *Cell phone ownership hits 91% of adults.* Washington, DC: Pew Research Center. Retrieved from http://www.pewresearch.org/fact-tank/2013/06/06/cell-phone-ownership-hits-91-of-adults/.

Stewart, M. G., & Walker, S. R. (2005). *Rethinking curriculum in art.* Worcester, MA: Davis Publications.

Taylor, P. G., Carpenter, B. S., Ballengee-Morris, C., & Sessions, B. (2006). *Interdisciplinary approaches to teaching art in high school.* Reston, VA: National Art Education Association.

Taylor, P. G., Ballengee-Morris, C., & Carpenter, B. S. (2008). *It is not easy being green: SecondLife.com, self-portraiture and identity.* National Art Education Association Convention, March 26–30, New Orleans, LA.

IV

FIELD REPORTS

9

Grey Literature at the Cummings Center for the History of Psychology, a Case Study

Jodi Kearns and Cathy Faye

ABSTRACT

Grey literature is material of limited circulation and of little control by commercial publishers, including items such as white papers, technical reports, conference programs, directories, meeting agendas, flyers, newsletters, and mailings. Recent pushes for international recognition of grey literature repositories indicate that organization of and access to grey literature is a useful practice for supporting historians and other researchers. The authors here present a case study of the more than twenty-five-thousand-item, and growing, collection of grey literature at the Cummings Center for the History of Psychology in which historians wade to uncover information of little-known or lesser diffusion for their research. The case study begins with a description of the institution that houses the collection, describes the scope and appeal of the grey literature collection, and addresses problems of organization and access with the solutions that were applied, including rapid mass digitization and metadata creation. This piece concludes with a discussion on the use of grey literature in historical research and education, and outcomes aligned to the organizational strategic plan.

GREY LITERATURE

Grey literature is material of limited circulation and of little control by commercial publishers (GreyNet, n.d.) and includes items such as white papers, technical reports, conference programs, directories, meeting agendas, flyers, newsletters, and mailings. De Blaaij (2008) claims that grey literature is not widely considered by historians in their research processes—a claim the authors aim to support by a grey literature citation analysis project in scholarly journals in history. Recent pushes for international recognition of grey literature repositories is made evident with the 2014 announcement of the Sixteenth International Conference on Grey Literature, the publication of the nine-page international directory of institutions peddling grey literature (see GreyNet, 2014), and the publication of a formal textbook dedicated to the study of grey literature (see Farace and Schöpfel, 2010). Almost half (47 percent) of the institutions and organizations listed in the *International Directory of Organization in Grey Literature* are in the United States (GreyNet, 2014), possibly indicating that organization of and access to grey literature in the United States is a useful practice for supporting historians and other researchers.

The authors here present a case study of the more than twenty-five-thousand-item and growing, collection of grey literature at the Cummings Center for the History of Psychology in which historians wade to uncover information of little-known or lesser diffusion for their research. The case study begins with a description of the institution that houses the collection, describes the scope and appeal of the grey literature collection, and addresses problems of organization and access with the solutions that were applied. This piece concludes with a discussion on the use of grey literature in historical research and education.

THE CUMMINGS CENTER FOR THE HISTORY OF PSYCHOLOGY

The Cummings Center for the History of Psychology (CCHP), located at the University of Akron in Akron, Ohio, is a unique institution that cares for, provides access to, and interprets the historical record of psychology and related human sciences. Its overarching vision from the strategic plan is "to explore what it means to be human." The CCHP houses a museum of psychology that showcases artifacts, documents, films, and photographs from the history of the human sciences. In 2013, the CCHP launched the Institute for Human Science and Culture, a multidisciplinary institute dedicated to understanding historical and contemporary issues in human sciences. The institute houses several collections, including the Ludy T. Benjamin Jr. *Popular Psychology* Magazine Collection and the David P. Campbell Postcard Collection. CCHP is also home to the Archives of the History of American Psychology (founded in 1965), comprised of a vast collection of artifacts, media, and documents, including the personal papers of many important psychologists. One of the largest collections of the archives is the collection of special interest grey literature documents around which this case study is based.

A team of seven librarians, archivists, and historians collaborate to provide access to collections through information retrieval tools, reference services, exhibit curation, and educational opportunities.

SCOPE AND SIGNIFICANCE OF THE GREY LITERATURE COLLECTION AT CCHP

The Special Interest Collection at the Cummings Center for the History of Psychology is comprised of a large and unique body of materials that documents the history of psychology and its place in American society from the late nineteenth century to the present. The collection is diverse, containing a variety of materials such as conference proceedings and programs, military technical reports, unpublished research reports, newsletters and directories from psychological organizations, popular magazines from the history of psychology, and unpublished theses and dissertations (Figure 9.1). The collection contains approximately twenty-five thousand documents and might in fact be the largest collection in the world of grey literature pertinent to psychology and its history.

Together, these materials provide an in-depth look at the many varieties of psychology that have emerged since the late nineteenth century, including industrial-organizational, educational, clinical, and social psychology. The collection also documents the ways in which psychology has both shaped and been shaped by American society, providing a unique window for viewing American history. For example, the collection contains roughly ten thousand technical reports of psychological research contracted by various branches of the U.S. Army, Navy, and Air Force. A sample document from these reports includes a World War II–era report on the psychological effects of oxygen deprivation or hypoxia at high altitudes. This work, conducted by psychologists for the U.S. Air Force, was never formally published and is therefore not readily available from other sources. The collection also contains conference proceedings of a variety of organizations. An 1885 booklet outlines the proceedings of the American Society for Psychical Research, an intriguing group devoted to the study of paranormal or psychic phenomena. Similarly, the collection also contains pamphlets advertising the Society for Freedom in Science dated between 1945 and 1962. The work of this society, comprised of a group of academics that opposed political participation of scientists in an attempt to dissolve Marxism, has much to contribute to contemporary understandings of science and society.

The scope of topics and available formats in the CCHP grey literature collection is expansive and exciting; historians, archivists, and researchers regularly uncover archival gems.

ACCESS TO DOCUMENTS

A significant part of the grey literature at the CCHP was a donation of a personal collection of materials belonging to psychologist Dr. Saul B. Sells. This donation came in eighty boxes, and materials in the boxes were without an obvious system of organization and item-level inventory. The staff at the CCHP knew this had the

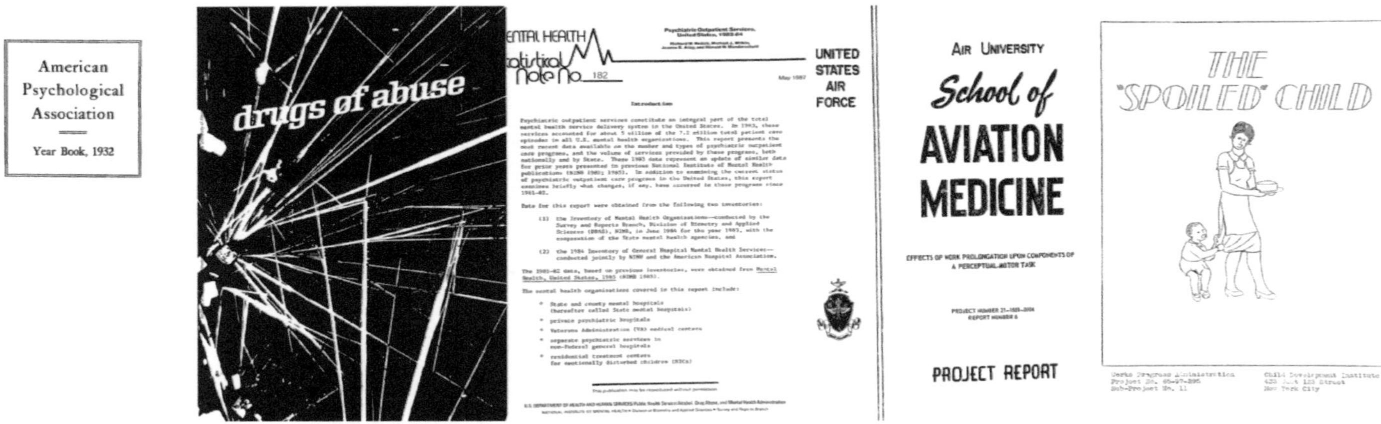

Figure 9.1. Grey literature documents at the Cummings Center for the History of Psychology.

potential to be a valuable resource to historians since the originator, Sells, made a significant contribution to the field of psychology. Staff knew that the collection included some military technical reports, but specific details remained hidden because limited staff resources left the collection in the shipping boxes for a decade. Like other unprocessed collections in archives, this collection was not available for research.

In addition to the unsorted, boxed Sells collection, other items donated that match the collection development policy were part of the special interest collection of grey literature to which few had access, even though it represented a rich body of multidisciplinary literature produced by both lesser known (e.g., Szondi Newsletter) and widely recognized (e.g., the Federal Aviation Administration) organizations, several of which no longer exist under their original auspices, such as the Society for Freedom in Science and the National Council of Women Psychologists. Some of these newsletters were in fact never formally printed; for example, newsletter issues from the Child Development Institute of the Works Progress Administration have hand-drawn covers, and some are comprised of typewritten and handwritten notes.

Even for those few items that were organized, such as newsletters of the Ohio Psychological Association and membership directories of the Society for the Psychological Study of Social Issues, a researcher needed to be on-site to access the single-user-at-a-time, off-line FileMaker database where descriptions of this special interest collection were kept.

SPONSORSHIP AND SHARING DIGITAL ASSETS

The American Psychological Association (APA) publishing group expressed interest in a collaboration with the CCHP and, together with the University of Akron legal team, forged a partnership. Private funding would provide the chance to change the visibility of this hidden collection in a way that both members of the partnership have a stake in the quality of the process and product (Kaufman & Ubois, 2007). In short, it took nearly two years for both parties to agree to the terms. The APA would fund a project to hire a project manager, to rent scanners and hire technicians to run them, and to generate digital assets that would be added to PsycNET databases (primarily PsycEXTRA and PsycBOOKS) and that could be available to all University of Akron students, staff, and faculty, with portions available to the wider public on CCHP websites. The project manager would organize students and documents; test for quality control of digitizations; and liaise between the CCHP, the APA, and the on-site technicians. Libraries across the world subscribe to PsycNET databases. PsycNET abstracts for each digitized document from CCHP collections would receive the credit: "This historic document is included through collaboration with the University of Akron, The Archives of the History of American Psychology, University Libraries." In turn, descriptions of digital objects placed on CCHP websites would receive the credit: "This document was digitized in partnership with the American

Psychological Association and is also available in APA databases, http://www.apa.org/pubs/databases/index.aspx." Increased access to materials and increased visibility in the global research community were an inevitable result.

In 2011, an article in *PsycINFO News* called this arrangement their "most valuable partnership" among its relationships with other institutions and that it "has stood head and shoulders above the rest" (APA, 2011). So the CCHP and the APA must have done a few things right with this partnership.

RAPID MASS DIGITIZATION

The APA contracted a vendor to put two high-quality, rapid book scanners on-site at the CCHP, each with its own technician to run the machine. The scanners, usually used for digitizing books, were capable of automatically capturing up to 1,600 page images with two mounted SLR cameras by turning pages with a robotic arm and a puff of air. In eight months, the contractors had digitized 1,922 rare and antiquarian books on one scanner (including image capture, image editing, and file processing), while the other scanner simultaneously captured images of nearly 15,000 grey literature documents—a project that continued through ten more months.

During rapid, mass digitization, several issues were addressed and resolved. First, the technicians were not archivists and required some archival instruction, such as not opening books and pressing on the spines to help the book fit into the scanner. Further, early in the process, the robotic arms were tearing paper, so the technicians turned every one of those thousands and thousands of pages to complete digitization. Finally, the scanners proved effective for scanning books in spite of the slower, unautomated page turning; however, they were much less effective for digitizing the grey literature because much of the collection was not in book form, while the scanners were specially designed for book scanning with the book cradle and camera mounts. Trifold flyers, stapled loose leaf, and oversized materials took longer to digitize with the contracted equipment intended for scanning bound pages.

In addition to scanning any materials in the public domain, the APA publishing team provided the CCHP project manager with a list of copyright owners with whom the APA held agreements to use and share their content in PsycNET databases. CCHP staff stuck strictly to the lists provided and did not make additional arrangements and decisions about copyright. As such, legal dilemmas were avoided, though much of the grey literature was not digitized, and remains so. After the initial eighteen months of rapid mass digitization, the rented scanners were removed. The technicians no longer worked on-site and continued to process images and files back at their headquarters. Digitization continued using flatbed scanners by CCHP staff and students. The process was ongoing and massive through May 2013, although the scanning after the initial eighteen months was no longer rapid and using flatbed scanners, but then digitization of special collections is not always technically avant-garde (Erway, 2011) and rapid. Though the partnership ended, CCHP digital projects continue to digitize documents in the public domain and on the preservation priority list.

ORGANIZATION, STORAGE, AND DIGITAL ACCESS

To keep a stocked queue of materials ready for the scanning technicians, the digital projects manager with one to three student assistants opened several boxes of the Sells grey literature and sorted items by organization and report number to prepare items for scanning. Each item received a unique barcode identifier that the technicians used to label each image captured for each item and to keep item images clustered on their system. With space for sorting only two to three boxes of grey literature at one time, it is not surprising that, in the end, several duplicate documents were needlessly, though unintentionally, scanned. Because the mass digitization was, indeed, rapid, the decision was made early on that metadata would not be created for each item prior to scanning. If metadata were created before scanning, duplicates would have been easily identified and removed.

The postscanning queue of grey literature was filed into a set of vertical files organized by corporate name, and these materials sat organized but without electronically available metadata while scanning continued. Borrowing from an earlier paper focused on the collaboration, Kearns, Faye, and Willis (2012) explain that "the rapid mass digitization of the grey literature forced the digitization team to worry later about descriptive and bibliographic metadata in order to maintain a constant availability of documents in the scan queue while the equipment was still under the rental agreement." After the eighteen months of rapid mass digitization and physical arrangement of original documents in vertical files, the whirlwind digitization ended. To date, around one-third of the grey literature documents digitized has been made available in APA databases and has been delivered back to the CCHP.

From 2008, when organization and digitization of the grey literature began, through the end of the partnership in 2013, more than twenty thousand digital objects were created from CCHP content in three collections: books, tests, and grey literature. At least three-quarters of the digital collections is grey literature. In 2012, CCHP initiated a contract with OCLC to license the CONTENTdm digital content management system. CONTENTdm permitted CCHP staff to create metadata for every digitized item and every item in the grey literature collection that did not qualify for digitization, such as materials not in the public domain and content belonging to organizations without a legal agreement to share services and materials. It took up through 2013 to complete metadata creation for every item in the CCHP special interest collection of grey literature, a project that began in February 2008. Once these records were created in CONTENTdm, the returned digital objects resulting from the partnership with APA were easily inserted into the existing records in CONTENTdm by searching title and author information against the records. There are currently around twenty-five thousand records in the special interest collection, with around 3,200 digital objects available, some resulting from the APA partnership, and some not. Where the numbers do not seem to add up, there is often a single record with no digital objects representing an entire run of a newsletter or serial print. Metadata for every item in the special interest collection of grey literature is searchable from a single interface on http://collections.uakron.edu/cdm/landingpage/collection/p15960coll1.

The grey literature collection continues to grow through new accessions and new records added weekly. Though the partnership with APA has ended, materials from this collection continue to be digitized if they are in the public domain and if they are at risk of deterioration.

GREY LITERATURE IN RESEARCH AND EDUCATION

Attributed to more increased visibility and access, the special interest collection of grey literature has enabled tens of thousands of direct searches since March 2012, according to CONTENTdm reports. Some of these searches have resulted in formal research requests, such as the following gathered from CCHP reference statistics:

- an historian of science researching the history of functional music found a requesting access to a digital copy of the 1944 newsletter *Industrial Music News*
- a researcher looking for documents on how the practice of hypnosis by psychologists was influenced by the U.S. government in the early 1950s was provided some 1950s newsletters from the Society of Psychological Hypnosis
- a mechanical engineer hunting for early documents about ergonomics found answers in the 1947 Aero Medical Laboratory report, *Analysis of Factors Contributing to 460 "Pilot-Error" Experiences in Operating Aircraft Controls*
- a doctoral student sent a request and received a copy of the *Foundations of Psychology: Visual Aids Manual* found in the special interest collection of grey literature to support research in the history of educational films in psychology

Grey literature materials are important resources for scholars studying psychology and its history. For those working on contemporary issues in psychology, the materials in this collection provide an incredible, untapped source of data and findings in psychology. Because a commercial publisher has not published the majority of the reports in these studies, they are not always taken into account when psychologists conduct literature reviews or meta-analyses in their fields. Understanding and summarizing existing studies on a topic is an important part of designing and testing hypotheses in psychological research. Increased access to unpublished studies like the ones found in the CCHP Special Interest collection would help researchers gain a fuller understanding of the state of knowledge on their topics and areas of research.

These topics are also useful resources for historians of psychology who make extensive use of archival materials in their attempts to trace and explore the history of more than a century's worth of research on human cognition, emotion, and behavior. These unpublished materials are an incredibly rich record of societies, institutions, research groups, people, and ideas in the history of American psychology. Some of these materials may exist in other repositories, but without a considerable degree of physical and intellectual organization, interested parties may have difficulty discovering, locating, and accessing them. Furthermore, for many of the documents in this collection, it is likely that the Cummings Center for the History of Psychology holds the sole existing copy.

ALIGNING DIGITAL PROJECTS TO ORGANIZATIONAL VALUES: OUTPUTS AND OUTCOMES

Large-scale organization and digitization projects yield tremendous benefits to patrons of collecting and research institutions, and, as such, provide sustaining returns for the organization. This particular project resulted in generating multifaceted access points to the world's most expansive (and, until recently, hidden) collection of grey literature, which has since been demonstrated to be of use to historians, scholars, researchers, and educators. Designing digitization projects, coordinating corporate partnerships, and making documents accessible to on- and off-site scholars will likely be most successful when these plans and workflows are aligned with the organization's mission and core values. That is, operationalizing your organization's strategic plan ought to enable a sustainable digitization program by providing an intellectual framework and motivation (Mirvis, Googins, & Kinnicutt, 2010.) The vast, sustaining outputs and outcomes of this particular project, then, can be neatly recapped in terms of CCHP core values: access, education, inclusion, preservation, and service.

Access

From 1965 through 2008, metadata for all documents, including those that now fall into the grey literature collections, were available only for searching on-site. Vast and detailed series of card catalogues indexing names and subjects were migrated to local-access FileMaker databases as CCHP entered the computer age, permitting searching across collections only for on-site and single searchers. Researchers and scholars would call to ask CCHP staff to search across collections for materials. Beginning in 2008, researchers could be redirected to PsycNET databases to discover grey literature materials. Later, beginning in 2012, this collection of more than thirty thousand documents would receive public records available in the CONTENTdm platform, including even those special interest records without an associated digital object. Public domain documents digitized during this project would mostly all eventually become available in this same system, now indexed by Google. Google indexing has enabled findability of both the CCHP and CCHP collections from its single, go-to search engine. It is no longer necessary for patrons to find CCHP materials by going to the CCHP repository or by contacting us directly.

Further, in contract with our corporate partners, all researchers, students, staff, and faculty of the University of Akron can have access to all materials digitized during this project. In future collaborations with other publishing organizations, CCHP would grant only nonexclusive rights to digitized CCHP content without limitations or restrictions on amounts of scanned documents that could be made public.

Education

We assume that the increased findability of documents in our collections, resulting from the rapid mass digitization project, metadata creation, and online digital access copy availability, is responsible for increased research requests satisfied in the grey literature collection. Increased access and visibility to grey literature documents of special interest has also increased requests for educational opportunities from local high school, college, and university teachers who have found us by Google or by ever-spreading word of mouth. For example, in 2013, CCHP received a grant from the Institute of Museum and Library Services to write curriculum for local high school teachers to help make it easier for them to justify bringing students on field trips to the CCHP. Funded by this grant, a new exhibit was installed. The "Measuring the Mind" exhibit displays some materials uncovered during the described project. Further, knowing precisely at the item level the grey literature available in the collection, these teachers have access to digital copies of thousands of primary sources to support their classroom learning.

Additionally, CCHP staff has provided archival information literacy instruction using these digital documents as examples for practice research and understanding about reading and using primary literature. Newsletters and directories, for example, are useful for understanding value in primary sources. Availability of these documents online or electronically by email makes these general archives learning activities effortless in planning.

Inclusion

Nearly fifty years after the founding of the Archives of the History of American Psychology, digital preservation, access, and stewardship have helped shape a small, on-site researching audience into a global usership, with visitors to the CCHP online repository including nations from six continents. Access and readership is no longer limited to American scholars, and it is open to patrons ranging from Girl Scouts, to community leadership groups, to interested student groups, and to historians, among others. Rapid mass digitization and organization has enabled the CCHP to open collections to the widest possible audiences interested in the history of psychology and related human sciences.

Preservation

This project and partnership resulted in both the digitized, captured content of the grey literature collection and the physical storage and arrangement of the documents.

All fifteen thousand digitized documents are now part of the CCHP digital repository, are backed up on University of Akron servers, and are stored on the server system at APA publishing. Additionally, the physical grey literature documents are housed in acid-free archival folders in vertical files and in an intellectual order, rather than in the moving boxes in which they were mailed to the archives years ago. It is necessary to understand that large-scale projects like the one herein described cannot only be about the resulting digital assets. Steps in the workflow include physical and intellectual organization for sustained retrievability, and physical and digital storage in order to sustain the life of the document and its digital surrogate.

Service

One consequence of the APA-CCHP partnership was the establishment of one staff position dedicated to managing digital projects. The APA paid for this position until the end of the project in 2013, although it continues to be partially funded through continuing collaboration and corporate partnerships with other publishing organizations. The Digital Projects Manager continues to lead a team of students and volunteers to populate the digital repository and to continue working on digitization projects that promote the strategic plan in compliance with the priorities listed in the CCHP Digitization Priorities Policy:

1. Research requests.
2. Photographs from collections currently being processed.
3. Materials requested by publishers and organizations paying for services.
4. Materials from any collection that require digitization for content preservation.
5. Other materials in all formats, especially the following:
    - Still image collections.
    - Special interest materials in the public domain (government publication, materials published before 1924, materials for which we own copyright).
    - Test materials in the public domain.
    - Moving images and sound recordings of research and public interest and of educational value, especially those in the public domain lists.

The University of Akron receives free of annual charge subscriptions to PsycEXTRA, PsycTESTS, and PsycBOOKS for anyone on the UANET domain. This gift to the students, faculty, and staff of the University of Akron resulted from the contract with the APA and saves the university libraries more than an estimated $20,000 annually. These funds, then, can be spent on additional library resources.

The initial project began in 2008 to digitize grey literature materials from psychology's history in order to populate a commercial database, but the outputs and outcomes have provided and continue to provide a service to scholarship by opening formerly unpublished materials of limited circulation to a global audience through digital diffusion.

This project has contributed considerably to the CCHP's ability to meet its mission and goals. However, it also provides a model for other institutions seeking to implement similar projects involving outside groups, organizations, or corporations. By carefully considering the needs of each institution, it is possible to design projects that benefit libraries and archives, their patrons, and corporate groups with an interest or stake in the archives' materials. In this vein, this project serves as a useful and successful model or prototype, encouraging and providing a platform for the creation of these kinds of collaborations across many institutions.

REFERENCES

(APA) American Psychological Association. (2011). PsycBOOKS: A historical partnership. *PsycINFO News, 30*(4), 5–6.

de Blaaij, C. (2008). The use of grey literature in historical journals and historical research: A bibliometric and qualitative approach. *Grey Journal, 4*(2), 14–20.

Erway, R. (2011). *Rapid capture: Faster throughput in digitization of special collections.* Dublin, OH: OCLC Online Computer Library Center, Inc. Retrieved from http://www.oclc.org/content/dam/research/publications/library/2011/2011-04.pdf.

Farace, D., & Schöpfel, J. (2010). *Grey literature in library and information studies.* Berlin, Germany: De Gruyter Saur.

GreyNet International. (n.d.). *Grey literature.* OpenGrey. Retrieved from http://www.opengrey.eu/about/greyliterature.

GreyNet International. (2014). *International directory of organizations in grey literature.* Grey Literature Network Service. Retrieved from http://www.greynet.org/internationaldirectory.html.

Kaufman, P. B., & Ubois, J. (2007). Good terms: Improving commercial-noncommercial partnerships for mass digitization. *D-Lib Magazine, 13*(11/12). Retrieved from http://dlib.org/dlib/november07/kaufman/11kaufman.html.

Kearns, J., Faye, C., & Willis, L. (2012). From unprocessed unknowns to digital diffusion: Uncovering grey literature at the Cummings Center for the History of Psychology. *Grey Journal, 8*(3), 154–60.

Mirvis, P., Googins, B., & Kinnicut, S. (2010). Vision, mission, values: Guideposts to sustainability. *Organizational Dynamics: A Quarterly Review of Organizational Behavior for Professional Managers, 39*(4), 316–24.

10

The Emerging Tradition of Digital Classics

Sarah A. Buchanan

ABSTRACT

Digital classics has steadily matured as a field situated between scholarship in classical studies and digital humanities. Globally, particular digital classics endeavors have addressed issues of professionalization, project dynamics, and terminology, prompting the recent formation of the Digital Classics Association (DCA). This chapter identifies seven major topical areas presented at the inaugural DCA conference in 2013 through a content analysis, and situates these within the ongoing activities of the new association. In viewing the digital classics field in the context of its own history, this analysis illustrates ways in which research today expands upon the existing corpus by applying technological approaches to advance and generate new knowledge about the ancient world.

INTRODUCTION

It might be said that there are at least as many definitions of digital classics as there are digital classicists. In addition to those so-called, there remain many classicists today who use computers who might not consider themselves a digital classicist. These issues mirror current debates taking place in the digital humanities—which we may tentatively consider a parent of digital classics—about the role of particular skills and uses of technology to carry out research in the classics. *Classics* research, too, resists compartmentalization, as so many successful projects in the digital classics are the fruit of collaborations between technologists and subject experts, humanists and scientists, and scholars and practitioners. So, too, has the naming of disciplines recently resurfaced in a way that provokes continued debate over efforts toward strategic positioning and presence in the academic world (Feeney, 2013). Thus, we see three issues—professionalization, project dynamics, and terminology—that complicate a common understanding of what digital classics is, and more significantly, where it is headed. This heterogeneous, global history of digital classics activities has inspired the recent formation of the Digital Classics Association (DCA), and a review of the presentations from its inaugural conference in 2013 will help illustrate the range of projects ongoing in the United States. Digital classics scholarship, broadly understood, involves the use and development of computational tools to aid in the study and exploration of Greco-Roman antiquity, a truly data-intensive enterprise. This chapter approaches digital classics as part of a broader conceptualization of the growing role of digital tools in academia, rather than as an academic specialty. In this manner, it adheres to the view, expressed by Gregory Crane and others, that strident efforts to delineate this area from broader efforts in the humanities are not only unnecessary but may be self-defeating. Crane's call for "an end of the history" posed an intervention in thinking by suggesting that theoretical development shifts away from a focus on the field's specialization and deep exceptionalism (Solomon, 1993) and toward a common recognition that digital capacity is not only impacting classical studies but also is rather part consequence of broader transformations in society and in the academy. As he argues, "There should not be a history of classics and the computer, for the needs of classicists are simply not so distinctive as to warrant a separate 'classical informatics'" (Crane, 2004). A decade since this observation, much, and yet little, has changed with regard to the converging needs of classicists and other humanists.

GLOBAL INITIATIVES

A multitude of terms can be found to describe roughly similar ideas as practiced in different countries—humanities computing, classical computing, digital classics, eClassics, e-philology, and digital heritage, to name a few (McCarty, 2001; Gouglas, Rockwell, Smith, Hoosein, & Quamen, 2012; Latousek, 2001; Babeu, 2012; Blackwell & Crane, 2009, para. 37; Pusceddu, 2010; Remondino & Campana, 2014). Continuing research examines the relationship between classics and information and communication technologies (Hardwick, 2000; Kanellou, Grantham, Rodríguez Echavarria, Gottlieb, & Pletinckx, 2008; Peru, 2014). The recent "Around the World Symposium on Technology and Culture," which featured presentations from twenty-five countries, exemplifies this terminological span and provides a global window into the conduct of digital humanities research in different university and research environments (Davies-Venn, 2013).[1] The varying uses of the above terms serve as an indication of the types of activities encompassed by this subject umbrella; in this chapter "digital classics" is used as an encompassing term for work being conducted in and across these areas. This section will briefly synthesize a selection of resources that collect further information on such activities.

Research in digital classics is generally concerned with "methods and digital practices that can add to the empirical understanding of facts about the ancient world, its literature and its people, or the continuing use of that heritage in later texts and ages" (Bodard & Mahony, 2010, p. 4). As the field has developed rapidly in the last decade or so, several key resources have emerged in the field that function as research *fora*:

- The Stoa Consortium for Electronic Publication in the Humanities (stoa.org), founded by Ross Scaife in 1997, remains a central collection of resources supporting open access classics projects.
- The Digital Classicist network (digitalclassicist.org), established in 2004, comprises a website and a wiki with which contributors build new collaborations and share methodological and technological approaches alike (Terras, 2010; Mahony, 2011).
- Antiquist (antiquist.org), established in 2006, is a "heritage computing community" that communicates through its website, listserve, and workshops.
- The Ancient World Online (ancientworldonline.blogspot.com), an online journal since 2009, collects open access material relating to the ancient world.
- The Forum for Classics, Libraries, and Scholarly Communication (FCLSC) (classicslibrarians.org), established in 2005, aims to support classics librarianship by providing space for colleagues to participate in the development and continuation of resources widely used in the classical discipline.
- The Digital Classics Association (dca.drupalgardens.com), formed in 2012, is, like the FCLSC, an affiliated group with the American Philological Association (APA).

Owing to the range of evidential material appropriated in the classics discipline—including archaeological, epigraphic, documentary, linguistic, forensic, and art historical evidence—classical scholars have assuredly adopted the label of interdisciplinarity. For example, the method of paleography as the study of scripts can be traced to 1708, but as a component of manuscript studies (to say nothing of papyrology and diplomatics) it is but one tool used by scholars and scientists alike working with ancient texts. Catalogs, codicology, and palimpsests also comprise key techniques within manuscript studies (Tchernetska, 2009). Studies using these four types of source materials—scripts, catalogs, books/codices, and palimpsests—have certainly been broadened with the introduction of digital systems. As illustrated by one thesis that traces the history of material conservation from the ancient Romans to the modern day, conservation principles have changed dramatically since the "destructive" restorations commonly performed on classics' source materials up to the eighteenth century (Hulmer, 1955). Classical scholars acknowledge that early work with palimpsests in the 1800s produced new textual discoveries, although today we regard these scholars' understanding of chemical properties and conservation practices as quite primitive. A wave of international conferences held at the turn of the twentieth century, as well as the pioneering work of Cardinal Ehrle—keeper of the Vatican Library and promoter of the International Conference of St. Gallo on the preservation of archival materials in 1898—helped elevate the practice of scientific analysis in restoration and the study of paper (Caldararo, 1987). Indeed, we see that classical scholars have long fashioned themselves experts in reading source texts and devising ways to organize and index author names. The twentieth century saw the launch of many resources that continue to enjoy wide usage in classical study—two of the most notable being the Perseus Project and the *Thesaurus Linguae Graecae*. A selection of publications have focused broadly on the digital classics, and specifically on these projects, including special issues of *Digital Humanities Quarterly* (Crane & Terras, 2009), *Digital Medievalist* (Bodard & Mahony, 2008), *Favonius* (Frischer, 1987), and papers from the Center for Hellenic Studies' Summer Workshop on Technology in 2003 (Blackwell & Scaife, 2004). Both Pritchard (2008) and Edmunds (1995) further examine the scholarly foundations laid by David Packard in the 1960s. These projects constitute key centerpieces in the historical progression of digital classics research, which has been characterized as having followed five phases since its start in the mid-twentieth century—first beginning with online access to texts, then scholarly corrections to those texts, then a concentration on markup languages, followed by digitized page images of texts, and finally a fifth and ongoing generation that is centered around facilitating user contributions in constructing digital collections (Stewart, Crane, & Babeu, 2007).

Even if from afar it seemed at one time that "we knew c. 1970 what there was of Greek literature" (O'Donnell, 1994), our knowledge of this—and indeed any—discipline is biased, however subtly, by the availability of the source materials accessible and available for close study. Digital technology has transformed the field of classical studies by enlarging the corpus of data (initially textual, but now also photographic, geographic, and multitemporal) that is "queryable" for a wider range of research questions. Babeu (2011) expertly synthesizes how different research disciplines *within* classics make extensive use of technologies and cyberinfrastructure to study as broad a range of materials as possible, noting in particular those of archaeology, art and architecture, epigraphy, geography, manuscript studies, numismatics, paleography, papyrology, philology, and prosopography. Digital archaeology, for example, continues to build on a tradition of computational tools to facilitate research at all of its stages—from fieldwork, to data collection, to publication and teaching (Watrall et al., 2013).

THE DIGITAL CLASSICS ASSOCIATION (DCA) AND ITS INAUGURAL CONFERENCE

The scholarly environment of activities and research in the digital classics is, as we have seen above, extraordinarily rich. In particular, online resources such as the Digital Classicist wiki make such efforts in the digital classics—both those full-fledged and those more exploratory—accessible to researchers situated physically around the world. In reflection of this existing (cyber)infrastructure, the initial seed for what would become the Digital Classics Association (DCA) was planted in early 2012. It was then, at the American Philological Association (APA) Annual Meeting in Philadelphia, that a discussion developed between Neil Coffee and Allen Romano (N. Coffee, personal communication, April 21, 2014; hereafter Coffee, 2014). Coffee and Romano's discussion focused on recent iterations of the Digital Classicist Seminars, many of which are held in London, at the Institute of Classical Studies (University of London).[2] As both scholars were based in the United States, they noted that very few American colleagues had participated in the seminars. Additionally, Coffee pointed to several projects that were at a point of maturation, and that would possibly benefit from receiving feedback from "the broader classical community." Coffee notes,

> Tools were being built that, in all likelihood, would have a determinative influence not just on the speed with which scholarship was carried out (as was the case, for example, with making it easy to find a text online), but on how evidence from the classical world would be interpreted. So, for example, it is possible that the Orbis project, with its (necessary) assumptions about how travel times and commerce worked, will become a de facto standard for understanding this part of the ancient world. The wider world of classical scholarship might want to participate in discussions around these tools as they are being constructed, to make sure they do their jobs in the best way, because resource constraints generally mean that the work will not be done twice, and even funding to repair or improve an existing digital resource is often difficult to find. (Coffee, 2014)

From their discussion of these issues, Coffee and Romano began to identify the scope for a proposed Digital Classics Association (DCA). Succinctly, "The motivation for founding the DCA was to bring the great work being done in different corners of the digital classics world into conversation, and especially to bring them to the attention of the wider world of classical scholarship" (Coffee, 2014). The colleagues discussed their proposal with Gregory Crane, who accepted the co-chair position with Coffee, and also with Charlotte Roueché and Christopher Blackwell, who formed the Steering Committee. Romano served initially as secretary-treasurer. Having formed interim leadership, the founders established a website for the DCA, wrote bylaws, and composed an application to the APA for an Affiliated Group Type II Charter.[3] These materials were shared with the classical community through a call for members, which was then posted in several online venues.[4] Through the website, the nascent group received about three hundred subscribers, according to Coffee. In addition to their work within the channels of the APA, the officers were also aware of the need to extend the discussion beyond the time constraints of the APA annual meetings, which are held in conjunction with the Archaeological Institute of America (AIA). Hence, in the fall of 2012, the DCA Steering Committee issued a call for papers for its inaugural conference, which would be held at the University at Buffalo, State University of New York, on April 5 to 6, 2013. Of this major activity, Coffee reflects:

> The conference was meant to try to bridge sub-disciplines in the classical world. Hence "Word" = literature & linguistics, "Space" = roughly, material culture, "Time" = history.

We couldn't get more than this in the title, but did mention philosophy in the cfp. (Coffee, 2014)

In addition to this statement of scope, on a practical level the conference location was determined by Coffee's ability to organize the event at his home institution. The DCA committee, working with graduate students in the University at Buffalo (UB) Department of Classics, notified proposers of their acceptance in the conference and published the conference program online in early February 2013.[5] The committee also shaped the inaugural conference by inviting participation from beyond their expected audience of classical studies scholars, including leaders from the digital humanities field (e.g., Geoffrey Rockwell and Matthew Jockers), educators (Monica Berti, Walter Scheidel, and Rebecca Schindler), and librarians.

Nearly simultaneous with the planning of DCA 2013, the committee also received word of its successful proposal for affiliation with the APA, and approval to host a paper session at the APA annual meetings for the next four years (2014–2017). The panel theme for the first session in 2014 (Chicago) was announced as "Getting Started with Digital Classics"; the due date for abstracts was set for March 29, the week before the DCA 2013 conference. As a joint colloquium, the speaker slots on the panel would be available to either APA or AIA members. Further indication of the breadth of the committee's initial work can also be evidenced by their outline of preliminary themes for the subsequent APA programs, which were announced as: "Making Meaning from Data" (2015), "Digital Resources for Teaching and Outreach" (2016), and "Digital Classics and the Changing Profession" (2017).[6]

The Topical Content of DCA 2013

The DCA 2013 conference presentations showcased an expansive range of areas within classical studies that, in sum, recalls those illustrated in Babeu's (2011) overview. The conference theme, "Word, Space, Time: Digital Perspectives on the Classical World—An Interdisciplinary Conference Organized by the Digital Classics Association," exemplified these focus areas and was further reflected in its choice of conference logo, a horizontal sundial featuring Roman numerals on the dial plate. The following content analysis (Table 10.1) of the topics covered at the conference provides one indication of the spread of research interests across the digital classics field. In Table 10.1, the research topics in the left column situate the individual presentation in a disciplinary area within classical studies. Both the posters and workshops, initially grouped as sessions three and seven on account of their format, have been integrated topically into the full breadth of the program. Note that the third column preserves the original session grouping assigned to the presentation by the conference program committee.

As seen in Table 10.1, a span of roughly seven research topics characterized the thirty-three presentations at the DCA 2013 conference: digital arts and architecture (two), literary and linguistic analysis (seven), natural language processing and ma-

Table 10.1. Content Analysis of DCA 2013 Research Topics

Digital Classics Research Topic	*Title of Presentation*	*Session Title at DCA 2013*
Digital Arts & Architecture	RomeLab: Performance on the ephemeral stage	5. Visualizing the Built Environment and Lived Space
	New approaches to mapping mythology: A digital collection	6. Instruction and Outreach
Literary & Linguistic Analysis	A stylometric study of Pindar's Odes	1. Mining Texts and Mining Images
	Getting started with Tesserae allusion detection	3. Posters/Demos
	Addressing Polytonic Greek in a digital context: A CD-ROM (and beyond) for Cretan renaissance literature	4. Textual Corpora and Conventions
	Cracking the code: A Coptic digital corpus for interdisciplinary research	4. Textual Corpora and Conventions
	Statistical methods for R	4. Workshops
	The ancient world in nineteenth-century fiction: A macroanalysis	8. Literary Criticism and Digital Methods
	Using Tesserae to extend the philological commentary	8. Literary Criticism and Digital Methods
Natural Language Processing & Machine Learning	Using Google Pagerank to detect text reuse	1. Mining Texts and Mining Images
	Data mining digital archives of figured Greek vases	1. Mining Texts and Mining Images
	Treebanking the world of Thucydides: Linguistic annotation for ancient history	3. Posters/Demos
	Distant reading alliteration in Latin poetry	8. Literary Criticism and Digital Methods
Pedagogy & Gaming	Dungeons and Discourse	3. Posters/Demos
	The Athens Minecraft Project	3. Posters/Demos
	Stepping joyfully beyond textbook: From visualizing to reliving the ancient world	3. Posters/Demos
	A guided Greek tutorial system based on John William White's *First Greek Book*	6. Instruction and Outreach
Prosopography & Periodization	Charting ancient ethnography: The OSU Herodotos Project	3. Posters/Demos
	Traversing time and space: Ontological analysis of traditional and new literacies	6. Instruction and Outreach

(continued)

Table 10.1. *(Continued)*

Digital Classics Research Topic	*Title of Presentation*	*Session Title at DCA 2013*
Semantic Web, Linked Data, & Bibliometrics	Fragmenta Historica 2.0: Quotations and text reuse in the semantic web	1. Mining Texts and Mining Images
	Classics and the semantic web	3. Posters/Demos
	Cataloging the classics: Linking bibliographic records and digital texts in the Forum for Classics, Libraries, and Scholarly Communication	4. Textual Corpora and Conventions
	Exploring citation networks to study intertextuality in classics	4. Textual Corpora and Conventions
Visualization, Archaeology, & GIS	Redrawing the map of the Roman world	2. Historical Mapping
	Stitching together ancient geography online	2. Historical Mapping
	Mapping antiquity a la carte: A GIS interface of the ancient world	2. Historical Mapping
	Traveling with Pausanias: Using Google Earth to engage students with ancient maps	3. Posters/Demos
	GIS mapping of fort and town settlements along Hadrian's Wall	3. Posters/Demos
	Environmental modeling and Pompeian houses	4. Workshops
	Virtualization for DH projects	4. Workshops
	Basics of ArcGIS mapmaking	4. Workshops
	Teaching spatial literacy in the classical studies curriculum	5. Visualizing the Built Environment and Lived Space
	Digital approaches to ancient cities: The Kalavasos and Maroni built environments project, Cyprus	5. Visualizing the Built Environment and Lived Space

chine learning (four), pedagogy and gaming (four), prosopography and periodization (two), semantic web/linked data/bibliometrics (four), and visualization/archaeology/ GIS (ten). Note that several presentations could possibly fit into more than one of the above topics, particularly those involving philology, network analysis, or historic archaeology. Unmistakably, we see that presentations on digital mapping and geography constituted nearly one-third of the conference, and in these were discussed such projects as ORBIS ("redrawing the map") (Meeks and Grossner, 2012a, 2012b; Dunn, 2012), Antiquity à-la-carte ("mapping antiquity"), and Pleiades ("stitching together")—together these and others served to advocate in form for the continued use of linked data and metadata standards for projects across both the classics and the broader humanities (Elliott, Heath, & Muccigrosso, 2012; Byrum & Williamson, 2006). Currently, digital classics projects such as Perseus, Pleiades, Pelagios, Papyri.info, and Nomisma.org all use linked data principles, a foundation that will support future expansion of their datasets. Secondly, the exploitation of machine learning technologies, particularly in applications for large quantities of texts and object metadata, was also covered in depth (Coffee et al., 2014). Textual analysis and access also saw significant coverage, with the Perseus Project alone cited as source data in at least four presentations (Smith, Rydberg-Cox, & Crane, 2000; Crane, 2011). Additionally, while both qualitative and quantitative methods are to be found, it may be interesting to note the relative absence of certain topics—pure philosophy, ancient religion and ritual, government and politics, other material culture studies (epigraphy and numismatics), and sociohistorical analyses such as on gender and health—though these may be present, but in a tangential way.

In addition to the eight sessions presented, there were opening remarks provided by Gregory Crane and closing remarks provided by Geoffrey Rockwell. In his remarks, Crane discussed his then newly announced work with the Open Philology Project based at the University of Leipzig[7] and called for classicists to devote renewed efforts toward making the outputs of their scholarship more open and accessible to readers outside of the English and European languages. In the business meeting portion prior to the start of the conference, Jeffrey Rydberg-Cox was elected to the position of the DCA's secretary-treasurer. The conference and an evening reception were held in the Center for the Arts overlooking Lake La Salle on UB's North Campus, and attendees also enjoyed a dinner in downtown Buffalo. The program schedule permitted all attendees (approximately one hundred) to attend all presentations, which contributed to a sense of shared community and collegiality.

WHAT SHOULD DIGITAL CLASSICS DO?

Digital classics has a future longer than its past. While the DCA 2013 conference showcased a great many research topics, there are surely untold dozens more being studied actively by the composite membership of the DCA, which now hovers around five hundred—an increase of 166 percent over just a year's time. In his closing remarks at the DCA conference, Geoffrey Rockwell encouraged the community to rededicate our efforts to supporting the use of "primitives" in Classical Studies—place, people, periods ("Word, Space, Time")—while still continuing to seek public input and participation through efforts such as crowdsourcing and virtual games (Rockwell, 2013; Francese, 2013a). Rockwell also provided further historical context to the questions posed by Gregory Crane's opening remarks by recalling previous efforts toward creating networks of scholarly resources for the classics, such as the Classicist's Workbench (Frischer, 1989), and the reading machines envisioned by Agostino Ramelli and imagined in the pages of *Science and Mechanics* (1935) and the comics section.[8] These inventions center on the persistent discipline of philology, and we should embrace the full breadth of scholarship sustained by this term rather than dismiss it for sounding too, well, antiquarian. Rockwell argued that "Classics is the test bed of the humanities," and as such, conferencegoers and classicists had the ability to participate in broader efforts in both the classical studies and digital humanities fields. Indeed, digital classicists should be encouraged by the interdisciplinary nature of work in this field. Digital classicists, cognizant of the historical trajectories visible in their field, would also be well served in taking a particular interest in archiving versions of their work and following digital preservation best practices. Current leaders in this area include the German initiative IANUS, which is developing a digital classics data repository, and likewise the ARCHES project for archaeological resources (Dally, Fless, & Förtsch, 2012; Degraeve & Bibby, 2013). Shortly after the conference, many participants contributed to the Day of DH 2013 by describing the projects and issues encountered in the course of their work.[9] Digital classics researchers are also engaged in efforts to explore the current and future scholarly infrastructures of peer review, promotion, and tenure (Francese, 2013b; Rockwell, 2012). Following a specific recommendation during the closing session, a page has since been dedicated to the topic of "Educational Resources" on the Digital Classicist wiki.[10] Related scholarly resources such as stoa.org, the *Bryn Mawr Classical Review*,[11] and *Digital Humanities Quarterly*—all mentioned by name during the conference—continue to receive new work from the conference community. Within the APA itself, the Digital Latin Library, a consortial effort launched in 2012 by three scholarly societies—the APA, the Medieval Academy of America, and the Renaissance Society of America—aims to enhance the corpus of digital resources from the post-Classical (800s CE) and early modern period, an era that was broached in the DCA presentation "The Ancient World in 19th Century Fiction."[12] Reflecting on the pace of change witnessed in the field of digital classics just over the last half-century, one constant that remains relatively unexplored is the role of classics librarians. Librarians have been an important part of many digital classics research projects, providing access to a greater amount of materials through shared digital resources than were previously available (Heverly, 2006). A more nuanced understanding of not only the historical presence of classics libraries but also the work of classics librarians today will undoubtedly aid in the future development of new academic initiatives in digital classics research.[13]

With the DCA planning to organize additional conferences internationally, the audience for digital classics research is only anticipated to grow. As the scope of the conference presentations indicates, digital classicists have a wide array of methodologies, topics, and disciplinary approaches to draw on in their future work. Some of this work has already been successfully presented at the 2014 APA/AIA Annual Meeting (five papers added the topics of historiography, photography, papyrology, and text reuse to those presented at DCA 2013), and this and future planned sessions will continue to build on the humble yet early beginnings of digital classics-related topics at this venue since 1966 (Brunner, 1993, p. 12). Digital classicists now find themselves equipped with a research infrastructure both here in the United States and worldwide that engages with broader developments in academia, in the digital humanities, and in classical studies, and they will be well served by the continuation of these efforts.

ACKNOWLEDGMENTS

Thanks to Neil Coffee for his generous comments and reflections. This research was partially supported by a University of Texas, School of Information, Professional Development Award.

NOTES

1. *Around the World Symposium on Technology and Culture*, Kule Institute for Advanced Studies, University of Alberta, May 31, 2013. Retrieved from http://aroundtheworld.ualberta.ca/the-archives/.

2. Digital Classicist Seminars (2006–), *The Digital Classicist.* Retrieved from http://www.digitalclassicist.org/wip/index.html.

3. *Affiliated Groups*, The American Philological Association. Retrieved from http://apaclassics.org/annual-meeting/145/affiliated-groups. While a Type I Group receives accommodations at the APA/AIA meeting for a business meeting and/or reception, a Type II Group also receives a panel or paper session listing on the APA Program.

4. Invitation to Form a Digital Classics Association, message of March 10, 2012, *The Digital Classicist List.* Retrieved from http://apaclassics.org/apa-blog/invitation-form-digital-classics-association.

5. *Word, Space, Time: Digital Perspectives on the Classical World*, DCA Conference 2013. Retrieved from http://www.classics.buffalo.edu/events/dcaconference/.

6. *Affiliated Groups—2013*, The American Philological Association. Retrieved from http://apaclassics.org/annual-meeting/145/affiliated-groups-2013#Digital.

7. *The Open Philology Project and Humboldt Chair of Digital Humanities at Leipzig*, Perseus Digital Library Updates. Retrieved from http://sites.tufts.edu/perseusupdates/2013/04/04/the-open-philology-project-and-humboldt-chair-of-digital-humanities-at-leipzig/.

8. *The Kindle of 1935*, Paleofuture. Retrieved from http://www.paleofuture.com/nofuture/2011/12/3/the-kindle-of-1935.html. *Libraries of the Future in "Our New Age."* Retrieved from http://www.smithsonianmag.com/history/sunday-funnies-blast-off-into-the-space-age-81559551/.

9. *A Day in the Life of Digital Humanities (Day of DH) 2013.* Retrieved from http://dayofdh2013.matrix.msu.edu/.

10. *Educational Resources*, The Digital Classicist Wiki. Retrieved from http://wiki.digitalclassicist.org/Educational_Resources.

11. The *Bryn Mawr Electronic Resources Review* (BMERR) has, since 2000, been subsumed by the *Bryn Mawr Classical Review*, although its archive is available from http://csanet.org/bmerr/.

12. *Digital Latin Library (DLL) Project*. Retrieved from http://apaclassics.org/publications-and-research/digital-latin-library-project.

13. For example, the Classics Library of the University of Texas, founded in 1966, comprises nearly 30,000 volumes and 180 journal subscriptions and supports one of the largest classics faculty in the nation. In addition to classical studies, it also supports interdisciplinary studies in archaeology, art history, comparative literature, and information history—all of which now have a presence in what we have termed the "digital humanities."

REFERENCES

Babeu, A. (2011). *"Rome wasn't digitized in a day": Building a cyberinfrastructure for digital classicists*. Washington, DC: Council on Library and Information Resources. Retrieved from http://www.clir.org/pubs/abstract/reports/pub150.

Babeu, A. (2012). Classics, "digital classics" and issues for data curation. In *DH Curation Guide: A community resource guide to data curation in the digital humanities*. Urbana-Champaign, IL: University of Illinois. Retrieved from http://guide.dhcuration.org/research-practices/classics/.

Blackwell, C., & Crane, G. (2009). Conclusion: Cyberinfrastructure, the Scaife Digital Library and classics in a digital age. *Digital Humanities Quarterly*, *3*(1). Retrieved from http://www.digitalhumanities.org/dhq/vol/3/1/000035/000035.html.

Blackwell, C., & Scaife, R. (Eds.). (2004). *Classics@: An Online Journal: Issue 2: Workshop on Technology and the Classics*. Cambridge, MA: The Center for Hellenic Studies of Harvard University. Retrieved from http://chs.harvard.edu/wa/pageR?tn=ArticleWrapper&bdc=12&mn=1324.

Bodard, G., & Mahony, S. (2008). "Though much is taken, much abides": Recovering antiquity through innovative digital methodologies: Introduction to the special issue. *Digital Medievalist*, *4*. Retrieved from http://www.digitalmedievalist.org/journal/4/DCintro/.

Bodard, G., & Mahony, S. (Eds.). (2010). *Digital research in the study of classical antiquity*. Surrey, UK: Ashgate.

Brunner, T. F. (1993). Classics and the computer: The history of a relationship. In J. Solomon (Ed.), *Accessing antiquity: The computerization of classical studies* (pp. 10–33). Tucson, AZ: University of Arizona Press.

Byrum, J. D., Jr., & Williamson, D. W. (2006). Enriching traditional cataloging for improved access to information: Library of Congress Tables of Contents projects. *Information Technology and Libraries*, *25*(1), 4–11. doi:10.6017/ital.v25i1.3324

Caldararo, N. L. (1987, Autumn). An outline history of conservation in archaeology and anthropology as presented through its publications. *Journal of the American Institute for Conservation*, *26*(2), 85–104.

Coffee, N., Gawley, J., Forstall, C., Scheirer, W., Johnson, D., Corso, J., & Parks, B. (2014, Spring). Modelling the interpretation of literary allusion with machine learning techniques. *Journal of Digital Humanities*, *3*(1). Retrieved from http://journalofdigitalhuman

ities.org/3-1/modelling-the-interpretation-of-literary-allusion-with-machine-learning-techniques/.

Crane, G. (2004). Classics and the computer: An end of the history. In S. Schreibman, R. Siemens, & J. Unsworth (Eds.), *A companion to digital humanities* (pp. 46–55). Oxford, UK: Blackwell. Retrieved from http://www.digitalhumanities.org/companion/.

Crane, G. (2011). *Working with text in a digital age: An NEH Institute for advanced topics in the digital humanities.* Tufts University. Retrieved from http://sites.tufts.edu/digitalagetext/.

Crane, G., & Terras, M. (Eds.). (2009). Changing the center of gravity: Transforming classical studies through cyberinfrastructure (special issue). *Digital Humanities Quarterly, 3*(1). Retrieved from http://www.digitalhumanities.org/dhq/vol/003/1/.

Dally, O., Fless, F., & Förtsch, R. (2012). Altertumswissenschaften. In H. Neuroth, S. Strathmann, A. Oßwald, R. Scheffel, J. Klump, & J. Ludwig (Eds.), *Nestor [Network of Expertise in Long-Term Storage of Digital Resources] Handbuch: Langzeitarchivierung von Forschungsdaten. Eine Bestandsaufnahme.* Boizenburg: Werner Hülsbusch. Retrieved from http://www.ianus-fdz.de/projects/ergebnisse/wiki/.

Davies-Venn, M. (2013, May 30). *UAlberta gets the world talking about digital culture.* University of Alberta. Retrieved from http://news.ualberta.ca/newsarticles/2013/may/ualberta-gets-the-world-talking-about-digital-culture.

Degraeve, A., & Bibby, D. (2013). *Archaeological archives and the ARCHES (Archaeological Resources in Cultural Heritage—A European Standard) project.* European Archaeological Council. Retrieved from http://www.european-archaeological-council.org/13-0-Archives.html.

Dunn, S. (2012, Summer). Review of ORBIS. *Journal of Digital Humanities, 1*(3). Retrieved from http://journalofdigitalhumanities.org/1-3/review-of-orbis-project-by-stuart-dunn/.

Edmunds, L. (1995, Fall). Review: Computers and the classics: The third phase. *Arion, 3*(2/3), 317–50.

Elliott, T., Heath, S., & Muccigrosso, J. (2012, Spring/Summer). Report on the Linked Ancient World Data Institute (LAWDI). *ISQ: International Standards Quarterly, 23*(2/3), 43–45. doi:10.3789/isqv24n2-3.2012.08

Feeney, D. (2013, September). *September 2013 President's letter: Moving towards the Association's new name.* American Philological Association. Retrieved from http://apaclassics.org/apa-blog/september-2013-presidents-letter-moving-towards-association%E2%80%99s-new-name.

Francese, C. (2013a, April 15). *What should Gregory Crane do? (DCA wrap-up).* Dickinson College Commentaries. Retrieved from http://blogs.dickinson.edu/dcc/2013/04/15/what-should-gregory-crane-do-dca-wrap-up/.

Francese, C. (2013b, August 27). *Neil Coffee on digital classics and peer review.* Dickinson College Commentaries. Retrieved from http://blogs.dickinson.edu/dcc/2013/08/27/neil-coffee-on-dh-and-peer-review/.

Frischer, B. (Ed.). (1987). Papers of the UCLA conference on classics and computing, Los Angeles, July 19–20, 1986 (supplementary volume). *Favonius: A Journal Devoted to the Classics and the Classical Tradition, 1.*

Frischer, B. (1989, May). The UCLA classicist's workbench. *Computing and the Classics, 5*(3), suppl. 1–4. Retrieved from http://newark.osu.edu/facultystaff/personal/jtebben/Pages/ComputingandtheClassics.aspx

Gouglas, S., Rockwell, G., Smith, V., Hoosein, S., & Quamen, H. (2012). Before the beginning: The formation of humanities computing as a discipline in Canada. *Digital Studies,*

3(1). Retrieved from http://www.digitalstudies.org/ojs/index.php/digital_studies/article/view/214/290.

Hardwick, L. (2000, August). Electrifying the canon: The impact of computing on classical studies. *Computers and the Humanities, 34*(3), 279–95.

Heverly, W. G. (2006, Spring). From scroll to database: What do classics librarians do? *Amphora, 5*(1), 16–17.

Hulmer, E. C. (1955). *The role of conservation in connoisseurship*. Doctoral dissertation, University of Pittsburgh. Retrieved from ProQuest Dissertations and Theses. (AAT 89163102).

Kanellou, D., Grantham, A., Rodríguez Echavarria, K., Gottlieb, H., & Pletinckx, D. (2008). Bridging the knowledge gap between cultural heritage and information and communication technologies professionals: The network of expertise. In A. Posluschny, K. Lambers, & I. Herzog (Eds.), *Layers of Perception.* Proceedings of the 35th International Conference on Computer Applications and Quantitative Methods in Archaeology (CAA), Berlin, Germany, April 2–6, 2007 (pp. 1–7). Bonn: Dr. Rudolf Habelt GmbH. Retrieved from http://proceedings.caaconference.org/paper/134_kanellou_et_al_caa2007/.

Latousek, R. (2001). Fifty years of classical computing: A progress report. *CALICO Journal, 18*(2), 211–22. doi:10.11139/cj.18.2.211-222

Mahony, S. (2011). Research communities and open collaboration: The example of the Digital Classicist wiki. *Digital Medievalist, 6.* Retrieved from http://www.digitalmedievalist.org/journal/6/mahony/.

McCarty, W. (2001). Poem and algorithm: Humanities computing in the life and place of the mind. In D. Fiormonte & J. Usher (Eds.), *New media and the humanities: Research and applications: Proceedings of the first seminar on computers, literature and philology, Edinburgh 7–9 September 1998* (pp. 1–9). Oxford, UK: Humanities Computing Unit, University of Oxford.

Meeks, E., & Grossner, K. (2012a, Summer). ORBIS: An interactive scholarly work on the Roman world. *Journal of Digital Humanities, 1*(3). Retrieved from http://journalofdigitalhumanities.org/1-3/orbis-an-interactive-scholarly-work-on-the-roman-world-by-elijah-meeks-and-karl-grossner/.

Meeks, E., & Grossner, K. (2012b, Summer). Modeling networks and scholarship with ORBIS. *Journal of Digital Humanities, 1*(3). Retrieved from http://journalofdigitalhumanities.org/1-3/modeling-networks-and-scholarship-with-orbis-by-elijah-meeks-and-karl-grossner/.

O'Donnell, J. (1994). Review [Review of the book *Accessing antiquity: The computerization of classical studies*, ed. J. Solomon]. *Bryn Mawr Classical Review*, 94.02.14. Retrieved from http://bmcr.brynmawr.edu/1994/94.02.14.html.

Peru, G. (2014, February 18). *Introducing digital classics.* Software Sustainability Institute. Retrieved from http://www.software.ac.uk/blog/2014-02-18-introducing-digital-classics.

Pritchard, D. (2008). Working papers, open access, and cyber-infrastructure in classical studies. *Literary & Linguistic Computing, 23*(2), 149–62. doi:10.1093/llc/fqn005

Pusceddu, C. (2010). *E-philology*. Digital variants. Retrieved from http://www.digitalvariants.org/e-philology.

Remondino, F., & Campana, S. (2014). *3D recording and modelling in archaeology and cultural heritage: Theory and best practices.* Oxford, UK: Archaeopress.

Rockwell, G. (2012, Fall). Short guide to evaluation of digital work. *Journal of Digital Humanities, 1*(4). Retrieved from http://journalofdigitalhumanities.org/1-4/short-guide-to-evaluation-of-digital-work-by-geoffrey-rockwell/.

Rockwell, G. (2013, April 9). Digital Classics Symposium in Buffalo. *Theoreti.ca*. Retrieved from http://theoreti.ca/?p=4739.

Smith, D. A., Rydberg-Cox, J. A., & Crane, G. R. (2000). The Perseus Project: A digital library for the humanities. *Literary & Linguistic Computing, 15*(1), 15–25. doi:10.1093/llc/15.1.15

Solomon, J. (Ed.). (1993). *Accessing antiquity: The computerization of classical studies.* Tucson, AZ: University of Arizona Press.

Stewart, G., Crane, G., & Babeu, A. (2007). A new generation of textual corpora: Mining corpora from very large collections. In *Proceedings of the 7th ACM/IEEE-CS Joint Conference on Digital Libraries (JCDL '07)* (pp. 356–65). New York: ACM. doi:10.1145/1255175.1255247

Tchernetska, N. (2009). Manuscript studies. In G. Boys-Stones, B. Graziosi, & P. Vasunia (Eds.), *The Oxford handbook of Hellenic studies* (pp. 747–62). Oxford, UK: Oxford University Press.

Terras, M. (2010). The Digital Classicist: Disciplinary focus and interdisciplinary vision. In G. Bodard & S. Mahony (Eds.), *Digital research in the study of classical antiquity*. Surrey, UK: Ashgate.

Watrall, E., Graham, S., Frey, J. M., Schopieray, S., Adams, B., Brock, T. P., . . . Pett, D. (2013). Current research & practice in digital archaeology. In *Digital Humanities 2013: Conference Abstracts.* University of Nebraska-Lincoln, USA, 16–19 July 2013 (DH2013). Lincoln, NE: Center for Digital Research in the Humanities. Retrieved from http://dh2013.unl.edu/abstracts/ab-376.html.

11

Perception of Researchers about Institutional Repositories to Archive Indigenous Scholarly Literature

A Case of Pakistan

Nosheen Fatima Warraich

ABSTRACT

Institutional Repositories (IRs) are digital archives providing free access to the intellectual output of academic and research institutes. This chapter aims to explore the perception of researchers about an institutional repository in the University of the Punjab (PU), Lahore-Pakistan. It also investigates the research output of PU faculty, the journals published by PU, and the availability of that output. It identifies gaps in present knowledge recording systems and suggests ways to adopt best practices in this regard. It is a qualitative study based on literature review, web content analysis, and a focus group with library and information science (LIS) researchers.

It is found that an IR is essential, especially in an institution that on an annual basis publishes 32 research journals, contributes over 350 research articles to international journals, produces 250 PhD theses, and completes 237 research projects. The findings show that LIS researchers and university teachers strongly agree with the existence of an IR. They also have some concerns about IR sustainability and currency. It is not a simple task to develop an IR as there are copyright, technological, and financial issues along with the need for trained human resources. Requiring long-term planning, an IR needs to be undertaken as a project rather than as a routine task. There is a need to plan it systematically and extensively because now IRs are more of an issue of policy decision than only a technological issue. It is also suggested that all researchers and teachers should be bound to submit their intellectual output (national and international articles, theses, conference papers, books/book chapters, research projects, presentations, and grey literature) to the university in digital format along with print format to develop a digital collection for the university.

INTRODUCTION

The emerging information society made the availability of intellectual content of an institution on the Internet critical for its visibility and image (Crow, 2003). The present digital culture in academia not only affected teaching but also research and its cycle from creation to dissemination. In this changing and challenging e-culture in universities, the existence of Institutional Repositories (IRs) needs no justification. IR is the face of a university that shows the university's original contribution to the body of knowledge and its impact on society. A university-based institutional repository is a set of services that a university offers to the members of its community for the management and dissemination of digital materials created by the institution and its community members.

Basically, an institutional repository is the collection and sharing of scholarly contribution of an academic institute through electronic means. The purpose of an IR is to store and disseminate the intellectual output of an institution to the community and the society at large. This is an emerging concept in the academia of third world countries (Chan, Kirsop, & Arunachalam, 2005), which are trying to follow the case of MIT, the pioneer of IR in universities. Access to scholarly literature is imperative to research productivity and a key factor in today's knowledge-based economy.

Before going into the detail of this study, we need to discuss how an institutional repository is considered a cultural heritage repository. For this study, the author used the following definition of cultural heritage (ICOMOS, 2002):

> Cultural Heritage is an expression of the ways of living developed by a community and passed on from generation to generation, including customs, practices, places, objects, artistic expressions and values. Cultural Heritage is often expressed as either Intangible or Tangible Cultural Heritage.

Cultural heritage is the result of human interaction with society that produces intangible or tangible demonstration that connects the past to the present. Cultural heritage can be distinguished in the:

- built environment (buildings, townscapes, archaeological remains)
- natural environment (rural landscapes, coasts and shorelines, agricultural heritage)
- artifacts (books, documents, objects, pictures)

The driving force behind all definitions of cultural heritage is that "it is a human creation intended to inform" (Feather, 2006). Feather supports the argument that creation of a university community that is "intended to inform" the present and future generations is to be considered part of a cultural heritage repository.

Artifacts, such as books and documents, objects, and pictures, are part of cultural heritage and can be placed into a cultural heritage repository. The current study proposed an IR in Punjab University that will consist of its members' contributions. This proposed IR comes under the category of a cultural heritage repository as PU is one of the oldest seats of learning in South Asia and has a rich cultural heritage in the form of artifacts (i.e., books and documents). PU has recorded evidences of cultural heritage for more than 130 years, and the collection is even richer than collections maintained in any other institution in the region. The university has rare articles, magazines, and documents that need to be added to an IR. Higher academic institutions are responsible for the generation of quality information because most of the research is being carried out in these institutions under academic domains. The University of the Punjab has a continuing share in the rich cultural heritage of the Indus valley civilization by producing quality research.

PU was established in 1882 in Lahore-Pakistan. It is one of the oldest and largest universities in South Asia. It has more than one thousand learned teachers and researchers whose research work is recognized and published nationally and internationally. Its academic departments published more than thirty-two research journals regularly, but with varying frequency from annually to quarterly. An institution with such research credentials needs to archive its published research not only to facilitate current researchers but also for future generations. There is no mechanism to archive this rich intellectual and scholarly communication and make it available to the research community as open source. The concept of institutional repositories is not new in the developed world (Groenewegen & Treloar, 2008; Rosenblum, 2008; Saw, Lui, & Yu, 2008). Even the developing South Asian countries have taken many initiatives regarding institutional repositories (Das, 2008; Das, Dutta, & Sen, 2007; Fernandez, 2006; Ghosh & Das, 2007).

McKenna (2012) discusses the dilemma of academic research publishing that is produced (created, reviewed, edited, and published) by academicians free of cost, but commercial publishers charge its access cost. The people from academia give their time, use their offices, and contribute as authors, reviewers, and editors of the journals, getting relaxation in workload just for academic prestige. They all contributed quality research that is either funded by their university or other national agency. Commercial publishers cash in all their efforts in monetary terms, and the institutions themselves have to pay millions of dollars to the publisher for their own research that is created and edited in their institution. Academicians even have to pay $40 to $50 for an eight- to ten-page article written by their colleague. McKenna discusses the example of JSTOR, which does not want (like other publishers) to provide open access to research, labeling this situation "locked in the ivory tower."

A census report of U.S. institutional repositories stated that the majority of the IRs had fewer than one thousand digital documents. Only four (8.3 percent) pilot-test IRs, and seven (19.4 percent) operational IRs contain more than five thousand documents. This project also mentioned that there is no relationship between IR size and age (Rieh, Markey, St. Jean, Yakel, & Kim, 2007).

PAKISTANI CONTEXT

The Higher Education Commission (HEC) of Pakistan has established the Pakistan Research Repository (PRP) to promote international visibility of research originating from institutes of higher education in Pakistan. This repository has already made the full text of over 1,600 doctoral theses available in high-quality digitized format. HEC also promotes open access to public-funded research results through its PRP. It is an open access digital archiving project of the HEC to increase international visibility of the results of research emanating from institutions of higher education in Pakistan. The aims of this service are to maintain a digital repository of the intellectual output of Pakistani institutions, to provide a single-entry access point to view this research, and to disseminate the scholarly literature as widely as possible. It provides Atom and RSS feeds for information to registered users on latest additions. PRP can be browsed by type of documents. Presently it has archived journal articles, conference papers, and PhD/MPhil theses and dissertations. Some other types of scholarly documents such as patents, monographs, books, and learning resources will be added in the near future. PRP has adopted a systematic mechanism for the collection and digitization of MPhil- and PhD-level theses submitted in Pakistani universities.

Significance of the Study

An IR is essentially an organizational commitment to the stewardship of print and digital sources produced by an institution or its member on any forum. It also includes long-term preservation where appropriate, as well as organization and access or distribution. PU has a rich scholarly literature (increased day by day) in all disciplines as it published thirty-two regular scholarly journals (most of them are HEC recognized). Its teachers published 1,061 research articles per year in international impact factor (IF) journals, which is almost doubled by the numbers of national and non-IF journal articles produced by the teachers each year. In this rich research culture, it is desired to assess the need of an Institutional Repository (IR) for its teachers and researchers to provide free access to this intellectual treasure of the institution.

Objectives of the Study

This study aims:

- to collect the data about the journals published by PU and their availability
- to explore the perception of researchers about an institutional repository in PU
- to identify gaps in the present knowledge recording system and suggest ways to adopt best practices in this regard

Research Design

This is a qualitative study based on web content analysis and a focus group with LIS researchers. To meet the first objective of the study about the journals published by different departments, colleges, or institutes of the university, the author collected information from the PU website and reviewed the webpage of all the departments of the university. The concerned department librarian and faculty members were also contacted to get journals' information. A qualitative approach is used to explore the phenomenon because it has the strength to understand complex organizational and social phenomena more clearly. Its "bottom-up" approach to local problems and issues allows complexities to be elucidated by those who are directly involved, rather than studied from a distance by remote researchers (Gorman, Clayton, Shep, & Clayton, 2005).

A focus group with nine LIS research students was conducted to reveal their perceptions regarding IRs. The researcher herself moderated the focus group and took notes during this process. The students all were invited for this focus group, and they provided their consent to participate in this study through text messages. They volunteered themselves for the study, but they were served with shawarma and cold drinks at the end of session.

DATA ANALYSIS

The quantitative data about journals was organized using MS Excel 2007. The qualitative data was also recorded. Thematic analysis was used to organize the data, and different theme and patterns emerged in this process.

Data Analysis and Interpretation

Data analysis revealed that there were thirty-two journals published by PU. More than half were HEC recognized and fell in the "X" and "Y" HEC categories. The data about these journals were tabulated according to their frequency of publication, their starting years, and the year of current issues published. Table 11.1 shows the starting year of the journals published by PU. Data show that three journals have been published since before the independence of Pakistan from British rule in 1947, and this fact made PU more prominent among the other universities in this territory. There was an addition of eight more journals in the next thirty years (1947–1977). The number of journals and scholarly communication received an impetus in the 1990s, and nineteen journals started to publish from different departments of PU in this decade; that is, from 1988 to 1997. From 1998 to 2007, there were only seven new journals to start publishing. HEC Pakistan encouraged journal publication and set a different measure to maintain the quality of journals. HEC set the criteria to categorize all these journals ranging from "W" to "Z" categories. "W" is the uppermost category that includes the Impact Factor journals, and "Z" category journals meet the minimum criteria to be HEC-recognized journals. As of 2013, PU was publishing thirty-two journals, and a significant number of the journals were published in two formats: print and electronic. Some journals are only published in e-format, and all journals are available full text on the PU website.

All the journals published by PU departments have different frequencies of publication, varying from quarterly to annually. Table 11.2 shows that a significant number of journals, eighteen (58 percent), have biannual frequency, followed by ten (32 percent) journals published annually. Only three (10 percent) journals are published quarterly. But the important question is currency of the journal rather

Table 11.1. Starting Year of the Journals Published by PU

Journal Published Since	*Frequency*
Before 1947	3
1948–1957	1
1958–1967	5
1968–1977	2
1978–1987	4
1988–1997	19
1998–2007	7

than frequency. Whatever the publishing frequency, journals are published regularly according to a set schedule or not.

It is worth mentioning that only ten (32 percent) journals have been published regularly, and their issues appeared in 2013. Among these ten journals, three are bi-annual and regularly published both issues in June and December. The other twenty-two (68 percent) journals are not following the publication frequency. Eight journals published their latest issue in 2012 but have not appeared yet as of November 2013.

Along with the national journals, PU teachers and researchers got published in international and Impact Factor journals. PU is the single university in Pakistan that gives monetary benefits to its teachers on the number of papers published every year. Teachers get an average of $200 for one published article (Impact Factor journals for sciences and HEC-recognized journals for social sciences). In the case of two authors, the monetary award is equally divided between both authors. Table 11.3 shows the increase in the number of research articles published by the PU community. In 2007 to 2008 it was 162, raised to 278 in 2008 to 2009. In 2010 to 2011, the number of articles was 352, which is more than double the 2007 to 2008 research productivity.

There are number of factors for this increase:

- University incentives for research
- Conducive work environment
- University higher authorities are keen and concerned for good quality research
- Ranking of university based on research output
- Peer pressure for producing research
- Prerequisite for faculty selection on higher position
- HEC policies
- Emerging research culture in campus

Table 11.2. Frequency of Journals Published by PU Departments

Journal Published	*Frequency*	*Percentage*
Annual	10	32
Biannual	18	58
Quarterly	3	10

Table 11.3. Number of Articles Published in International Journals

Journal Published	*Frequency*
2007–2008	162
2008–2009	278
2010–2011	352

Perception of Researchers about an Institutional Repository in PU

An IR is the digital archive of a university intellect and scholarship. However, *only* archiving the research and scholarship in a systematic way does not fulfill the function. The most important function of an IR is its dissemination to the community free of cost. The present digital culture in academia not only affects teaching but also research and its cycle from creation to dissemination. In this changing and challenging e-culture in universities, the existence of an IR needs no justification. IR is the face of a university that shows the university's original contribution in the body of knowledge and its impact on society.

In order to assess the perception of researchers about an IR in PU, a focus group was conducted with nine LIS researchers who all were working professionals in public and private sector university and medical college libraries on October 18, 2013. The respondents' ages ranged from twenty-five to forty, and, among the nine respondents, four were from PU.

After the researcher explained the operational definition of an IR, the floor was opened for their comments. The researcher took notes of the whole session and tried to keep them on the relevant points that she had made before the session. The researcher herself organized the textual data from the session, and themes and patterns emerged from this data. In theme discovery, more is better. It is not that all themes are equally important. Investigators must eventually decide which themes are most salient and how themes are related to each other. But unless themes are first discovered, none of this additional analysis can take place. Analyzing text involves several tasks: (1) discovering themes and subthemes, (2) winnowing themes to a manageable few (i.e., deciding which themes are important in any project), (3) building hierarchies of themes or code books, and (4) linking themes into theoretical models (Ryan & Bernard, 2003). For Strauss and Corbin (1990), the links between expressions and themes are "conceptual labels placed on discrete happenings, events, and other instances of phenomena." Themes, or categories, are the classification of more discrete concepts.

As for as reliability (consistency) assessment is concerned, "there is no single set of categories [themes] waiting to be discovered. There are as many ways of 'seeing' the data as one can invent" (Dey, 1993, pp. 110–11). How do investigators know if the themes they have identified are valid? There is no ultimate demonstration of validity, but we can maximize clarity and agreement to make validity more, rather than less, likely. First, theme identification involves judgments on the part of the investigator. If these judgments are made explicit and clear, then readers can argue with the researcher's conclusions (Agar, 1980).

The focus group respondents were asked about the existence and justification of IR in PU. They all were in favor of an IR and opined that there should be, rather, *must* be an institutional repository for researchers to access the indigenous literature along with research published by the PU community in international journals, books, or proceedings. One of the respondents argued that university institutional repositories should contain the types of cultural artifacts (i.e., pictures, rare newspapers, and documents) presented in the Punjab University library (PUL). In fact, PUL has the richest cultural artifacts, including manuscripts and old, rare Urdu and English papers that are not available in the archives and museums of the region. Adding those materials to an IR will enhance the visibility of this digital collection, and the IR will become an institutional cum cultural heritage repository. The university should feature its distinguished collection, whether acquired or created by its members.

Two respondents had serious concerns about copyright and legal issues. Other respondents opined that there are many publishers that allowed authors to include their work in IRs. Open access to IRs enhances the number of citations of a journal and its articles. Some publishers are not in favor of IR because it is contradictory to their commercial interest.

Four respondents emphasized that most institutions take on IR initiatives ambitiously without proper planning, so ultimately the IRs are not maintained and sustained. All of these respondents were working LIS professionals and have had this type of experiences in their institutions. They opined that it should not be a one-time effort. Instead, it is a continuous process. They strongly suggested that the retrospective conversion should be done on a project basis with separate staff and budget head. Developing an IR is not the library's or archives' routine task; it must be treated as discrete phenomenon.

When they were asked about the utility of an IR for researchers, they unanimously agreed that it is useful and beneficial for the research community rather than supporting and facilitating their research endeavors. But one of them pointed out that it would be helpful for research and researchers if IRs provided complete and updated information. This is an important issue that was discussed in detail. It was also explored that repository success is based on the submission of intellectual content by the authors and there is a need to conduct an authors' needs assessment survey. Three questions are important in this regard:

1. Do authors agree to submit/share their research with the community?
2. Are authors competent enough for self-archiving?
3. Are the library staff willing to share rich cultural artifacts in an IR?

One participant suggested that researcher/teachers are bound to deposit their work in the repository—if they do not submit, they will not get any reward on it from the university. In other words, researchers have to submit in the repository to get any benefit of their work. In this way, the repository will receive more records and provide access to more information sources.

The respondents were also in favor of DSpace (developed by MIT libraries) and EPrints (already used in HEC research repository) programs to initiate an IR. Both are open source software and have customization features according to individual needs. One of the respondents is supporting Fedora (also an open source system) to develop an IR. There are open source communities to support and guide about these programs. Due to the advancements in technology and open source software (i.e., EPrints and DSpace, etc.; see Wise, Spiro, Henry, & Byrd, 2007), the development and maintenance cost of an IR is comparatively more economical now than in the past, so now IRs are affordable. There are different standards available for IRs, such as open archives and metadata harvesting protocol, among others.

The next question was, if the IR is so essential, then who is responsible to maintain it, and what is the criteria for adding items in it? All of the respondents agree that LIS professionals with IT skills should be responsible for the IR in any organization. They opined that an important issue is continuous support of the administration and technological facilities. This is a laborious task and continuous process that needs patience. Some decision makers thought this was an IT professional job, but IT professionals are not fully aware of knowledge generation and dissemination processes and are unable to do this job. LIS professionals should take assistance from IT professionals and management professionals in the planning and maintenance stage. In the context of PU, the research office with the collaboration of the Quality Enhancement Cell and the PU library will be responsible for this IR project.

Two respondents focused on the cut points to enter the data in IRs—deciding the time frame and deadlines to meet it. Realistic estimation is necessary to work smoothly. Commonly, current archiving is the first focus, followed by retrospective archiving.

This is a very important point—what will/should be done to plan the retrospective archiving? There we need maximum data to make intelligent decisions. They suggested retrospective archiving in chronological cum faculty-wise order. There should be five-year plans for all kinds of retrospective archiving. Another participant suggested that teachers should be involved in this process and they should update their own pages with the link to full text. This will save the cost of data entry by library staff. All teachers are bound to maintain and update their pages in the repository.

Respondents discussed the question of what are the benefits for teachers who do all the exercise. How are they motivated to submit their work in an IR? According to the respondents, the following are some potential benefits to motivate teachers to share their intellectual effort with the community:

- Enhance research visibility
- More number of hits and citations
- Better image of the university
- Disseminate to a wider audience
- Motivating young researchers

The literature establishes that there is a low number of items in IRs. Even in the United States, a significant number of repositories have less than 1,500 items (Rieh et al., 2007). To avail the full benefits of a repository, it is necessary to archive maximum institutional intellect in it, and the teachers are the important stakeholders in this system. Teachers should facilitate and assist in adding their research to the IR.

The next issue is the financial resources of the project, or what will be the budget allocation policy? There are budget needs for high-tech hardware, software customization and installation, security (i.e., backup), sustainability, and staff training for this project. There should be a separate budget for the IR, and it should not be taken from the regular library budget.

The success of an IR depends on two points—one is technological and the other is sociological. The former is comparatively easier to manage than the latter.

Seven respondents had concerns about the stability of an IR. They opined that it is a good idea, but there is a need to develop a process to do it in a systematic way to make it a permanent feature of the university. This is not a one-time effort; it is as cyclic and continuous a process as the research creation itself. Respondents emphasized long-term planning on a permanent basis and touched on policy decisions. One of the respondents gave her own example that she added a clause in the UN library policy to submit a PDF copy of a book to get an ISBN number. These types of initiatives would add the number of records in the repository.

PROPOSED MODEL FOR IR IN PU

This work will be done in a systematic way in all faculties. Dean's offices, the PU research office, and the Quality Enhancement Cell are responsible for collecting the data, and Mainly Library will organize all these collected research pieces.

There are three methods to deposit the research in the IR. First, there is self-archiving, in which all the faculty members provide interfaces to update/upload their research and its bibliographic information. In the second method, library staff collects and enters the research of faculty members. The third option is harvesting, in which the system automatically searches and updates the required information in the IR. All teachers should submit their publications (i.e., research papers in national and international journals, books, book chapters, conference papers funded by PU or HEC, research projects funded by PU, presentations, etc.) in the soft form to get the benefit from it (Figure 11.1). To plan an IR, the words of Lynch (2003) are the guiding principles:

> This is an area where I believe universities need to invest aggressively, but where they also need to implement thoughtfully and carefully, with broad consultation and collaboration across the campus community (with intellectual leadership from the faculty and the library working in partnership) and with a full understanding that if they succeed they will permanently change the landscape of scholarly communication.

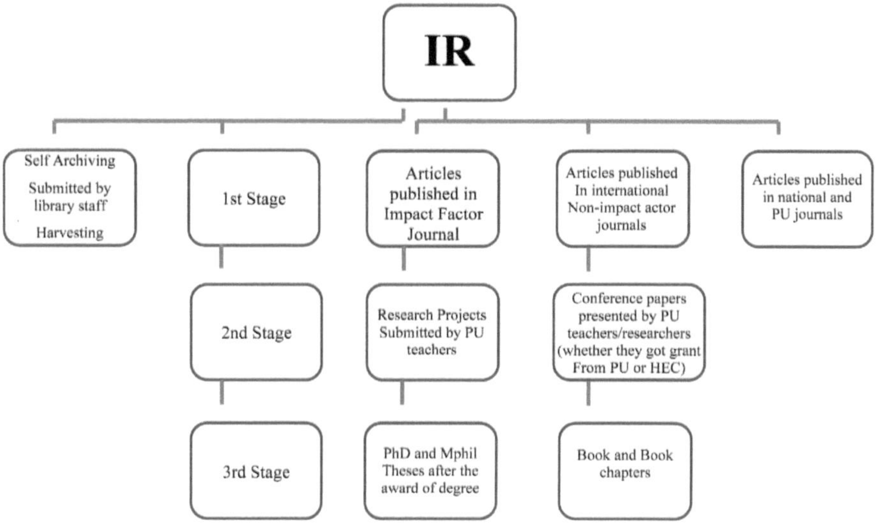

Figure 11.1. Proposed model for IR in PU.

CONCLUSION

The findings of this study show the potential of an IR in a university with good research productivity and the presence of cultural artifacts in its library. Punjab University published 32 research journals and produced 250 PhD theses. Its teachers get published in more than 350 research articles in international Impact Factor journals and completed 237 research projects annually. Along with this research productivity, the university library has rich cultural artifacts that need to be archived for better visibility on the web. This is an ideal situation to plan an institutional cum cultural heritage repository to archive the rare documents and research produced by university faculty/researchers.

REFERENCES

Agar, M. (1980). Getting better quality stuff: Methodological competition in an interdisciplinary niche. *Urban Life, 9*, 34–50.

Chan, L., Kirsop, B., & Arunachalam, S. (2005). Open access archiving: The fast track to building research capacity in developing countries. *SciDev Net.* Retrieved from http://www.scidev.net/global/communication/feature/open-access-archiving-the-fast-track-to-building-r.html.

Crow, R. (2003). *The case for institutional repositories: A SPARC position paper.* Washington, DC: Scholarly Publishing & Academic Resources. Retrieved from http://www.sparc.arl.org/sites/default/files/media_files/instrepo.pdf.

Das, A. K. (2008). *Open access to knowledge and information: Scholarly literature and digital library initiatives; the South Asian scenario.* New Delhi, India: UNESCO. Retrieved from http://portal.unesco.org/ci/en/files/26393/12075628443open_access_book_en.pdf/open_access_book_en.pdf.

Das, A. K., Dutta, C., & Sen, B. K. (2007). Information retrieval features in Indian digital libraries: A critical appraisal. *OCLC Systems & Services: International Digital Library Perspectives, 23*(1), 92–104.

Dey, I. (1993). *Qualitative data analysis: A user-friendly guide for social scientists.* London, UK: Routledge.

Feather, J. (2006). Managing the documentary heritage: issues from the present and future. In G. E. Gorman & S. J. Shep (Eds.), *Preservation management for libraries, archives and museums (pp. 1–18).* London, UK: Facet.

Fernandez, L. (2006). Open Access Initiatives in India—An evaluation. *Partnership: The Canadian Journal of Library and Information Practice and Research, 1*(1). Retrieved from https://journal.lib.uoguelph.ca/index.php/perj/article/view/110#.U7_zy_ldWuI.

Ghosh, S. B., & Das, A. K. (2007). Open access and institutional repositories—A developing country perspective: A case study of India. *IFLA Journal, 33*, 229–50.

Gorman, G. E., Clayton, P. R., Shep, S. J., & Clayton, A. (2005). *Qualitative research for the information professional: A practical handbook* (2nd ed.). London, UK: Facet Publications.

Groenewegen, D., & Treloar, A. (2008). The ARROW project: A consortial institutional repository solution, combining open source and proprietary software. *OCLC Systems & Services: International Digital Library Perspectives, 24*, 30–39. doi: 10.1108/10650750810847224

(HEC) Higher Education Commission, Pakistan (n.d.). *Pakistan Research Repository.* Retrieved from http://eprints.hec.gov.pk/.

*(ICOMOS) International Cultural Tourism Charter (*2002). *Principles and guidelines for managing tourism at places of cultural and heritage significance.* ICOMOS International Cultural Tourism Committee.

Lynch, C. A. (2003, February). Institutional repositories: Essential infrastructure for scholarship in the digital age. *ARL, 226*, 1–7. Retrieved from http://www.arl.org/resources/pubs/br/br226/br226ir.shtml.

McKenna, L. (2012, January 20). Locked in the ivory tower: Why JSTOR imprisons academic research. *The Atlantic.* Retrieved from http://www.theatlantic.com/business/archive/2012/01/locked-in-the-ivory-tower-why-jstor-imprisons-academic-research/251649/.

(PRR) Pakistan Research Repository. (n.d.). *Welcome to Pakistan Research Repository.* Retrieved from www.eprints.hec.gov.pk.

Rieh, S. Y., Markey, K., St. Jean, B., Yakel, E., & Kim, J. (2007, November/December). Census of institutional repositories in the U.S.: A comparison across institutions at different stages of IR development. *D-Lib Magazine, 13*(11/12). Retrieved from http://www.dlib.org/dlib/november07/rieh/11rieh.html.

Rosenblum, B. (2008). Developing new skills and expertise to support digital scholarship and scholarly communication. Proceedings of the IFLA General Conference and Council, Canada, August 10–14, 2008 (pp. 1–7). Munich, Germany: De Gruyter Saur.

Ryan, G. W., & Bernard, H. R. (2003). Techniques to identify themes. *Field Methods, 15*(1), 85–109.

Saw, G., Lui, W. W., & Yu, F. (2008). A library odyssey. *Library Management, 29*, 51–56. doi: 10.1108/01435120810844649

Strauss, A., & Corbin, J. (1990). *Basics of qualitative research: Grounded theory procedures and techniques*. Thousand Oaks, CA: Sage.

University of the Punjab (n.d). *Home: University of the Punjab*. Retrieved from www.pu.edu.pk/journals.

Wise, M., Spiro, L., Henry, G., & Byrd, S. (2007). Expanding roles for the institutional repository. *OCLC Systems & Services: International Digital Library Perspectives*, *23*, 216–23. doi: 10.1108/10650750710748522

V

REVIEWS

12

Allied Media Conference

An Interchange Leading to Possibilities for Another World; Review of the 16th Annual Allied Media Conference, June 19 to 22, 2014, Detroit, Michigan

Celeste Â-Re

The Allied Media Conference (AMC) draws an assemblage of technologists, artists, educators, and activists to engage in critical discourse for strategic planning, to create learning spaces, and to showcase multimedia applications used in community sustainability and digital justice work. Hosted by the Allied Media Projects network, AMC was first held as the Midwest Zine Conference at Bowling Green State University in 1999. Expanding from a do-it-yourself (DIY) print media conference to inclusion of digital media, the forum was incorporated as Allied Media Projects in 2002 and relocated to Detroit in 2007 (Hartman, 2014; Lewan, 2014). AMC is imbued with DIY ethics. As a component of the Allied Media Projects incubator network, AMC is guided by the network mission to "cultivate media strategies for a more just and creative world" (AMP, 2014a). Modeled on the network principles that every problem a community faces has people working proactively to decipher it and that "the most effective strategies are ones that work in situations of scarce resources" (AMP, 2014b), AMC provides an opportunity for interdisciplinary problem solving in a collaborative environment.

This 2014 (Figures 12.1 and 12.2) convergence at Wayne State University brought together 1,900 attendees participating in skills-share sessions and workshops

Figure 12.1. AMC 2014 banner.

Figure 12.2. AMC 2014 opening ceremony.

centered around eleven tracks, accompanied by practice spaces and strategic development panels. The themes of the serial sessions, or tracks, were (AMC, 2014a):

- Abundant Bodies Media
- Building Better Futures through Play
- Creative Placemaking/Placekeeping
- I ♥ Print Media
- Liberation Technologies for World Building and Survival
- Media Strategies for Transforming Justice
- Research Justice
- Resourcing and Sustaining Our Movements
- The Sound Track
- Watch This! Surveillance, Security, and Organizing
- Youth Media and Movements

RESEARCH JUSTICE

Grounded in community-based media intervention and participatory action research frameworks, the AMC multidisciplinary platform offered practical exchanges relevant to cultural heritage informatics (CHI) scholarship and pedagogy. The focus of many of the presentations in the Research Justice (RJ) track related directly to subject areas inherent to the CHI sector (cultural literacy, data lifecycle management, digital curation, digital divide, folksonomies, and heritage preservation). The daylong RJ network gathering was an unconference, interlacing brainstorm sessions and group discussion. This event provided an effective way to parse the contours of RJ investigation and analysis. Activities yielded definitions of research justice and research injustice, outlined principles for conducting RJ projects, and identified RJ collective build-out and strategies for networking. Etherpad notes (AMC, 2014b) can be accessed at the Allied Media Conference website for further information.

As a progressing doctoral student, I found the sharing of practical insights on community assessment, cultural resource mapping, and data visualization refreshing. Two RJ breakout sessions, "Counter-Mapping 101" and "Community Surveys for Community Power," proved useful to my discovery of resources for CHI methodology. "Counter-Mapping 101" was particularly instructive, offering discussion of concepts, methods, and hands-on experience.

"Counter-Mapping 101"[1]

"Counter-Mapping 101" workshop attendees began by developing a concurrent definition of a map as a visual representation of information obtained through surveying ideas and relationships. Lize Mogel, artist and counter-cartographer, described the narrative layers of a map as a history of space as well as environmental and cultural inventory, and examined the concept of spatial justice and the power of maps as authoritative tools in decision making. Mogel pointed out that, because mappers are oftentimes not connected to the areas they are mapping, omissions of information occur.

Seguing from Mogel's recommendation for a more democratic use of mapmaking tools, Laura Harjo, a professor of Community and Regional Planning at the University of New Mexico, and Chris Schweidler, cofounder of Research Action Design, defined counter-mapping as a counternarrative to "normal" cartography, which may or may not use the Cartesian coordinate system. They drew upon indigenous cartography as examples:

- Drawing on the ground
- Performance cartography
- Coded maps for knowledge encryption
- Map biographies of historically unrecognized peoples

Two counter-mapping case studies were presented: a crime data counter-mapping project and a blexting field survey. I selected the field survey exercise, which featured analysis of the Detroit Blight Removal Task Force's use of data generated through the Motor City Mapping blexting, a blight texting app (Loveland Technologies, 2014) and mapping database. The blexting tool is a mobile application created for collecting photographs of parcels of land tagged with condition descriptors. Workshop participants identified stakeholder issues and methods to support complementary mapping.

The presenters concluded the workshop with a scenario and three questions for consideration when incorporating tactical approaches to mapping: after generating a map of a community, consult with stakeholders and compare the representation with information held by the community members. Are there similarities or differences? What is on the map, and what has been left off the map? Do the differences or missing information indicate an apparent bias?

DIGITAL STEWARDSHIP

The hallmark of AMC 2014 was the network topology panel—DIY Wireless Internet Mesh Networks. At standing room capacity, this session identified resources, offered hands-on ethernet cable making, and highlighted workflows involved in "creating inexpensive local Wi-Fi that allows users to connect their devices directly with each other . . . whether or not it is connected to the Internet" (Byrum & Nucera, 2014). The workshop is the product of an ongoing collaboration between the New America Foundation's Open Technology Institute and digital stewardship initiatives based in Brooklyn (Red Hook WiFi) and Detroit (Allied Media Digital Stewards). The objective of this partnership is to provide training and promote community technology, public computing, and skills development as solutions to address the digital divide in the United States (and globally).

I spoke with one digital steward, Monique Tate, about her involvement with the project. Tate is the community outreach coordinator at Data Driven Detroit and a technologist who entered the domain after having worked for over twenty years in the corporate sector at one of the top three automotive finance companies. A long-standing community activist and self-described "displaced worker," Tate was introduced to Allied Media Projects' digital steward initiative in 2012 when she participated in a neighborhood forum on community technology. At the assembly she met Diana Nucera, director of Allied Media Projects' Detroit Digital Stewards project. Upon completion of a twenty-week digital steward training, Tate continued working with a network of alumni to build a mesh network infrastructure in her community in the Morningside neighborhood of Detroit.

The Morningside Mesh slogan, "connecting neighbors one block at a time," reflects the process required to build the infrastructure in the 2.1-square-mile area (City Data, 2014). The digital stewards continue to develop the network three years after the inception of the program. Describing the process, Tate stated:

> We inquired with AMP [Allied Media Projects] about building an open mesh network in the neighborhood. Compuware had sponsored the building of a home by Habitat for Humanity in the community; part of Compuware's mission was to see Internet access provided in addition to the building of homes, bringing technology, community, and corporate partners to the table. We pursued activity as a partner and brought the information back to the community association.

Impressed by the diversity (age, "race," gender) of the digital steward presenters (and AMC attendees overall), I expressed my experience of not finding many people of color represented at tech conferences and inquired as to AMC's success at inclusion. Tate's response was illuminating:

> That is what you tend to find in the tech field, but the digital steward program is very diverse. That's the point. When you're offering something like this through urban communities you have to tap the part of the population that is being missed and overlooked. [AMP] makes a conscientious effort to reach out and remember the underserved. It's part of the dynamic, interacting and engaging with underserved communities linked through the digital justice coalition network. It's grass roots.

More information about the DIY workshop and details about the installation of the AMC conference-wide wireless mesh network can be found on the Open Technology Institute blog (Gunn, 2014).

CONCLUSION

This review highlights only three events of the over two hundred sessions and variety of interesting themes addressed during the four-day AMC conference. The AMC 2014 Social Media Parallel Universe (AMC, 2014c) can be accessed on the AMC site for blog posts, audio, and video coverage of the conference. I believe the strategies evolved through the AMC process have the potential to impact contributions in standards, best practice, pedagogy, and ethics policy development in the CHI sector.

ACKNOWLEDGMENTS

The author would like to thank the University of South Carolina School of Library and Information Science and the Cultural Heritage Informatics Leadership Fellow program for providing funding to attend AMC 2014.

NOTE

1. Counter-Mapping presenters included: Lize Mogel, An Atlas of Radical Cartography; Chris Schweidler, Research Action Design, Research Justice Collective; Jessica McInchak, Data Driven Detroit; Kat Hartman, Civic Data Design Lab fellow at MIT School of Architecture + Planning; and Laura Harjo, University of New Mexico.

REFERENCES

(AMC) Allied Media Conference. (2014a). *AMC 2014 program book*. Retrieved from http://amc.alliedmedia.org/amc2014-program-book.

(AMC) Allied Media Conference. (2014b). *Research justice network gathering etherpad notes*. Retrieved from https://etherpad.alliedmedia.org/p/14548#Research%20Justice%20Network%20Gathering.

(AMC) Allied Media Conference. (2014c). *AMC 2014 social media parallel universe*. Retrieved from http://alliedmedia.org/news/2014/08/26/amc2014-social-media-parallel-universe-our-big-round-posts-blogs-video-and-audio.

(AMP) Allied Media Projects. (2014a). *Mission*. Retrieved from http://alliedmedia.org/mission.

(AMP) Allied Media Projects. (2014b). *AMP network principles*. Retrieved from http://alliedmedia.org/amp-network-principles.

Byrum, G., & Nucera, D. (2014, September 29). Scaling community technology. *Meeting of the minds*. Retrieved from http://cityminded.org/scaling-community-technology-11677.

City-Data. (2014). Morningside neighborhood in Detroit, Michigan (MI), 48224 detailed profile. Retrieved from http://www.city-data.com/neighborhood/Morningside-Detroit-MI.html.

Gunn, A. (2014, July 21). The 2014 allied media conference magicnet: Third time's the charm. [Web log comment]. Open Technology Institute. Retrieved from http://oti.newamerica.net/blogposts/2014/the_2014_allied_media_conference_magicnet_third_time_s_the_charm-118636.

Hartman, K. (2014, June 17). *Allied media projects and the global relevance of Detroit's grassroots tech scene*. Model D. Retrieved from http://www.modeldmedia.com/features/16yrsofAMP061714.aspx.

Lewan, A. (2014, June 6). *Jenny Lee*. Detroit Urban Innovation Exchange. Retrieved from http://www.uixdetroit.com/people/jennylee.aspx.

Loveland Technologies. (2014). *Motor City mapping: Blexting*. Retrieved from http://makeloveland.com/.

13

SCFM 2014 Conference Review

Porchia Moore

INTRODUCTION

Organized on December 18, 1970, the South Carolina Federation of Museums (SCFM) is an advocacy group representing museum professionals and their subsequent museums and cultural heritage institutions across the state of South Carolina. SCFM's major goal is to strengthen professional standards and increase awareness of museum interests among state representatives. The ensuing mission for the organization is to serve, represent, advocate, and promote the best interests of South Carolina museums, thereby strengthening professional standards and procedures, facilitating communication, fostering inclusiveness, and increasing professionalism and the sustainability of institutional resources. Since its inception, SCFM has organized its annual statewide conference, which centers on thematic subjects of importance relevant to the advancement of museums and the edification of museum professionals' knowledge and skill set.

The annual conference attracts an average of 120 to 130 participants working in various stages in their professional careers, including emerging professionals, midcareer professionals, museum veterans, and museum retirees, as well as museum enthusiasts. The majority of SCFM attendees comprise those employed in the cultural heritage sectors focused on public history, art, preservation, and historic house museums and plantations. Accordingly, attendees identify as working in the capacity of curators, executive directors, collection development, graduate students, and professors; in addition to those employed as educators, (park) interpreters, administrators, and programming coordinators within various museum departments are included, to name a few.

THE CONFERENCE REVIEW

The 2014 SCFM Conference commenced in historic Camden, South Carolina, from March 12 to 15, 2014, with the theme "Let's Talk Museums and Communities in Conversation." Subsequently, four conference buzzwords were chosen that presenters were asked to use as a guide to shaping proposals for the conference. The thematic buzzwords were *diversity*, *community*, *sustainability*, and *conversations*.

The Historic Camden Archive and Museum served as the main venue for the Registration and Exhibitor's hall. The remaining conference locations were spread throughout downtown historic Camden at historic venues, such as Camden City Hall, and historically registered locations such as the Mills Court House and the Price House. Approximately one hundred participants from across South Carolina attended and represented important cultural heritage institutions such as the Columbia Museum of Art, Historic Spartanburg, the Gibbes Museum of Art, the State Museum, Historic Columbia Foundation, various historic sites and plantations, and the Agricultural Museum of South Carolina. SCFM has established a much-anticipated tradition for the first day of the conference. Participants have the option to choose one of two daylong workshops. The first option is the highly popular Traveling Workshop, and the second option is the White Gloves Gang. The Traveling Workshop allows a set number of attendees to take a bus tour of the region and visit numerous museums and cultural heritage sites of interest. The SCFM 2014 Traveling tour visited the following cultural heritage sites:

- The National Steeplechase Museum
- Holly Hedge and Gardens
- Bloomsbury House and Kitchen
- Bethesda Presbyterian Church and DeKalb Monument
- Bonds Conway House
- Historic Camden

The second option, the White Gloves Gang, occurs simultaneously and invites collections care professionals or those interested in collections care to dedicate the day to caring for neglected projects and cultural heritage objects at a selected museum. The chosen museum for SCFM 2014 was the National Steeplechase Museum, which is dedicated to educating the public about the exquisite history of horse culture and horse racing in Camden, South Carolina. The White Gloves Gang completed numerous projects, including:

- Rehousing archival material
- Mount making
- Cleaning cultural heritage objects
- Inventory and numbering

The South Carolina Federation of Museums went to great lengths this year to attract diverse types of cultural heritage institutions since many past institutions represented consisted largely of historic house museums. As a result, it was expedient to see the inclusion of a first-time participant, the Avery Research Center for African-American History and Culture, which was the first interaction with the organization in the history of SCFM. The Avery Research Center presentation, "I'm Building Me a Home: The Avery Research Center and the African American Museum Tradition," examined the history of the African American museum in the cultural landscape and the role that African American museums play both in the African American community and for nonblacks outside of the community.

There were several compelling presentations throughout the conference. Two standout sessions focused on community partnerships and collaboration, which quickly arose as a thematic point of interest for the majority of attendees. The first session, "The 'Artistic' Language: Foreign Language Tour Programs in SC," consisted of a partnership between the Education Department at the Columbia Museum of Art and various members of the Columbia College Foreign Language Department. The copresenters discussed the strategic plan between the art museum and the college to provide art tours in French and Spanish to art museum visitors by employing the foreign language and translation expertise of graduate students and professors. The Historic Columbia Foundation presented the second session of note with their session, "Engaging Columbia Communities," which outlined the success of their Institute of Museum and Library Services grant-funded project, the Manns-Simmons Community Engagement Project. The presenters explained the challenges and execution of the yearlong endeavor that helped foster interest in both history and local cultural heritage by pairing local area C. A. Johnson High School students with community seniors. The goal is to increase historical inquiry as a result of students' work in collecting oral histories. Therefore, these efforts help to contextualize local historic sites throughout the predominately African American community and increase participation in visitation within the many historic house museums managed by Historic Columbia.

In keeping with the thematic buzzwords of communities and conversations, there were two sessions of note. The first was "The Art of Healing," a collaboration between the Gibbes Museum of Art and Roper St. Francis Hospital, which created programming that evokes healing for hospital patients by using art therapy. The second session of note was a major collaboration between the Smithsonian, Family Tyes, Lowcountry Africana, Daniel Island Historical Society and residents, the Edisto Island community, and other local stakeholders. The project seeks to make material culture accessible through various unique engagement efforts.

Two more conference highlights focused on the challenges and delights of technology, and postconference surveys heavily suggested that the desire to learn more about technology was at the forefront of conference attendees' minds. The graduate students at the University of South Carolina's School of Library and Information Science program (USC SLIS) enrolled in the special topics course, Emerging Technologies in Cultural Heritage Institutions, provided a hands-on workshop that instructed participants on low-budget, high-tech ways to incorporate digital engagement using 123D Catch, a free, downloadable app that allows the user to scan a museum object and quickly upload the image to an institution's website, thereby increasing the cultural heritage institution's digital access. This topic of the importance of digital immersion, access, new media, and technologies was continued in the "Emerging Professionals" session. The session was a joint collaboration between the College of Charleston's Arts Management Program and USC SLIS. The USC SLIS session became somewhat provocative as it became clear that a genuine disconnect occurred between emerging professionals and veteran museum employees who had polar ideas regarding how to move South Carolina museums forward in the area of new technologies. As a result, the strong desire to continue this discussion has led to the formation of an outside-of-conference workshop where emerging professionals will be paired with veterans to share lived experiences regarding working in the cultural heritage sector. A second workshop will also take place outside of the conference that will allow the emerging professionals (USC SLIS students) to teach important new media technologies such as social media, data management systems, 3D printing and scanning, and web design.

There were two sessions that garnered high attendance and praise: (1) "Riot Incite: A Sustainable Museum's Controversy and How They Are Using It," executed by the Agricultural Museum of South Carolina; and (2) the "Museums and Non-Profit Law" session given by a University of South Carolina Law School professor from the Pro Bono program. The "Riot Incite" program was especially profound because the presenter encouraged using controversial topics as a means to increase interest, advocacy, and participation in a museum rather than shying away from controversy, thereby inviting a lively, engaging conversation regarding collection development and the need for institutional paradigm shifts.

In this vein, it was most rewarding to witness the revolutionary session presented by the Historic Columbia Foundation's presentation, "Telling a New Story: Negotiating the Change in Focus at the Woodrow Wilson Family Home." The presenters expounded upon how they made the paradigmatic shift from a traditional staid, unchanging historic house museum with similar nationwide thematic tropes and narratives to an upfront exploration of Reconstruction, which acts as the fulcrum narrative alongside the story of President Woodrow Wilson. Because historic house museums, particularly those centered on the lives of former U.S. presidents, often are mired to one central patriotic narrative, this move to change the narrative of the Woodrow Wilson House is at once bold and has the potential to revitalize these types of cultural heritage museums. The potential for this project to operate as a model for presidential house museums across the country is monumental. The conference ended with the keynote luncheon speech given by keynote speaker, artist, writer, synesthete, and curator Carol Steen of New York. Steen spoke about experience of synesthesia, famous synesthetes, and urged attendees to think about culturally responsive ways to address synesthesia in the cultural heritage sector.

CONCLUSION

As libraries, archives, and museums continue to observe the multifaceted ways that new media technologies alter and reconfigure their missions, institutional goals, and collective visions for cultural heritage, conferences such as SCFM have the capacity to function as creative colloboratories at a time when many museums are under threat of increased closings. There is tremendous potential for the SCFM conference to situate South Carolina museums and employees into significant national conversations regarding preservation, archaeology, and expansion projects, particularly since there has been a booming interest in thano-tourism, eco-tourism, and slave dwelling projects from across the globe pertaining to the institution of slavery, as well as renewed interest in art, culture, and foodways related to southern life. The overall impression at having attended the conference is that cultural heritage professionals are hungry for opportunities to increase skill sets (particularly as it relates to new media and new technologies), eager to learn more about ways to partner and collaborate, and are extremely invested in learning how to foster engagement and grow their institutions through increased participation and access digitally and physically. It became very clear that South Carolina museums are lagging in the use of technology in cultural heritage institutions, and SCFM has dedicated itself to moving South Carolina museums into the forefront of this audience demand. The major benefits for having attended the conference were the social networking opportunities, the chance to hear about the successes and challenges associated with projects within institutions one might not have been privy to, and the unique experience of learning about regional cultural heritage and the rich history of horse culture in historic Camden, South Carolina. Moving forward, SCFM seeks to increase membership and interaction within the organization and continue to provide an exceptional conference experience to statewide cultural heritage professionals.

14

Digital Preservation—Not a "One Size Fits All" Solution

A Critical Review of *Preserving Digital Materials* by Ross Harvey, Second Edition, 2011

Carol Lynn Price

The first edition of *Preserving Digital Materials* by Ross Harvey was published in 2005. By 2011, the digital environment had undergone such significant developments that Harvey revised his work and published a second edition. Preservation, once the sole responsibility of libraries, museums, and archives, now impacts virtually everyone who uses information. In the second edition, Harvey outlines the issues, strategies, and challenges to digital preservation and emphasizes major directives that change the preservation framework for the future.

As author, librarian, and educator, Ross Harvey has been an advocate for archives and preservation throughout his career. A former newspaper librarian, his interest in preservation was sparked by the deterioration of newspapers at the National Library of New Zealand. He is published widely in the fields of bibliographic organization, library education, newspaper history, the preservation of library and archival material, and most recently, digital preservation (reseaRch interests, 2014).

For the past five years, Ross Harvey was a visiting professor at Simmons College where he was instrumental in developing the online Digital Stewardship Certificate, training students in creating and managing a sustainable digital repository, library, or archive (Moyer, 2013). Currently, he is an adjunct professor at Royal Melbourne Institute of Technology in Victoria, Australia. In 2007, Ross Harvey was awarded a Fellowship of LIANZA (Library and Information Association of New Zealand Aotearoa) for his outstanding work as a teacher, researcher, writer, and lecturer (reseaRch interests, 2014).

The 2005 edition was Harvey's first book on digital media. In 2010, he wrote *Digital Curation: A How-to-Do-It Manual*, which focused on preventing the corruption or obsolescence of digital materials. At the time, it was the most updated volume on digital preservation; however, Harvey revises much of this information in the second edition of *Preserving Digital Materials* (Harvey, 2012). Harvey's purpose for writing both editions was to write a concise handbook and reference for practitioners and others who need to understand how preservation is changing within the digital world. He makes it clear that this book is not a "how-to" manual, but rather a management tool for digital preservation activities. According to Harvey, digital preservation is the single most serious issue for information professionals today. From his new research findings, he hopes practitioners will improve current preservation practices. Harvey sees digital preservation as a global concern, and unlike the first edition, this book covers the economics of preservation and the skills and education needed by practitioners worldwide.

The digital environment is redefining preservation and requiring new strategies and practices. The terminology used to describe preservation is no longer appropriate in the digital world and has different interpretations among practitioners. Harvey believes digital curation and digital stewardship are more acceptable terms since they describe the whole preservation process of creation, collection, organization, and dissemination. Users of digital materials need to know that the digital record is stable and trustworthy, yet it is inevitable that digital records will be altered due to the nature of digital preservation. The ideal condition would be to keep the digital materials as close to the original as possible. As a result, it becomes necessary to define the characteristics, essential elements, and significant properties of the materials, and to determine what levels of change are acceptable. Historians once used letters and correspondence as a source of historical information, but today much of this documentation occurs in digital formats such as emails, blogs, tweets, and social media. How will this change the way information on personal communication is archived? Harvey questions how quickly emails will become inaccessible. Individuals are storing their personal photographs, videos, diaries, and journals on digital media confident that they will be able to access this information indefinitely. In the past, the creation, reproduction, and distribution of print information was very distinct, but digital technology makes this path indistinguishable. Now the publisher is the creator and the distributor.

Libraries, archives, and other cultural heritage institutions encounter new technical, organizational, fiscal, and legal challenges in taking on the preservation of digital holdings. With these challenges comes the need to involve all creators of information, especially the new stakeholders. Harvey expands the arena of stakeholders to include the commercial and private sectors, search engine and gaming companies, government agencies, hardware and software developers, publishers, and virtually all producers of information. Libraries cannot do it all, and Harvey maintains that cooperation and collaboration among all stakeholders is the most efficient solution to digital preservation.

Harvey sums up the difficulty of preserving digital media as the three modes of digital death—the instability of storage media, obsolescence of storage, and the accessibility to technology. He warns that we must preserve digital items as they are created, or run the risk of losing them. The challenge in digital materials is reformatting and monitoring changes in technology to maintain access to the information. Harvey's concern is that these activities will add another burden to preservation departments where funds and personnel are already strained. As with all new developments, Harvey insists that an organizational commitment must be made for digital preservation to become an integral part of operations and not funded as special projects.

Readers of *Preserving Digital Materials* may be overwhelmed by all there is to know about how to preserve digital materials, almost to the point of fatigue. A short list of the issues that Harvey raises on digital preservation include the increasing amount of materials that need to be digitized; changing file formats, hardware, software, and other technology; and the decision-making process for preservation selection. Chapters include an array of techniques, strategies, opinions, research studies, models, and preservation initiatives. At times, Harvey's rhetoric becomes frustrating when he describes various methods of preservation only to follow with their limitations or failures. For example, he implies that migration is the preferred preservation strategy for most digital archives, then he presents a list of arguments against using migration. Similarly, the extensible markup language (XML) is considered a viable archival data format, but while it is an excellent option for email's simple data structure, it is not the preferred format for more complex kinds of materials since it loses the document's original formatting and layout. Harvey was right when he said there is no "one size fits all" solution.

Harvey admits a decision not to preserve is usually final. Readers learn that the first email sent in 1972 was not saved, and if it had been, it was on magnetic tapes that fall apart after seven or eight years. Alternatively, due to obsolete formats, there is no longer access to the data with identity information of prisoners of war or missing-in-action soldiers from the Vietnam War or on the herbicide information to analyze the impact of Agent Orange. He claims that there is no way to know how much digital information has been lost or compromised and cautions us against getting too overwhelmed by selection decisions, assuring us that we will never get it completely right.

In his last chapter, Harvey projects the state of digital preservation for the future. His areas of concern have not changed much since his first edition. These challenges cover a range of options from developing standards and policies to securing funding and finding solutions for digital preservation. He is encouraged by our technical progress and suggests that the social, political, and economic issues will become perpetual areas to be monitored and addressed through further research and collaboration efforts if there is to be consistent achievement and mutual goals.

Harvey is an expert on digital preservation, and readers will find his book is a valuable reference to define terminology, strategies, and techniques for digital preservation. The twenty-page bibliography is a valuable addition; however, he regrets that some of the links may suffer from "link rot." One clear message that prevails throughout the book is *collaboration*. Digital preservation is expensive and resources are scarce, so practitioners need to join forces and use one another's strengths and talents. Since the first edition, Harvey reports that many more libraries, museums, and archives have developed sustainable digital solutions and preservation policies.

This action is good news since these organizations have implemented preservation budgets, software tools, and the use of skilled personnel. Harvey says that he did not write a how-to manual, but it is an excellent working guide to digital preservation—at least until the third edition comes out.

REFERENCES

Harvey, R. (2011). *Preserving digital materials* (2nd ed.). Berlin; Boston, MA: DeGruyter Saur.

Moyer, J. (2013, June 27). [Web log message]. Retrieved from http://simmons.edu/gslis/for/current/news/blog/2013/06/fond-farewell-to-ross-harvey-by-jennifer-moyer.php. reseaRch interests. (n.d.). *Ross Harvey*. Retrieved from http://elibank.net.

Ross Harvey. (2012). In Contemporary Authors Online. Detroit, MI: Gale. Retrieved from http://ic.galegroup.com/ic/bic1/ReferenceDetailsPage/ReferenceDetailsWindow?failOverType=&query=&prodId=BIC1&windowstate=normal&contentModules=&display-query=&mode=view&displayGroupName=Reference&limiter=&currPage=&disableHighlighting=false&displayGroups=&sortBy=&search_within_results=&p=BIC1&action=e&catId=&activityType=&scanId=&documentId=GALE%7CH1000206681&source=Bookmark&u=usclibs&jsid=7f3778d056bd985c133565a74c8cfbb0

Index

About the Editor

Samantha K. Hastings joined the faculty at the University of South Carolina, School of Library and Information Science as director and professor in August 2006. Previously, she directed the digital image management program of study at the University of North Texas, School of Library and Information Sciences and served as interim dean 2004–2005. She holds a MLIS from the University of South Florida, Tampa, and a PhD from Florida State. Her research interests in the retrieval of digital images, cultural heritage, telecommunications, and evaluation of networked information services influence how she views the changing roles for information professionals. She has worked as a consultant and built full-text and image databases for accountants, dentists, doctors, lawyers, and county and state governments. Along the way, she has worked to help public libraries and museums connect to the Internet and share their cultural objects in a digital environment. Her current research explores the use of three-dimensional digital objects in learning environments. She served as president of the American Society for Information Science and Technology (www.asist.org) in 2004 and served five years as the acquisitions editor for the ASIS&T Monograph series, published by Information Today, Inc. She is currently president of the Association for Library and Information Science Educators (ALISE). Recently, she launched a new annual review for Cultural Heritage Informatics with editor Charles Harmon of Rowman & Littlefield.

About the Contributors

Celeste Â-Re is a PhD candidate in the Cultural Heritage Informatics Leadership program at the School of Library and Information Science, University of South Carolina. Her research focuses on issues related to disprivileged, underserved, historically disenfranchised, and raced learning communities.

Sarah Buchanan is a doctoral student in information studies at the University of Texas at Austin. Her research interests include the archival arrangement and description of special collections, museum archaeology, digital classics, and the digital humanities.

Laura-Edythe Coleman is a doctoral candidate focusing on museum informatics at the School of Library and Information Science, Florida State University. Her research examines cultural heritage institutions in communities reconciling civil conflict and explores the role of information in the creation of individual and collective identities.

Andrea Copeland is an assistant professor at the Department of Library and Information Science, School of Informatics and Computing, Indiana University at Indianapolis. Her research interests include public libraries, digital preservation, and information behavior.

Jessica Dame, a handheld art project assistant, holds her MLIS from the School of Library and Information Science at the University of South Carolina. While a graduate assistant in the Hollings Special Collections Library, Jessica completed a summer internship with the Archives of American Gardens within the Smithsonian Gardens in Washington, D.C.

Liya Deng is a doctoral candidate and Cultural Heritage Informatics Leadership fellow at the University of South Carolina School of Library and Information Science. Her research agenda lies at the interpenetration of culture and information technology, focusing on the impact of modern technologies on the preservation and dissemination of cultural heritage through the creation of digital libraries, archives, and museums.

Cathy Faye is the assistant director of the Drs. Nicholas and Dorothy Cummings Center for the History of Psychology at the University of Akron. In addition to her research in the areas of social psychology and the history of science, she is one of the editors of *Nineteenth Century American Asylums: A History in Postcards*, published by the University of Akron Press.

Karen Heid is an associate professor of Art Education at the School of Visual Art and Design, the University of South Carolina. She actively supports schools with professional development, teaching art, and building learning communities while continuing to create art.

Dick Kawooya is an assistant professor at the School of Library and Information Science at the University of South Carolina. His research interests include information policy and law, particularly in the area of copyright/intellectual property rights in both national and international contexts; information ethics; information in society, and the foundations of library and information services.

Jodi Kearns is the digital projects manager at the Drs. Nicholas and Dorothy Cummings Center for the History of Psychology at the University of Akron. She holds three graduate degrees in library and information science, including an MS in library science and a PhD in philosophy in interdisciplinary information science from the University of North Texas.

Porchia Moore, a PhD candidate at the School of Library and Information Science at the University of South Carolina, is a recipient of the Cultural Heritage Informatics Leadership fellowship and is earning a certificate of museum management from McKissick Museum. Porchia's research explores the intersection of critical race theory and museums, demonstrating both the need and the opportunity for cultural competency to transform museum participation.

Jennifer Burek Pierce is an associate professor at the University of Iowa School of Library and Information Science. Her research considers what happens when ideas once shared face-to-face are committed to print, including how communities of readers are understood in light of the books and materials made available to them and made by them.

Carol Lynn Price is a doctoral student at the School of Library and Information Science at the University of South Carolina. Her latest project with the Byrne-Diderot Library at the American College of Building Arts is creating a digital exhibit on Christopher Werner (1805–1875), a prolific wrought iron manufacturer and craftsman in Charleston, South Carolina, during the mid-nineteenth century.

Tonia Sutherland holds a doctorate from the University of Pittsburgh's iSchool and is currently the lead researcher for the Collaborative for Historical Information and Analysis in the World History Center at the University of Pittsburgh. Global in scope and comparative in nature, Tonia's research and teaching interests include information stewardship, policy and ethics, theories and cultures of collaboration, critical information studies, community and cultural informatics, and digital humanities.

Simon Tarr, an associate professor in media arts at the School of Visual Art and Design at the University of South Carolina, is also working toward a PhD at the School of Library and Information Science. Simon continues to create films and perform live VJ shows at conferences, festivals, and clubs from Tokyo to New Orleans.

Tucky Taylor is the department head of Circulation, Reserves and Educational Films at Thomas Cooper Library, University of South Carolina. Her research interests include copyright and intellectual property issues.

Stan Trembach is a PhD student in the Cultural Heritage Informatics Leadership program at the University of South Carolina, School of Library and Information Science. He is interested in exploring ways in which modern technologies contribute to the preservation of historically and culturally valuable artifacts, and, in general, how the advent of new technologies has impacted the library world and library users.

Nosheen Fatima Warraich is an assistant professor in the department of Library & Information Science at the University of the Punjab, Lahore, Pakistan. Her research interests include human resource management in libraries, digital libraries, and the application of quantitative research in library and information science and digital libraries.

www.ingramcontent.com/pod-product-compliance
Ingram Content Group UK Ltd.
Pitfield, Milton Keynes, MK11 3LW, UK
UKHW040910190926
475560UK00008B/86

9 781442 250116